Female Roles in East German Drama 1949 - 1977

European University Studies

Europäische Hochschulschriften
Publications Universitaires Européennes

Series I

German Language and Literature

Reihe I Série I

Deutsche Sprache und Literatur
Langue et littérature allemandes

Bd./Vol. 483

PETER LANG
Frankfurt am Main · Bern

Katherine Vanovitch

Female Roles in East German Drama 1949-1977

A Selective History of Drama in the G.D.R.

PETER LANG
Frankfurt am Main · Bern

CIP-Kurztitelaufnahme der Deutschen Bibliothek

Vanovitch, Katherine:

Female Roles in East German Drama : 1949 - 1977 :
a Selective History of Drama in the G.D.R. / Katherine
Vanovitch. - Frankfurt am Main ; Bern : Lang, 1982.
(Europäische Hochschulschriften : Reihe 1, Dt.
Sprache u. Literatur ; Bd. 483)
ISBN 3-8204-5737-2
NE: Europäische Hochschulschriften / 01

ISSN 0721-3301
ISBN 3-8204-5737-2

Druck und Bindung: fotokop wilhelm weihert KG, darmstadt

CONTENTS

PREFACE

The wave of research into the history of women in literature over recent years has pursued two, often overlapping courses. As part of the feminist quest to unearth the forgotten path of 'herstory', that is, history made and interpreted by women, a number of books have appeared which seek to rehabilitate women writers, identifying and questioning the social and aesthetic premises which first condemned them to oblivion, and providing new material for the debate surrounding the specific nature of feminine consciousness. The other course has been to consider the roles played by female characters in literature itself - characters created, in the main, by men - and to explore these roles for what they can illustrate about the changing lives of women and the social attitudes reflected through the vision of the author.

My own work, a doctoral dissertation submitted to the University of Cambridge in 1980 and reproduced here with a few formal amendments, has pursued the second course, simply because drama in the German Democratic Republic has been dominated by male writers. However, I hope that in presenting these writers in their literary and socio-historical context I can also make a contribution to the evaluation of gender as an influence in the process of artistic creation.

This book is intended to play a further role. When I began my research, I was only too aware of the lack of material, especially in English, which could provide a useful introduction to students of East German literature. Of course, this work is far too limited to be considered a literary history, but I hope that the selection of authors presented will provide undergraduates and others with some insights into the evolution of drama in the GDR, without resorting to the rather sterile and unreadable techniques so often encountered in a reference volume. Although my theme is esoteric, many of the trends which have determined the function of female characters apply to the development of drama in general, so that the present work can serve as a starting point for broader acquaintance.

In an attempt to convey the cultural context in which East German dramatists have written, I have drawn extensively on secondary material produced in the GDR. Details of those books and articles that were of particular value are listed in the Bibliography, along with other sources of ideas and information which I have found useful and also the editions of works referred to in the text. What cannot be formulated in such a specific manner is the wider research which I was able to carry out during a year spent in Berlin (GDR), sifting through magazines and newspapers of both literary and social interest, watching plays - and audiences - and talking to people inside and outside the theatrical world. I should like to express my gratitude to those who made my stay possible at a time when the formalities of cultural exchange between our two countries were minimal. At the same time, I should like to thank all those people, especially my mother and my supervisor, Dr Peter Hutchinson of Selwyn College, Cambridge, whose considerable practical and moral support enabled me to combine parenthood with completing my dissertation.

Chorleywood, 1981

INTRODUCTION

Recent research into the function of female characters in European and North American literature over the centuries has traced the evolution of traditions which are closely related to the social role of women in our culture, traditions which modify in response to shifts in this role and to changes in literary mood and form. *(1)* In general, there are two conventions which have persisted. The first is the overwhelming definition of female characters in terms of their relationship to men in love, marriage and motherhood - even where this occurs by default, that is, in the portrayal of the emancipated woman attempting to escape amorous or marital norms. Since the social definition of male characters is far more diverse, women have not only had fewer roles to play: their functions have also tended to be subordinate, and more strictly limited to the domestic and romantic tasks assigned to their gender. The second convention is a recurring identification of female characters with a moral principle, be it tolerance or self-sacrifice, motherliness or domesticity, eroticism or chastity. These qualities are predominantly associated with their status as wives and mothers, sweethearts and mistresses, and it is not unusual for them to be presented in symbolic, even idealized form.

In spite of their political commitment to sexual equality, left-wing writers in Germany before the Second World War did little to challenge these literary conventions. In proletarian art, both written and visual, the 'typical' worker is male. In the novels of Willi Bredel and his colleagues in the *Bund Proletarisch-Revolutionärer Schriftsteller*, the working-class woman is a shadowy figure, supportive to the men in her life and their party. *(2)* Bertolt Brecht borrowed two symbolic images from tradition, the Prostitute and the Mother, and made extensive use of them in his critique of mercenary, uncaring capitalist society. The Prostitute, a new variation of the amorous female, had emerged over the latter stages of the nineteenth century as a sad and sordid comment on the cheapening of urban life in industrialized Europe. In Naturalism She was an index of poverty and squalour. In Expressionism She became a demonic principle (in the mould of Wedekind or Strindberg), or else a romanticized victim and outcast of the Establishment. Brecht exploited this asocial aspect in his earlier works, and later the theme of humiliation through prostitution became an allegory for the struggle to survive. Under the influence of Maxim Gorky, who inspired a strong current of Mother symbolism in Soviet Russia, Brecht reinterpreted the maternal role traditionally played by female characters. Gorky's Mother first enters politics because of a basic desire to protect her revolutionary son. Once involved, she frees herself from this passive, subordinate role by recognizing that the Revolution serves her own interests, too. The East German scholars Sigrid Damm and Jürgen Engler, who describe the traditional image of womanhood in literature since Goethe as principled humanity in an evil world of men, observe how this mother reverses her conventional supportive function by becoming a main motor in building the conditions for social advance. *(3)* Nonetheless, this character still identifies 'her' interests as those which derive from her motherhood. Her commitment to peace and better conditions are an extension of her compassionate care for her son. Her motherliness is a social programme. It was this symbolism, not the practicalities of parenthood, which Brecht was to adopt for his own drama.

While it is true that the world of work has always played a small part in the lives of most fictional characters, the restricted definition of female figures in terms of their domestic and romantic relationship to others has been especially pronounced. Exceptions have been few, and even when literature has turned to sectors of the population where women are employed outside the home this has not been afforded much attention as an influence in their lives. Since the Industrial Revolution began to set its seal on the nuclear family as we know it today, by separating the productive from the domestic economy, philosophers, theoreticians and jurists have been particularly anxious to polarize the spheres of male and female experience. From Immanuel Kant, through Arthur Schopenhauer and Friedrich Nietzsche to Otto Weininger, we encounter the view that women are passive, not active, that they are emotional, not intellectual (although they may be instinctively moral - an abstraction from their preoccupation with the welfare of others), and that they belong in the home and not 'at work' (that is, in paid employment). *(4)* These distinctions were applied with fanatical rigidity in Nazi ideology between 1933 and 1945, and were endorsed by their literature - to which posterity has paid little attention.

The history of the German Democratic Republic (GDR) brought some substantial new influences to bear on social images of womankind. The right to work, along with equal pay for equal labour, was established for women in the Soviet-Occupied Military Zone in 1945. Whilst the extreme economic hardship of the post-war period and the demands of reconstruction were the two most pressing factors in spiralling female employment, Marxist theory also sees productive labour as the basic right and need of every individual, and the most significant force in personal development. In the culture which subsequently evolved, work therefore came to be the normal expectation of most women, a trend which was encouraged by the concerted agitational function of contemporary art and literature. In those early years, writers who were conscious of the effects of labour, under socialist relations of production, on the lives and opportunities of women, made political and productive activity an essential part of female characterization. However, writers who concentrated on other topics tended to introduce female characters only where they were required in relation to male characters.

Although this discrepancy faded away in the course of time, any detailed study of female roles in the literature of the GDR must start from the premise that the cultural status of women cannot be deduced solely from works devoted to the *Frauenfrage*. The general movement towards a pattern of characterization which is not based on gender alone can best be observed against a cross-section of both central and subsidiary roles throughout East German history. After all, women in the GDR have not completely abandoned domesticity to discover their identity in economic and political life. They are caught, rather, in a duality between the productive and reproductive spheres, as workers/citizens <u>and</u> housewives/mothers, and I have tried to outline some of the sociological ramifications of this elsewhere. *(5)* It is when women appear in subsidiary roles, that is, roles reduced to a single function in a play or a novel, that their traditional orientations have been most tenacious.

With the consolidation of a socialist economy, particularly in the sixties, literature moved away from its preoccupation with themes from production and began to explore intimate relationships in more depth. Parallel to this, the political and cultural hegemony of socialism brought about the demise of the positive hero with straightforward goals, in favour of greater self-questioning by literary protagonists. These tendencies encouraged the growth of an East German *Frauenliteratur*. However, whereas in the West we are witnessing a minority current of feminist writing alongside, separate from and usually in direct opposition to what Mary Allen has called the 'necessary blankness' - the notable absence of purposeful, independent female characters in most literature - in the GDR there is no such polarity, and the boundaries of *Frauenliteratur* are imprecise. The novels and short stories of Christa Wolf, Irmtraud Morgner, Gerti Tetzner, Brigitte Reimann, Elfriede Brüning, Christine Wolter, Helga Schubert and Helga Königsdorf, and the interviews with women collected and edited by Maxie Wander and Sarah Kirsch, most of which have attracted the attention of Western feminists and left-wing academics, betray certain similarities with the 'weibliche Ästhetik' of the West German *Bewegung schreibender Frauen* and sister movements in Britain and the United States - the self as both subject and object, concern for the redefinition of love and of human relationships in general, challenges to the traditional values of female dependence and male dedication to work. But these preoccupations are not exclusively those of women writers, and East German literary critics include amongst *Frauenliteratur* the works of Günter de Bruyn, Manfred Jendryschik, Karl-Heinz Jakobs, Volker Braun, and even Eberhard Panitz, and if several East German women have shown a predilection for prose fantasy, this is also a technique adopted by Braun, de Bruyn and Ulrich Plenzdorf. *(6)* As Eastern and Western critics alike have often illustrated, plumbing the depths of changing female identity is a process closely interwoven, in the GDR, with plumbing the depths of changing human relationships in the sense of Karl Marx's *Ökonomisch-philosophische Manuskripte* of 1844:

> Das unmittelbare, natürliche, notwendige Verhältnis des Menschen zum Menschen ist das *Verhältnis* des *Mannes* zum Weibe . . . Aus dem Charakter dieses Verhältnisses folgt, inwieweit der Mensch als *Gattungswesen*, als *Mensch* sich geworden ist und erfaßt hat . . . In ihm zeigt sich also inwieweit das *natürliche* Verhalten des Menschen *menschlich* oder inwieweit das *menschliche* Wesen ihm zum *natürlichen* Wesen, inwieweit seine *menschliche Natur* ihm zur *Natur* geworden ist. *(7)*

A society in which the fields of male/female encounter are broadened by equal opportunity in education and employment should, one might expect, help to break down cultural images of gender-specific activity - held by both sexes - which brand people as 'men' and 'women' before defining them as individuals. This should deepen the understanding that both men and women have of women (and of men), with a beneficial effect on the portrayal of women by male and female authors alike.

The question of male and female consciousness in writing is not a simple one. It is tempting to suspect that women writers are, on the whole, more likely to articulate female experience in their construction of female characters. But then again, authors creating characters have long been usurping territory which is not, strictly speaking, their own: as Heiner Müller confessed, 'Ich bin kein Bauarbeiter Ingenieur Parteifunktionär'. *(8)* A man may pass perceptive comments on the female condition while, throughout the history of fiction, certain women have been able to internalize a patriarchal vision of womankind, as the escapist tradition from Wilhelmine Karoline von Wobeser to Barbara Cartland testifies. The sex of the observer is a weighty factor, but only one factor in literary formulations of gender.

In the world of theatre, there have been few women playwrights. This is still the case in the GDR, in spite of the numerous successful women poets and novelists. Women's traditional inclination towards literature which is self-expressive - letters, diaries, confessional novels and poetry - may well account in part for this anomaly. It is a tradition which has arisen both from socio-economic conditions which, in the past, have not encouraged professional authorship amongst women, and from the ontogenetic implications of the thorough training in empirical psychology and sympathy which a woman receives in her roles as wife and mother. When a woman turns to fiction-writing, I would venture to suggest that this experience leads her to approach her characters in a more differentiated and conciliatory manner and to reject the rather more abstract and polarized structures on which drama tends to be based. *(9)* Any proclivities of this nature are certainly reinforced by the unsocial hours of theatre life, which militate, in the GDR too, against the participation of women with families. There are few women producers, although many women drama graduates work as advisers. In a society where dramatists frequently emerge through the theatre ranks, this will, of course, influence the process of selection. In fact, all the playwrights discussed in this work are men. The only woman who consistently published plays for theatre is Hedda Zinner, who began her political and literary career in the Weimar Republic. After the war, she continued to write anti-fascist plays in which most of the protagonists are men, with the exception of *Ravensbrücker Ballade* (1961), a drama about the women's concentration camp with a wartime thematic. Since the sheer wealth of potential material has demanded rigorous selectivity, Zinner was disqualified on the grounds that her work indicates very little about the cultural image of women in the GDR itself. Berta Waterstradt's play *Ehesache Lorenz* (1958) was similarly discounted on the grounds that the author underwent her apprenticeship under the aegis of the BPRS rather than in the GDR.

A shadowy figure in the reference tomes is Inge Müller. With her husband Heiner, she was the co-author of *Die Korrektur*, *Der Lohndrücker* and *Klettwitzer Bericht*. But she is not entered under her own name in the *Theaterlexikon* and emerges from most literary histories as an appendage, so that it is impossible to draw on any material currently available to reconstruct a picture of her individual contribution to what are known as the works of Heiner Müller. That Inge had some claim of her own to authorship is evidenced by the manuscripts she left at her suicide in 1966, and we know that her radio play *Die Weiberbrigade* - also unpublished - served as the basis for what must surely be the most provoking treatment afforded the *Frauenfrage* in East German drama: Heiner Müller's *Die Weiberkomödie*.

The lack of women playwrights expressing their female experience is certainly a factor in the warnings that Jack D. Zipes and Helen Fehervary have given about a new kind of idealization of women in drama. Zipes, noting the predilection of comedy writers for female exemplary protagonists, concludes that 'die exemplarische Frau zur komischen Muse des Sozialismus geworden (ist), die Stimmung und Lust schafft, damit günstige Zustände für gesellschaftliche Veränderungen entstehen können'. *(10)* His essay marks the first Western contribution to the subject of female characters in the drama of the GDR. It concentrates on the direct translation of women's social position into dramatic roles, rather than providing an analysis of the dramatic structures within which these roles operate, and his brevity inevitably encourages generalizations. He sees the image of women promoted by comedy as tending to reinforce a wider 'Verdinglichungsprozeß', in which women are instruments of social progress but subject to the economic priorities of a predominantly patriarchal society. Fehervary, whose résumé of female functions in East German literature is as stimulating as it is cursory, fears that women have become idealized, in the dramatic tradition deriving from Friedrich Wolf's 'positive hero', Anna, as asexual achievers. Of Brecht's followers, she argues that they 'in many respects portray more convincing female characters', but which are 'still their male author's projections, their attempt to explain their own insufficiency . . . which does not mean that Braun's and

Müller's characters are not part of our (women's - *K.V.*) referential context; historically, we are still moving and reacting within that'. *(11)*

Part of my intention has been to identify, in more detail, images of womanhood in East German drama, and to relate these to their social backcloth, observing how each author assimilates or challenges concepts of female personality. There is, after all, a complex connexion between social realities and cultural, including literary, images. Such an investigation, moreover, may assist in widening our response to the works of East German playwrights, since the potted summaries that have appeared both east and west of the Elbe suggest a society consisting almost exclusively of five-year plans and party apparatuses.

At the same time, however, I share Barbara Einhorn's belief in the necessity for more structural analysis of literary texts from the GDR, and her reservations about the dismissive implications of an entirely sociological approach:

> Until quite recently . . . many Western critics felt strongly that it was not possible to write 'good' literature within the constraints imposed by the cultural-political framework and, in particular, by the theory of Socialist Realism. Thus, they felt, one should, if one insisted on coming to grips with this mass of writing, deal with it, analyse and interpret it purely as a sociological phenomenon. *(12)*

The concept of Socialist Realism has grown broader and more sophisticated with the evolution of both artistic production and academic reception in the GDR, and the modification of narrative perspective and decline of 'Schematismus' which Einhorn traces in the structure of novels is paralleled, in drama, by decentralization of the protagonistic function and by a shift in the battlefronts of dramatic conflict.

A new impetus to Western structural investigation of East German drama came in 1974 with the publication of *Sozialistisches Drama nach Brecht. Drei Modelle: Peter Hacks, Heiner Müller, Hartmut Lange* by Wolfgang Schivelbusch. This book does not lapse into formal analysis for its own sake, but shows instead the relationship between dramatic form and the social assessment which those three dramatists seek to project. As his Brechtian yardstick implies, Schivelbusch is dissatisfied with the demise of the class contradiction which he sees reflected in mollified dramatic conflicts, so that his critique expresses his own scepticism towards the political theory of non-antagonistic contradictions. Any commentator writing about the GDR from beyond its borders must be caught in the same predicament: the dual responsibility of observing the internal laws of East German society whilst appraising them as an outsider. I have tried to moderate the dilemma to some extent by drawing largely on secondary sources from the GDR in order to convey something of the cultural climate in which East German playwrights live, work, perceive and relay. Moreover, although the absence of a conflict can be as illuminating as its presence, comprehension of the GDR can be served as much by a record of the social problems which do inspire writers as those which do not.

A study of female roles in East German drama can fulfil two purposes. It can register attitudes towards women, the changing part played by women in society, and the problems which they are considered to encounter. It can also throw some light on the dynamic of drama itself, showing how conventions of plot and character are established, developed and superseded. After all, female characters in plays are not women. They are artificial constructs operating within an artistic ritual which has its own limitations. However much a playwright may try to create the impression of a rounded personality, a character is and remains an abstraction, susceptible to stereotyping and offering a partial response to a situation (plot). Positive female protagonists composed by male writers are acutely ironical: the literary convention of the woman who breaks down rigid barriers between political activity and private morality to become a social visionary, while it derives from real female experience, has taken shape, in the drama of the GDR, under the auspices of men. The superior feminine insight of Johanna, Dascha, Tinka and Heloisa is the humanitarian insight of Helmut Baierl, Heiner Müller, Volker Braun and Stefan Schütz. The question whether this amounts to flattery or reification of the female sex can only be outstripped (not answered) by an acknowledgement that the dramatic role is a device which collapses culturally determined intellectual and emotional stimuli into a symbol. The manner in which these symbols are reinforced or challenged and reconstituted can only be examined by reference to both dramatic structures and social ideas. *(13)*

I have therefore started this investigation with two chapters which set the scene for the development of female roles in East German drama. The first is a summary of Marxist classics and historical influences which contributed to the formulation of SED policy on the status of women, and the second is a brief description of the cultural, and specifically theatrical, climate in which East German drama germinated after the war. As for the ensuing study, I have tried to make it representative. The *Henschel* stage library in Berlin contained at the time of my research about three hundred plays written in the GDR (discounting the substantial children's theatre), which offered about a thousand parts for women. Over a quarter of the *dramatis personae* were female, and this proportion is slowly growing, although not so much because characters are being defined as individuals rather than men or women, as in deference to women's participation in new areas of social life. However, whilst I have tried to cut a chronological and stylistic section through the drama of the GDR, some of my choices will inevitably seem arbitrary. On the whole, I have used plays which are particularly well known in the GDR itself, either to the general public or to specialists, if not both. Where an author has attracted the attention of his colleagues rather than theatres and audiences, as in the cases of Rolf Gozell, Stefan Schütz and, to some extent, Heiner Müller, I have tried to sketch some of the expectations with which audiences have learned to receive drama in the GDR, along with the difficulties that these expectations can create for the innovator. As Bertolt Brecht, the source of much wisdom, observed during rehearsals for Erwin Strittmatter's *Katzgraben*, 'das Theater ist wie ein Schwimmer, der nur so schnell schwimmen kann, wie es ihm die Strömung und seine Kräfte erlauben'. *(14)*

Chapter 1

THEORETICAL AND HISTORICAL BACKGROUND TO THE *FRAUENFRAGE* IN 1949

In *Die deutsche Ideologie,* Karl Marx suggested that the first division of labour was that between men and women in the family. This created the first property relationships and also the first ideological distinctions between one class of people and another. Around 1880, August Bebel, Friedrich Engels and Clara Zetkin, founding Marxist members of the *Sozialdemokratische Partei Deutschlands* (SPD), used this historical materialist basis to interpret the considerable anthropological studies of colonized societies which were flowing back to Europe. Their deliberations led to the publication of two books which presented an analysis of historical changes in the function and status of women, and also a socialist perspective for the future: Bebel's *Die Frau und der Sozialismus* and Engels's *Der Ursprung der Familie, des Privateigentums und des Staats.* These works argue that social formations are conditioned by the production and reproduction of the means of subsistence (through labour) and of human life itself (in the family). The family has existed in many forms as the means of production, and social relations in general, have developed. In the earliest societies, a child would have many fathers, and sometimes many mothers. Paternity only became a crucial institution as gentile property gave way to private property, and mother right to father right. Women's domestic work lost its significance in comparison with men's labour in obtaining a livelihood. Engels and Bebel deduce from this that women can only be rehabilitated with equal rights by joining men in the social production of wealth. Engels sees new opportunities for women's emancipation in the advent of the large-scale industrial economy, 'die nicht nur Frauenarbeit auf großer Stufenleiter zuläßt, sondern förmlich nach ihr verlangt, und die auch die private Hausarbeit mehr und mehr in eine öffentliche Industrie aufzulösen strebt' (p.158).

In other words, capitalism has provided a potential foundation for women's emancipation with its efficient, large-scale means of production, but the social relations of capitalism exploit women as second-class citizens. Female labour is a low-paid reserve, less skilled, less likely to be politically organized, and readily available as a cheap substitute for machinery or male labour. Working men are therefore often hostile to women, regarding them as unfair competition. At the same time, women are expected to perform a double shift by continuing to take responsibility for household work. Although housework is essential to maintaining the labour force, it is hardly socialized, and is thus inefficient and unrewarding, condemning women to isolation and drudgery.

All this, Bebel and Engels contend, can be overcome by socializing the means of production under the control of the working class itself, so that all production will be for need and not for profit. Women must have equal economic and legal status. Since this will mean that women are no longer dependent on marriage for support, the basis is laid for free choice in marital relationships, with both partners now self-sufficient and able to dissolve their bond should it cease to be meaningful. What Engels calls 'die individuelle Geschlechtsliebe' (p.67), a physical relationship between two people which freely expresses emotional and intellectual sympathies of a complex and fulfilling nature, is a relatively recent phenomenon, which has only become possible at this higher level of civilization. It was not the inspiration for monogamy under feudalism and capitalism, which was an economic development, a cellular form of civilized society embracing a similar class antagonism.

Bebel goes into exhaustive statistical detail concerning patriarchal abuse of monogamy under capitalism, explaining rape, illegitimacy and prostitution as consequences of women's relegation to objects of male pleasure. He links these male privileges with class exploitation, showing, for example, how landlords in rural areas impose their will on local girls. Such incidents, he notes, often end in illegitimacy, and even infanticide, for which the victim of this seduction is held entirely responsible.

Bebel did not believe in the necessity for formal marriage ceremonies in socialist society, since any relationship between two people would be a private matter and the result of their own inclinations. Whilst Bebel's personal preference seems to have been for long-term stable relationships - and in this he was typical of many traditional Marxist thinkers, from Engels to Lenin - he also makes a plea in his book for uncensored individual freedom. Morality should not be a rigid code which may only be broken in secret:

> Der Mensch soll unter der Voraussetzung, daß die Befriedigung seiner Triebe keinem anderen Schaden oder Nachteil zufügt, über sich selbst befinden. *Die Befriedigung des Geschlechtstriebs ist ebenso jedes einzelnen persönliche Sache wie die Befriedigung jedes anderen Naturtriebs.* Niemand hat darüber einem anderen Rechenschaft zu geben und kein Unberufener hat sich einzumischen (p.516).

Bebel's arguments concerning 'natural' behaviour are, nonetheless, a little inconsistent, due to a teleological streak which impairs his dialectical materialism. For example, having described the social reasons which led to widespread homosexuality amongst the Greeks, particularly the men, he then judges this practice to be 'unnatural'. But by what standards? A similar tendency to enable preconceptions to creep into his prognosis is evident in his views on the social function of women in socialism. He assumes, amongst other things, that bringing up children will automatically continue to be the duty and desire of women:

> Die Frau ist also *frei*, und Kinder, die sie besitzt, verkürzen ihr diese Freiheit nicht, sie können ihr nur die Freude am Leben vermehren. Pflegerinnen, Erzieherinnen, befreundete Frauen, die heranwachsende weibliche Jugend stehen ihr in Fällen, in welche sie Hilfe braucht, zur Seite (pp.519-520).

It does not, apparently, occur to him that men might wish to commit themselves to fatherhood, and this means that Bebel offers no guidance in the debate about the sexual division of domestic labour in early socialism, when the socialization of housework is still at a low level. He is, nevertheless, a firm proponent of this socialization, frequently extolling the virtues and efficiency of communal kitchens.

A similar prejudice emerges in Bebel's dismissal of certain occupations as unwomanly, a prejudice shared by Engels in his condemnation of British capitalism, *Die Lage der arbeitenden Klasse in England*. Bebel expresses admiration for the healthy young lasses of Sparta and certain African tribes, who participated in wrestling, games, and even war alongside men, but, like Engels, he goes on to confuse rejection of the harmful effects of industrial labour on the *human* body under capitalist conditions with a contemporary middle-class disapproval of certain types of *female* labour:

> Es ist wahrlich kein schöner Anblick, Frauen, sogar im schwangeren Zustand, mit den Männern um die Wette beim Eisenbahnbau schwer beladene Karren fahren zu sehen oder

> sie als Handlanger, Kalk und Zement anmachend oder schwere Lasten Steine tragen, beim Hausbau zu beobachten, oder beim Kohlen- und Eisensteinwaschen. Dabei wird der Frau alles Weibliche abgestreift und ihre Weiblichkeit mit Füßen getreten, wie umgekehrt unseren Männern in vielen verschiedenen Beschäftigungsarten jedes Männliche genommen wird. Das sind die Folgen der sozialen Ausbeutung und des sozialen Krieges. Unsere korrupten sozialen Zustände stellen die Dinge auf dem Kopf (pp.264-5).

Whilst few would dispute that pregnant women should enjoy some form of protection from heavy and dangerous jobs, such as now exists in all the socialist countries, the 'Naturschranken' which no sex can overstep (p.280) are never clearly defined by Engels or Bebel, and are still the cause of much debate in those societies.

Bebel does, however, engage in a powerful attack on contemporary preconceptions of the female psyche, explaining how women's social position has long prevented them from unfolding their intellectual and creative talents to the same degree as men. In the same way, he analyzes the phenomenon of fashion and women's concern for their appearance in terms of their economic need to find a husband, the competition for scarce males, the cultural impropriety of females being active and obvious wooers, and, in the case of the more comfortable classes, their lack of alternative preoccupations. There will be, he maintains, no economic legitimation for 'Repräsentation, Tand, Flitter und kostspielige Vergnügungen' (p.200) in socialism:

> Es sind hier wieder *rein ökonomische und soziale Ursachen,* die eine Eigenschaft, bald bei dem Mann, bald bei der Frau hervorrufen, die man als gänzlich unabhängig von sozialen und ökonomischen Ursachen anzusehen gewohnt ist. Daraus darf man weiter schließen, daß, sobald die Gesellschaft in soziale Zustände kommt, unter denen jede Abhängigkeit des einen Geschlechts vom anderen aufhört und beide gleich frei sind, *die Eitelkeit und die Modetorheiten ebenso verschwinden werden wie viele andere Untugenden, die wir heute für unausrottbar halten, weil angeblich sie den Menschen angeboren sind* (p.187).

The implications of this approach are that behaviour patterns considered to be instinctively masculine or feminine are, in fact, socially determined, and just as ephemeral as economic formations.

This did not mean that traditional ideology would be quick to change, as Lenin emphasized. He acknowledged to Clara Zetkin after the Russian Revolution that even staunch Bolsheviks were the creatures of a discriminatory culture:

> Unfortunately, we may still say of many of our comrades, 'Scratch the Communist and a philistine appears.' To be sure, you have to scratch the sensitive spots, - such as their *(sic)* mentality regarding women. *(15)*

Lenin repeated Marx's belief that a society can be evaluated in terms of its attitude towards women. Unlike many of his colleagues, who saw women's emancipation as an inevitable result of the proletarian revolution rather than a component factor within it, Lenin felt that 'the experience of all liberation movements has shown that the success of a revolution depends on how much the women take part in it' (p.62), and 'the proletariat cannot achieve complete liberty until it has won complete liberty for women' (p.81). The thorny question which faced the Russian Revolution was, however: what exactly constitutes 'complete liberty for women'?

Although the new Soviet power gave women equal rights, equal pay for equal work, access to divorce, maternity benefits, and a number of other basic improvements in their lives, many party members and trade unionists viewed any attempts by women to organize together and formulate their own demands with considerable suspicion. Socialization of housework, therefore, although it had the support of Lenin, was not a priority, and the early ventures with communal canteens, laundries and creches were not actively encouraged once the civil war was over. Moreover, the general economic and political climate was not conducive to discussion of new ideas, and the significance of the nuclear family in the lives of women was questioned less and less, after initial enthusiasm for a new communist morality in relationships became increasingly marginalized. The works of Alexandra Kollontai, the only woman in the first Bolshevik government and a firm advocate of autonomous women's organization, posed many searching questions about human relationships and the collective ethic. Her views were not nearly so libertarian as her enemies consistently insinuated, but when Stalin's accession to power put the finishing touches to her political isolation, they passed into oblivion. *(16)* Even Lenin, who was nothing like so conventional as his successor, expressed his disquiet about the interest in sexuality and marriage shown both amongst young Russians and in the women's groups of the SPD. Since connexions between German and Russian revolutionaries were very close, Lenin's opinions, and also the social structures established in the Soviet Union, were an influence on the thinking of German Communists over the next decade.

In Germany itself, the women's policy of the SPD had pursued a wavering course, reflecting the degree of political contention within the party. Zetkin, Bebel and Engels had developed a strategy for women which was based on involving them in the productive force to free them from dependence on men. The Lassallean tradition, meanwhile, condemned female labour as a capitalist iniquity. At the turn of the century, women increased their sway in the party as their numbers in the industrial workforce grew, and the demand for women's right to work was almost unanimous. But other demands affecting women tended to be reformist, restricted to the realms of protective labour legislation - about which the party was never satisfactorily united - and universal suffrage. Unlike the middle-class feminist movement, which has a long history in Germany, the Social Democratic women's movement saw the capitalist system, rather than male privilege, as the main enemy, and it was often exhorted by its leaders to channel its energies less into campaigning on its own issues than into particular tasks for the party machine that were seen as women's work, such as electoral preparations. This, and the SPD's chauvinist stance during the First World War, diverted a considerable proportion of women into new left-wing groups, including the *Kommunistische Partei Deutschlands* (KPD), which gave them more scope to seek radical solutions to the specific problems of their sex and conducted a vociferous abortion campaign in the twenties. In the SPD (and to some extent in these other parties) women continued to be relegated from the political decision-making to the social work. Although the SPD did not renounce its commitment to women's right to work, equal pay and equal education during the mass unemployment of the Weimar Republic, these demands were less clearly reiterated as the party tried to work within the capitalist framework it had accepted in the post-war election. Moreover, women were coming under increasing pressure from predominantly male trade unions to cede their jobs to the millions of unemployed men. The voice of radical socialism, which saw the cure for economic ills in a society where productive labour was the right and duty of all able-bodied citizens, was now rarely heard in the SPD. The left was split, and there was no force powerful enough to stop the ascendancy of Hitler's National Socialists.

Although there were signs of economic recovery before Hitler took power, the Nazi campaign against 'Doppelverdienertum' made some impact on the unemployment statistics, since women whose husbands were working were assumed to have no right to a job. The policy was popular with certain circles. The trade unions, on the whole, accepted the move as a solution to their members' unemployment, and the Church, whose influence had been strong in the Weimar Republic, found that it corresponded nicely to its own conception of a woman's place. The Nazis made great capital of the opportunity they were giving women to exercise their 'natural' function, and, as things were, working wives and mothers certainly had unenviable problems in combining their tasks. The Nazis therefore claimed to be revitalizing the German family, and their women's organization ran classes and discussions in domestic crafts, a useful channel for propagating political and economic policy: to match the austerity of an economy preparing for war, women were urged to prepare simple, cheap and wholesome food, to abhor cosmetics, and to bring up their children in the spirit of German patriotism.

And yet it is hard to judge the success of Hitler's policy for women. The major resistance to it came from working wives themselves. It was not organized resistance: women merely refused to give up their jobs voluntarily, indicating that they could not afford to or were not interested in the domestic alternative. In any case, as the war effort mounted, Nazi policy became contradictory. Women were called back, first into the munitions industry (an ironic violation of the image of life-bearing motherhood), and then as the principal upholders of the home front.

The Nazis had a further interest in keeping women at home for as long as the economy permitted. A country at war needs children, especially when the war is aimed at colonization. There were financial and moral incentives for childbearing, and the new divorce laws were justified in terms of the unlikelihood of an unhappy marriage producing offspring. Furthermore, in an effort to promote racially sound children, mixed marriages could be annulled easily. Birth control was strictly opposed, except in the case of 'undesirables', and Hess and Himmler even endorsed illegitimacy, so long as the children were of racial value, thus invoking the wrath of the Church. Himmler also had plans for promoting bigamy after the war, to cope with the shortage of males. Campaigns against abortion and homosexuality were stepped up, although such things were tolerated in non-Aryans. *(17)*

By the time of their defeat, the Nazis had therefore conducted a long and vehement public relations exercise in favour of the nuclear family. They stressed the myth that this was the age-old, natural base for German society, drawing largely on Nietzsche, who had quite definite ideas on the subject of gender roles: 'So will ich Mann und Weib: kriegstüchtig den einen, gebärtüchtig das andere.' *(18)* At the same time, the collapse of fascism left in its wake high female employment, something that had existed in Germany since its industrial revolution and which was fairly well established in the social expectations of many women. As the early post-war years dragged on, with the menfolk returning in trickles from captivity or still recovering from their wounds, the women continued to provide a vast reservoir of labour to clear the rubble and restore order and provisions to the towns and countryside.

Immediately after the war, local *Frauenausschüsse* were set up throughout the Soviet-Occupied Zone to organize as many women as possible to play an active part in the economic and social tasks facing the war-torn population. In 1947 they were amalgamated into the new *Demokratischer Frauenbund Deutschlands* (DFD), committed to peace and the eradication of fascism, and closely related to the *Sozialistische Einheitspartei Deutschlands* (SED), the party which represented the merger of Communists and Social Democrats.

The women's policies of the SED in the latter half of the forties were mainly directed at equal pay for equal work, broadening the professional and educational opportunities for women, and establishing their equal rights in financial and marital affairs. Much of their approach was tutelary: extensive social welfare programmes were inaugurated to alleviate the poverty of women and children in particular; women received paid time off work for domestic duties; protective labour legislation was introduced and ante-natal care was improved. The legal disadvantages of illegitimacy were also abolished. In line with the overall moderation of its demands in the interests of a broad, anti-fascist alliance, the party refrained from any challenge to the nuclear family as the basic functional unit of society. Socialization of household labour was not, in any case, an economic priority under the harsh conditions of *Aufbau*. However, in 1949 the party called for greater attention from the whole membership to the status of women, allocating a female comrade to each department to raise women's demands in connexion with all new policies and their execution. The *Frauenabteilung*, which advised the party on women's policy, also formally assumed responsibility for direction of the DFD.

In all their work amongst women, the SED and DFD stressed the importance of women's involvement in overall progress against the devastation of the war and the reconstruction of a peaceful, progressive and united Germany.

Chapter 2

THEATRICAL LIFE AFTER THE WAR

> Am Anfang der Spielzeit 1945/46 war es über dem Theatertrümmermeer Berlins wüst und leer. Es gab keine Textbücher, selbst nicht der Klassiker. Durch Zeitungsannoncen wurden Hebbel- und Shakespeare-Ausgaben gesucht. Waren schon in den Herbsttagen die zehn bis zwanzig Kilometer Anmarschwege zu Proben - etwa vom Grünewald bis zum Hebbel-Theater - mit äußersten Schwierigkeiten verbunden, so mußten sie im Winter oft bei bitterer Kälte zu Fuß oder mit dem Fahrrad überwunden werden. Im Januar probierten wir *Professor Mamlock* bei zehn Grad Kälte im Kulissenabstellraum des völlig zerschossenen Schiller-Theaters. In Mänteln und in dicken Wollschals gehüllt zog es uns mit einem unwiderstehlichen Drang zu einem kleinen Kanonenöfchen, das in der Mitte des monumentalen Raums eine mehr symbolische Wärme ausstrahlte. Und dennoch hat das Berliner Theater ein äußerst reichhaltiges, ja vielleicht zu buntscheckiges Repertoire gezeigt. *(19)*

****

When Dönitz capitulated on 8th May 1945, Germany found itself in a state of material and cultural disorder. Industry was at a standstill, agriculture severely disrupted, schools and theatres widely destroyed, and food, drinking water and electricity in scarce supply. Moreover, the vast Nazi propaganda machine had at last been silenced, leaving millions disorientated and demoralized. For progressive and humanist artists and intellectuals returning from exile in those early months of the post-war period, the most urgent task was to find new inspirations for the world of culture, to combat the ideology of chauvinism and militarism, and to bring fresh hope and perspectives to the German people. Paul Rilla was lenient in his appraisal of the twelve-year fascist interlude as a 'kulturelles Niemandsland, tauglich nur, um zu pädagogischem Abschreckungszweck besichtigt zu werden: das Niemandsland einer in aller Geschichte beispiellosen nationalen Selbstzerstörung'. *(20)* Others were more damning:

> Wir fanden ein Volk in Agonie vor. Das ist die Wahrheit. Es war vom Gift einer Verzweiflung gelähmt, die einer Mischung der Schocks der Bombennächte und Kriegsereignisse, des eingebleuten Kommunistenschrecks und dem Bewußtwerden eigener Mitschuld an all dem, was über Deutschland gekommen war, gleichkam. *(21)*

The new cultural forces which were to determine the course of theatrical life over the next few years were disparate but, in the Soviet-Occupied Zone, two major influences can be identified. The first consisted of various non-Marxist humanists working in the theatre as critics, producers and playwrights, who were actively committed to democratic anti-fascism and to the rebirth of progressive German culture, men like Herbert Jhering, Paul Rilla, Günther Weisenborn and Fritz Westen, who had close personal and professional contacts with Communists such as Friedrich Wolf, Wolfgang Langhoff, Fritz Erpenbeck, Maxim Vallentin and Johannes R. Becher, and who were able to forge a cultural alliance with left-wing political forces and the Soviet Military Administration. The second major influence was the KPD itself, which had begun preparing its cultural policy for post-war Germany in exile in Moscow.

KPD policy had by now broken with the sectarianism of the twenties. The reasons for this derived not only from a critical assessment of the party's own past, but also from the contemporary situation. In the thirties, European Communist Parties had already been revaluating the role of the Comintern and Stalin's condemnation of social democracy as the main enemy of revolution. In Germany, his policy had split the opponents of fascism and helped Hitler to power, whilst in France and Spain there had been experiments with popular front alliances. Dimitrov, Togliatti and Gramsci had elaborated Lenin's theory of democratic alliance for advanced industrial conditions, and these principles were debated at the VIIth World Congress of the Comintern in 1935. Congress demanded support for bourgeois intellectuals in their movement against cultural reaction, thus facilitating their transition to the socialist cause in the struggle against fascism. The demand was reiterated at the International Congress on the Defence of Culture in Paris in 1935, at the International Writers' Congress of 1937, and at the KPD's own Congresses in 1935 and 1939. Indeed, this decade saw many bourgeois writers collaborating on international literary magazines published in Moscow, which acted as a centre for discussions between Communists and other cultural workers during Hitler's period of power.

But the cultural policy in the Soviet-Occupied Zone was not simply aimed at winning over a few intellectuals to support working-class hegemony. Germany was not in a revolutionary situation. The more immediate task was to liquidate fascism, and this called for the combined strength of democrats of all kinds. At the international level, the Soviet Union had reason to believe that, having disposed of Hitler, the West would turn its aggression towards the socialist countries. It was thus more important to consolidate a united but politically neutral Germany in mid-Europe, rather than to create an explosive front between the two systems.

Considerations of this nature led the KPD to adopt a conciliatory policy that stressed the progressive potential of national German culture, breaking with the left-wing agit-prop tradition of the Weimar Republic in favour of continuity with the humanist classics. Similarly, the KPD modified its former economic demands in the hope of uniting all sectors of the population which might oppose the rehabilitation of fascists. The plans with which German Communists returned in 1945, plans for schools, publishing, theatre and cinema, and mass cultural activity, were conceived in Moscow in 1943 and 1944 with these aims in mind.

In two essays published in 1943, 'Deutsche Sendung - Ein Ruf an die deutsche Nation' and 'Deutsche Lehre', Johannes R. Becher, far from calling on Germans to break altogether with their sinister history, had urged them to seek out what was progressive in their heritage and to rediscover the humanism of their traditions. This was an appeal that anti-fascist theatre personalities were able to echo when the stages began to be played again - impressively in the circumstances - in June 1945. The editors of *Theater der Zeit*, which appeared from 1946, and Paul Rilla, writing in the *Berliner Zeitung*, stressed the need for a drama that would help provide orientation in rebuilding Germany. They turned to the classics and to new, realist plays on topical subjects, rejecting the fatalistic French existentialism that was predominant in Western zones as 'die Flucht aus der bösen Gegenwart und "Vordergrundwirklichkeit" in die abgründige Innenwelt, in das an sich selbst sich berauschende Ich'. *(22)* Works of the latter kind, which professed to deal with ahistorical human problems, pandered, they felt, to pessimism, unconstructive remorse, and theories of German 'Misere'. Herbert Jhering, broadcasting as head *Dramaturg* of the *Deutsches Theater* for the series *Stimme des Kulturbundes*, spoke of an audience eager to learn from the past:

> Diese Arbeitsmenschen wollen ernst genommen werden. Dieses Publikum hat Lust und Willen, geändert zu werden. Es will über sich selbst hinaus, ist neugierig auf sich selbst . . . Es will sich selbst wieder entdecken . . . Änderung durch Bestätigung, das ist es, was das neue Publikum vom Theater verlangt. *(23)*

The promotion of classical realist works, then, was not just a concession to the taste of bourgeois humanists. The particular approach of those classics which quickly became popular on the stages of the eastern zone - plays by Schiller, Shakespeare, Lessing and Goethe - was felt to correspond to the needs of the day. If theatre's aim was to clarify German history, then there was a case for looking to literature in the realist, rather than the modernist mode, although the application of these categories was sometimes simplified and questionable, as the suspicion addressed towards Brecht testified. Moreover, it was not merely a matter of finding the right texts, but of the interpretation they were given by progressive producers. Productions of eighteenth-century works tended to stress the Enlightenment philosophy of the unity of *Geist* and *Tat*, of acting on one's ethics, rather than succumbing to the more fatalistic conception of *Geist* subjugated by *Macht*, which was more likely to be reflected on western stages. The many *Faust* productions encouraged during Goethe's bi-centenary in 1949 confronted the pathos of Nazi interpretations, which identified the hero as Germany longing for power, by emphasizing the historical conflicts at work. Langhoff's *Iphigenie auf Tauris* and various productions of *Egmont* and *Götz von Berlichingen* were inspired by the same motives. Shakespeare, discredited by the Nazi critic Langenbeck for not portraying the omnipotence of destiny, was rehabilitated as an historical playwright by Gustav von Wangenheim's *Hamlet* in 1945. But the most popular classic of this first post-war season was Wisten's *Nathan der Weise*, at the *Deutsches Theater*, which opened on 7th September at 4.30pm to avoid the curfew. The reasons for this choice, after twelve years of systematic anti-Semitism, were self-evident. Lessing's rationality and Paul Wegener's interpretation of the Jew Nathan, a sympathetic performance without melodrama, combined to reintroduce racial tolerance onto the German stage.

Progressive producers and critics saw the importance of conquering the oversentimentality and phrasemongering rhetoric of Nazi acting methods, although at the same time they recognized the potential which audience empathy could offer their cause. Thus in their reviews they frequently called for a delivery of the words that would enhance the clarity of argument, breaking down the Nazi - and Wilhelminian - tradition of pathos, much in the manner of the Otto Brahm school, but without its fatalism. Jhering was particularly concerned that audiences of the time were so used to the fascists' 'Propagandaaugenblick' that they found it difficult to follow plays where history was shown to be more complicated, with different characters presenting different points of view *(24)*, and he scouted eagerly for young actors who combatted the conventions of 'Phrasenverschleiß':

> Der Wiederaufbau bedeutet: Regeneration der Schauspielkunst aus einem Geiste der Bescheidenheit, bedeutet ihre Erfrischung, Verjüngung, Vereinfachung vom Erlebnis der Zeit her und ihren Anschluß an die geistigen und gesellschaftlichen Kräfte überhaupt, die berufen sind, ein neues Deutschland aufzubauen. *(25)*

Another way of countering the Nazi emphasis on Fate was to draw attention away from a central figure and highlight the social forces influencing the action. In this, anti-fascists were keen to stress the differences between naturalism and realism. If naturalism in the theatre meant concentrating on accurate but superficial detail in movement, speech and setting, realism implied an attitude which should emerge from the production as a whole, based on comprehending the social world and informing the work and its characterizations. Both reasoned and emotional responses, mutually dependent, could legitimately be invoked to reinforce the humanist ethic.

In this context, Stanislavsky's method acting aroused substantial interest. Maxim Vallentin, Ottofritz Gaillard and Otto Lang founded a Stanislavsky School in Weimar in 1945, and Gaillard's book sold widely. Wolf's aphorism, 'der Mensch - das ist die Wahrheit!', epitomized the humanist approach to the dramatic character as a total personality placed in its social environment, and this was the premise adopted by Dr Erich Nippold in the standard manual *Theater und Drama*. Stanislavsky urged his pupils to 'know' their characters in depth and to exploit the verbal and mimetic arts to the full in order to project this total personality. The actor was trained to use detailed knowledge of the character, together with moral and social compassion, to make the drama more accessible to the audience. The humanists applied this method to accentuate the enlightening function of classical drama and of contemporary realism, drawing on the actor's committed, dynamic presentation of a character to encourage the audience to feel, think and act in empathy.

The crucial difference between Stanislavsky's understanding of the total personality and that of Max Reinhardt, revered as he was, lay in its integration of the social context. This appealed to progressive humanists who believed that people could change history and who therefore dismissed ahistorical absolutes, as the editors of *Theater der Zeit* were at pains to point out:

> Wer also . . . in der Seele einer türkischen Haremsfrau der Feudalzeit die gleichen oder nur ähnliche Handlungsmotive sucht . . . wie in der Seele einer modernen, ihren Lebensgefährten frei wählenden Europäerin, der wird in dem (allerdings weit verbreiteten) Irrtum befangen bleiben, es gebe - abgesehen vom grob Körperlichen - 'ewige', 'zeitlose', 'allgemeingültige' Lebensäußerungen. Er wird zwischen Aischylos und Strindberg, zwischen Shakespeare und Kleist, ja letztlich zwischen Sternheim und Meyer-Förster keine weltweiten grundsätzlichen, sondern nur formal-ästhetische Unterschiede erkennen. *(26)*

The language of anti-fascist theoreticians in the forties betrays an affinity with the aesthetics of Schlegel, Schelling, Hebbel and Schiller. It is quite clear from newspapers and magazines of the time that this continuity with early, progressive bourgeois writers far outweighed concern with the proletarian theatre of the twenties. Brecht did not return to Berlin until October 1948, and although he was welcomed as a dramatist with a firm class position his techniques made a more limited impact on the theatre. Similarly, the Soviet works that were produced in the Soviet-Occupied Zone were chosen from the optimistic realist tendency rather than from the more experimental repertoire of Mayakovsky and other formal innovators. This, then, was the climate in which East German drama was born.

The new *Zeitstück* made a difficult entrance. Western critics in particular were scathing of the 'Politisierung der Kunst', and many producers in the eastern zone were also unwilling to encourage young writers concerned with contemporary problems, as that was not a role they were used to playing. Leading anti-fascist critics, and notably the editors of *Theater der Zeit*, often lamented the dearth of good new plays and the inability of aspiring playwrights to find a satisfactory realist form for topical themes. There was an unimaginative obsession with two subjects - the returning soldier, and the condemnation of war - and in April 1947 Erpenbeck commented sadly in his editorial that, of all the plays that had been sent to him, half dealt with the one and half with the other, although there had also been one play about a working woman and one about women's equality. The standard, moreover, was rather low.

The main criticism that progressive essayists and producers were echoing concerned the tendency to moralize in a generalized fashion, without placing the recent past into a historical context which might enable the audience to understand what had happened in social terms. The criticism is endorsed by the GDR's recent reference work, *Die Geschichte der Literatur der Deutschen Demokratischen Republik:*

> Die Zeichnung des Antifaschisten erfaßte vornehmlich sein moralisches und ideologisches Profil, seine verantwortungsbewußte Haltung gegenüber dem gesellschaftlichen Ganzen. Demgegenüber trat die soziale Charakteristik der Bühnenfiguren oftmals zurück: sie unterblieb sogar in vielen Fällen (p.119).

These reservations were extended even to plays that were quite popular in the earliest repertoires, such as Fred Denger's *Wir heißen euch hoffen* (1946) and Annemarie Bostroem's *Die Kette fällt* (1948). Progressive adherents to catharsis and theatre of illusion were certainly in favour of moral clarity and a definite attitude to right and wrong in these works, but they realized nonetheless that empathy without a historical perspective could be dangerous. *Zeitstücke* should not only provide the audience with emotional and moral stimulation, but also explain the social forces that had been at work in Nazi Germany and the issues that had to be decided in the post-war period.

Chapter 3

FRIEDRICH WOLF:
DER SCHARFE GEGENSATZ ZWISCHEN FASCHISMUS UND HUMANISMUS

Until 1949, playwrights who owed their allegiance to socialism were unwilling to choose dramatic themes that might be considered endemic to the Soviet-Occupied Zone. From the pages of *Theater der Zeit*, from newspaper reviews, and from the activities of leading cultural workers in the *Kulturbund* and other suprazonal movements, it is clear that anti-fascists in the East were loathe to do anything that could contribute to a sense of separatism and to partition of the regions under Allied control. Their policy was to see German drama as a whole, applauding commendable plays and productions wherever they appeared. After all, most German writers, whether they were veterans returning from exile or young beginners struggling to express themselves in the moral turmoil, were preoccupied with fascism and its war. That was an experience common to Germans across the country. In any case, the chaos and uncertainty of those years made it difficult enough for authors to project the present, let alone the future course of their society.

When Friedrich Wolf returned from exile in 1945, he, too, was writing plays about complicity with fascism: *Was der Mensch säet* (1945), *Die letzte Probe* (1946) and *Wie Tiere des Waldes* (1947). As a critic, he participated in the debates about contemporary drama throughout Germany. As a cultural politician, he was an active member of the *Kulturbund* and a founder of the new *Volksbühne* and the *Deutsche Film-AG* (DEFA). It was only in 1949, the year of Germany's division, that he completed the script for his first drama to deal with a specifically East German conflict, *Bürgermeister Anna*, which DEFA filmed before its stage première in Dresden in 1950. Non-committally, the play is set in 'ein Dorf in Deutschland' (p.196) in 1946, but in fact the constellation of political forces it depicts is drawn from a proto-socialist context. Its major themes - the replacement of private gain by community interest, and equality of opportunity and social acknowledgement for women - would certainly have been more topical in a society undergoing a transition to socialism. Furthermore, this play marks a departure from certain principles of Wolf's earlier drama, since its function is no longer one of opposition, but one of example.

Wolf started writing as an Expressionist, and even after his conversion to a form of critical realism he adhered to dramatic conventions that were popular with spiritually committed Expressionists: in particular, the trajectory of a hero figure, in conflict with an adversary or adversary forces, towards an ultimate moral decision, for which the author seeks audience identification by emotive means. Wolf valued the immediacy of the relationship between stage and auditorium for the direct impact that his protagonists were able to make on the public. He wanted the decision taking place on stage to be infectious, to rally the audience in emotional and moral support for the commitment it demanded. Like many Expressionists, he believed in the special power of collective experience which the theatre could offer.

Wolf based a theory of catharsis on these early tenets, and he traced its evolution in historical terms. The fear and terror which Aristotle aroused among the Greeks was rooted in their philosophy of Fate, whilst the pity and fear which Lessing sought to elicit during the Enlightenment was influenced by the principle of human tolerance and understanding. For Wolf, in an age which demanded affirmation of the new society in its struggle against the old, catharsis was 'sofortige innere Entscheidung'. *(27)*

Tension was an important factor in creating this catharsis. The plot had to be linear, causal, spinning a web of difficulties around the hero(ine) and so catalysing the decision that would resolve the conflict. The emotional suspense would be fostered by a range of devices to draw sympathy for the protagonist, who would combine a number of agreeable qualities - such as youth, innocence, kindness - and in many cases a romantic plot, which the audience would want to see happily ended, was intertwined with the main conflict.

Wolf intended his audience to view the protagonist in a slightly critical light, and he usually achieved this by attributing ambiguous, curable characteristics such as naivety or petulance. His attitude to the relationship between stage and audience was nothing like as radical as Brecht's. Wolf was a long way from the critical *Rauchertheater* developed by his contemporary and, after the foundation of the GDR, when literature began to disseminate socialist ideas, their differences emerged markedly, as their discussion of *Mutter Courage* testifies. Wolf, who used his protagonists to set an example, felt strongly that Mutter Courage should have recognized her mistakes on stage. For Brecht, it was more important that the spectators themselves would evaluate her mistakes. *(28)* Brecht did not permit his audience the luxury of a passive reception dominated by empathy, but encouraged it, rather, to enjoy sitting in judgement over the aims and motivations of his protagonists. He was less inclined to hide the complexities and contradictions of society and personality than those dramatists who relied heavily on a central conflict between right and wrong, as Wolf openly did:

> Der scharfe Gegensatz zwischen Faschismus und Humanismus, zwischen Kriegstreibern und Friedenskräften ist nicht die Erfindung eines Schwarzweißmalers, sondern eine schwarzweiße Tatsache! *(29)*

For Wolf, too, socialist theatre relations required the emancipation of the audience, but not in its relationship to the stage so much as in the patterns of patronage which governed repertoire and the composition and behaviour of theatre-goers. Through the *Kulturbund* and the *Volksbühnebewegung*, he worked for closer links between the working classes and the theatre. Trade unions were involved in allocating subsidized tickets to their members, and work brigades often visited the theatre together before discussing a play, sometimes with the author present. Playwrights were encouraged to give talks in public halls and factories to bring their work closer to the mass of the people and to hear their views, and working people were invited to pursue their own creative potential by writing or acting themselves. In this way, drama was to become the affair of ordinary people, reflecting their lives and attitudes - although the classics still dominated listings in those earliest years. The concept of theatre for an intellectual or fashionable minority was challenged.

There can be little doubt that these new structural links between working people and the theatre as an ideological apparatus enabled socialist ideas to be propagated and discussed more widely, but this does not justify the assumption, fostered by West German critics during and even after the Cold War, that the stage was simply a transmission belt for SED policies. This approach is inadequate, like the vulgar Marxist 'conspiracy theory', to explain the cultural relationship between the SED, individual writers, and the general population. Playwrights and theatre workers who were members of the party were, quite naturally, influenced in their work by the policy they helped to formulate, but at the same time a dramatic product betrays elements of the author's personal priorities and interpretation of those policies. It would be wrong, too, to counterpose mechanistically the party - with a message to convey - and the rest of the people - who simply receive it. The relationships between the population and the SED, between party members and party leaders, and between German communists and external influences are complex ones, which deserve a fuller analysis than they have enjoyed to date. For the purposes of this investigation I would maintain simply that the reflection and projection of new social images in East German drama, and specifically the definition of women, was affected by the manner in which economic and cultural pressures were perceived by dramatists at the time, both as agents of contingent policy and as particular products of their environment.

Moreover, if drama itself is an index of these perceived priorities, then so is its reception. The themes which capture the attention of reviewers and literary historians illustrate the cultural perspective from which these people write. *Bürgermeister Anna*, for example, was described at the time, and is still described in reference works today, as being 'about' the fight for a school, rural backwardness, a soldier returning from war to a different world, the conflict between old and new social forces, and the capabilities of women in production and administration. *(30)* And yet an analysis of the text also reveals a substantial thread of comment and comedy relating to the treatment of women as sexual objects, personal possessions and domestic slaves, which is barely touched on by the whole critical reception of that play in the GDR. This would suggest that, whether because of social taboos or because of an economistic understanding of female equality, or an unholy alliance of the two, neither producers nor spectators responded to this particular cue.

Indeed, if we look at East German manuals of social psychology, we repeatedly encounter the view that personality develops first and foremost *in production*, which is taken to mean *in paid employment*, and that women only enter the social arena as true subjects of history once they are permitted to take jobs. Wolf's challenge to patriarchal prejudice has been seen, correspondingly, in Anna's socio-economic victory as mayoress, rather than in his criticism of certain male attitudes towards women at the level of personal relationships. The base/superstructure approach which then dominated orthodox Marxism placed the economic moment well to the fore in the dynamics of social change, often to the detriment of ideological reappraisal of more intimate morality. The superior significance which the public world carried in comparison with the private world seemed to reflect the philosophy of the male breadwinner, who comes home seeking refuge from serious problems, with his meals and slippers appearing like clockwork and his lady wife soothing his furrowed brow. The politics of the reproductive sphere - that is, not merely child-bearing, but also the provision of nutrition, recreation and education - are obscured to him, and his domestic life, of which his wife is a *part*, survives in relative isolation from the historical world outside, or at most assumes secondary status.

Friedrich Wolf himself was not economistic in his concern for women's rights, as he had demonstrated before the war. As a doctor, he had, for example, been centrally involved in the campaign against Paragraph 218 of the Weimar Constitution, which prohibited abortion. His play *Cyankali* (1929) took up this question, raising at the same time other male abuses of his heroine's social vulnerability, abuses that he elaborated in *Tai Yang erwacht* (1930). After the war, Wolf was soon demanding the right to abortion again, ostensibly on the grounds that, however much Germany needed children to replace its depleted population, the poverty of the time constituted a threat to infant health. This was no time to bear children who could not be fed and warmed. Wolf's argumentation, like that of the Hamburg women's conference in 1946, was based, not on the concept of an individual woman's right to choose, but on a scale of priorities with an underlying social ethic. Like Bebel, he felt that a society should not encourage the birth of children until it could provide them with a decent environment in which to grow up.

Helen Fehervary is surely a little too hasty in dismissing Wolf when she contends that Anna's liberation only supports the patriarchal structure, swallowing her up, alongside other heroines of those years, into male-orientated production. *(31)* There was, firstly, nothing new about the idea of women with jobs. Both Hete *(Cyankali)* and Tai Yang, Wolf's pre-war heroines, were workers. In the Weimar Republic as in China, it was essential to family survival that these women should work. What was new in *Bürgermeister Anna* was the lesson that working women could develop skills and responsibilities, and also that they might challenge the previous objectives of the productive workforce by fighting to establish their own priorities. Hete and Tai Yang represent the cheap, unskilled labour to which the overwhelming majority of women had been confined by capitalist economics. The war gave women a chance to prove themselves: Anna learns the mason's trade, but in peacetime she has to struggle for acknowledgement of her abilities and her social ideals against the returning male workforce.

Wolf had always observed backward male ideology concerning women. In *Tai Yang erwacht* he portrayed the prejudice of an old trade unionist, Chu, who doubted Tai Yang's capacity to withstand torture:

> CHU: Ob eine Frau das aushält?
> TAI *ruhig:* Frauen gebären Kinder, auch das tut nicht immer gut (p.176).

Chu's disparaging remarks were reinforced for the *Deutsches Theater* production of 1949 in the new version of the seventh scene:

> CHU: Was das Mädchen sagt, verdient keine Erwägung (p.195).

Tai Yang was constructed to refute views of the eternal feminine as something frail. She was courageous and endured great suffering, but her historical conditions did not give her a chance to develop qualities like Anna's of initiative and political leadership. Wolf's characters relate clearly to their social context. That is the key to his kind of realism. Anna's personality indicates the new opportunities opened up to women by a combination of post-war factors known, at the time, as 'die neue Mode'.

The idea of sending women home altogether after the war would have been totally irrelevant in the countryside, where they worked on estates or family smallholdings just as the men did, often contributing back-breaking labour, such as potato-picking. But the war granted women access to skilled trades, and the new social relations afterwards enabled them to put these to permanent good use. Anna's village needs a school, so, instead of being made redundant by a private employer, Anna builds one. The forces that be (personified by the Landrat) have no objections in principle: the only contradiction here is between the district plan and spontaneous initiative at a time of material shortages.

The artistic tradition whereby women have so often represented humanity frustrated in men's corrupt society is related to the ideal of 'motherliness', which is gentle, loving and protective. The ideal is a somewhat virtuous and uncomplicated version of reality, but then it was not constructed by mothers. Along with other socialist writers such as Gorky and Brecht, Wolf subscribed to this reverence for motherhood, which he saw tinged with pain. *(32)* He ascribes the most progressive and caring aspirations, symbolized by the school, to the village women. It is the mothers of today and tomorrow who identify with socialism. Even so, Wolf does not make this identification absolute, and the play begins with a reminder that mothers should not have to be the only parents to take responsibility for their children. The opening passage quickly shows the social contradictions implied in the view that women make progressive demands while men carry out the productive labour:

MUTTER DREWS: Ob wir uns nicht überheben mit dem Bau?	Women are not considered capable of building.
MUTTER RAPP: Sollen sie mitheben! Sind schließlich zur Hälfte auch ihre Kinder.	Shared responsibility should mean shared work.
MUTTER UCKER: 'Zur Hälfte'? Und ich sag: Kaum der kleine Zeh! Was kümmert den Mann so'n Wurm? Gemacht und fertig! Wer aber muß sich's Gehirn dann durchhecheln, wo Schuh und Strümpf hernehmen, wenn die kleinen Bälger im Schnee in Nachbardorfs Schule sollen?	But men do not recognize their responsibility for children.
MUTTER DREWS: Mein Gott, Marie, war doch nie anders; da beißt die Maus keinen Faden ab.	This is held to be an unalterable state of affairs.
MUTTER UCKER *zörnig:* Wer beißt keinen Faden ab? Bist du 'ne Maus und schlupfst gleich ins Loch, wenn der Lehmkuhl, der fette Kater, mit den Augendeckeln klappert? Unser Dorf baut die Schule, und müßt der Hahn die Eier dazu legen, wie deine Anne sagt! (p.197)	This is *not* an unalterable state of affairs. If men will not solve the problem, women will break out of their 'natural' role. Women will build.

However, there are times when Wolf's care in breaking down rigid notions about the two sexes and their social behaviour runs into conflict with some of the farcical situations which he sets up. Comedy can be a conservative force in so far as it frequently arises out of stock incidents. This calls for a certain amount of stereotyping, and a stereotype, which invites lampooning, does not emerge as alterable. Wolf is thus guilty of formal contradictions. For example, Ohm Willem and Hans are two men whose support for Anna undermines the idea that village interests divide according to gender, a polarization that Lehmkuhl incites to disguise his reactionary power bid as a defence of the male sex. And yet Wolf uses a conventional comedy situation, a physical battle between the sexes on the building site, and the audience laughs to see a big, strapping woman put a whimpering man across her knee and spank him. These subsidiary characters, the village men and women, are defined as archetypes. Mutter Ucker, for example, is 'eine stämmige, draufgängerische Person', Mutter Drews is 'etwas müde und abgearbeitet', and Mutter Rapp is 'fest und ruhig' (p.197), and the men are their counterparts. These figures confirm a conventional sense of normality, which the battle scene stands firmly on its head. Its farcical humour derives, in fact, from this very incongruity. Anna, meanwhile, is constructed by Wolf to discredit the suspicion that women's emancipation means a straightforward reversal of patriarchal supremacy. Lehmkuhl's language insinuates matriarchal tyranny - 'Weiberwirtschaft' (p.218), 'kreuz und quer kommandiert' (p.208), 'am Bauplatz angetreten' (p.208) - because the concept of equality in relationships is alien to him and does not serve his purpose. His language is an effective tactic in worrying the men, whose proud masculinity causes them to dread subjugation as a slight upon their dignity. Anna and the young couple, Hans and Ursel, try to prove that the 'neue Mode' is comradeship, not subservience.

A similar contradiction arises from Wolf's treatment of flirtation. Anna teases Ohm Willem in scene i by suggesting that she might flirt with Lehmkuhl in order to obtain his tractor, an idea which Willem finds natural. In itself the incident is comic because of the way Anna provokes the jealousy of this elderly gallant. But later, in the more serious scene iv, Anna condemns flirtatious behaviour as a relic of the corrupt past. A theatre company anxious to draw attention to outmoded gender-orientated practices of this kind might have attempted to highlight such discrepancies to make an audience feel discomfort at its own laughter. But if this was ever tried during the play's popularity, it was certainly never noted for posterity.

In *Bürgermeister Anna*, Wolf broke with his previous tragic mode, and he seems to have been influenced in his transition to comedy by the satirical tradition. The political context for this shift was the beginning of the *Aufbau* period in the GDR, when Wolf, along with many of his contemporaries, was attempting to replace the vacuum left by fascism with progressive ideas. People needed new perspectives if bleak fatalism was to be overcome, and so the new culture was optimistic. The desire to promote socialism against a backcloth of anti-communism, a desire which overshadowed concern for internal socialist debate, was most widely expressed in an exemplary mode of literature, through a positive hero(ine).

Wolf develops three brands of comedy in *Bürgermeister Anna*. The farcical function is borne by the subsidiary villagers, but the protagonist and antagonist each provide their own distinctive humour. On the one hand, Anna's wit is one of the features that endear her to the audience as a positive heroine of the exemplary type, and it brings a cheerful levity to the play. Lehmkuhl, on the other hand, is the butt of satire, which, in Wolf's subsequent definition, calls for total rejection of its victim. *(33)* Satire, he suggested, took as its material 'die typischen Zufallserscheinungen', whereas pure comedy 'meist einzelne kleinere menschliche Schwächen, Torheiten und Verdrehtheiten lachend entlarvt und zu einem versöhnenden Schluß gelangt'. This means that Anna and Lehmkuhl cannot have equal dramatic status, because Lehmkuhl is a caricature. Although his actions are cunning, his reasoning lacks sophistication, and that is significant on two counts. First, his extremity, such as his absurd behaviour in the coffin and his desperate recourse to arson, expose his objectives to the otherwise gullible peasants. This catalyses the reactions of the men in general, and Jupp in particular, and leads all too easily to a happy ending. Anna is able to triumph over reaction and to be reconciled with her beloved, and in this way succeeds as a female in office, vindicating Wolf's belief in female potential:

> Wer hätte zum Beispiel gedacht, daß zwanzig- bis fünfundzwanzigjährige junge Mädchen die Arbeit eines früheren amtsgewaltigen Dorfpaschas heute als Bürgermeisterinnen bewältigen könnten? Daß solch ein junges hellköpfiges Mädel, wie die Anna in meinem Stück, mit einer ganzen Männerhorde von Haustyrannen, kriegsgeschwollenen Heimkehrern und anderen Herren der Schöpfung mit so viel List, Klugheit und Charme fertig würde? *(34)*

Anna 'proves' her ability to administrate, but it is not entirely her doing that the wayward men are tamed. Confrontation is ultimately avoided, apart from initial verbal battles and minor skirmishes, as Lehmkuhl destroys his own case. Anna wins her battle against the district authorities, but Lehmkuhl is conveniently rendered harmless by his crime.

Secondly, the reactionary ideology expressed by the former landowner on the subject of women cannot fail to antagonize the audience. It is aggressive in its Biblical rhetoric, its lies and sneering epithets, and it scarcely conceals his ulterior motive: to regain his old power. Moreover, the men who are swayed by him are negative. Most of them are archetypally stupid and narrow-minded, while Jupp is motivated by misguided jealousy. Lehmkuhl's views are so crude that they could never persuade an audience, and he condemns himself further by blatant immoral outrages, such as offering Jupp money to buy a prostitute. His attitude to women is cynical, which, in effect, means that anything he says or does will be identified as wrong, without any discussion or practical illustration of *why*, for example, prostitution and pin-ups are undesirable in socialism.

Lehmkuhl's views are 'proved' wrong where women's economic role is concerned. He exhorts the village men to confine their wives to the home, but events in the play argue that women can perform useful and humane tasks in the community, and that their status should be higher than that of a dog or a domestic slave. In fact, women's new role in society makes them more interesting companions for men.

The battle of ideas regarding a woman's place also takes place at the level of verbal debates in the confrontations between Anna and Jupp. From the perspective of the audience, Anna has the advantage. She is the central figure and is seen to do good from the very beginning, whereas Jupp makes a late entrance and is hampered, as a newcomer, by his inability to comprehend certain changes. Anna's patient reasoning and social vision make her more attractive than the boastful young warrior. Jupp nevertheless manages to pose some crucial questions to Anna that make her consider the dilemmas of her own position: must she choose to be either an overworked mayoress or a loving wife, and will any children of hers ever make use of the school she is fighting to build? In breaking with habit and constructing a protagonist who is fundamentally positive throughout the play, Wolf creates a new function: Jupp is neither protagonist nor antagonist, but moves between these two characters generating further conflicts. On the one hand, Anna and Lehmkuhl are static poles in the main contradiction between the new and the old, and it is Jupp who personifies the reappraisal and commitment Wolf is asking of his public. On the other, Jupp also has a fruitful contribution to make in putting Anna's ideals to the test.

Jupp is not a caricature like Lehmkuhl, although his language illustrates patriarchal values. Women, for example, should be possessed and dominated:

> Was ein richtiger Fahrer ist, der liebt sein Fahrzeug wie 'ne Braut und gibt es nicht einem anderen ab (p.208).

He treats Anna like a military objective:

> Wir haben schon andere Festungen genommen (p.209).

Her civic function is at first a joke and then a perversion of normality:

> Haben die Weiber die Hosen an und stecken die Männer in Weiberröcken? (p.217).

In any case, if Anna can do the job, it must be easy:

Das kann wohl jeder (p.211).

He finds it hard to envisage Anna having interests of a productive or political kind, and when she warns him that there have been changes in his absence, he can only think of one reason:

Bist mit 'nem andern gegangen? (p.210).

Jupp, in his resentment, is natural prey for Lehmkuhl, especially as the landowner bribes him with the prestige position of tractor driver. But Jupp is not a hardened patriarch. His first jealous inability to acknowledge Anna's skills and aspirations does not mean that he is prepared to reduce women to sexual commodities, as Lehmkuhl would like. In fact, he cannot tolerate weak, submissive women such as Anna's sister, Grete, even though he uses her to threaten Anna with infidelity. Jupp is therefore able to learn to respect Anna as he watches her at work.

It is a difficult battle for Jupp, which Anna can only win if she breaks down the illusions - which her defiance of Jupp to some extent encourages her to share - about the irrelevance of emotional needs to a woman with political responsibility. There is much discussion of the idea that, for women as well as men, personality unfolds socially, in politics and production. When Jupp returns, Anna insists that the war has changed her, that being a mayoress is an extension of her social drives, and that Jupp cannot have his old Anne back simply by divesting her of office. She tries to explain her wartime experiences to show how the need to work opened new dimensions to her personality. When Jupp's attitudes begin to modify, he justifies his desire for Anna to leave her job by arguing that this would enable her to relinquish a great burden - a stark contrast to his earlier disdain. Later still he confesses that he was motivated by wanting her to have more time for him. By this stage he has begun to see that political and domestic life might co-exist, but Anna has to reaffirm yet again the value of social commitment:

JUPP: Entweder ist man Frau und Weib, oder man ist ein Stein und Bürgermeisterin!
ANNA: Weshalb denn gleich 'entweder - oder', Jupp? Und 'pfui, ein Stein!' und 'zum Teufel, Bürgermeisterin!' Jeder Mensch hat doch sein Leben, Jupp, und muß sein Leben achten; sonst ist er nichts wert (p.273).

If the love plot is to end positively, which it does, then Jupp must face the fact that female personality cannot be truncated:

Anne, Mädel, Bürgermeisterin . . . geht das denn alles zusammen? (p.281).

Wolf does not use his play to argue morally that women who are only housewives are repressed, or that they should extend their interests. His subjects are women whose wartime experiences *have* changed their self-image and their expectations. However, not all the women in the play have Anna's freedom to make new claims on their menfolk, as Mutter Haverkorn complains:

Meinen Mann will ich! Jawohl, 'die Schule' . . . ich weiß, aber was nutzt mir die Schule wenn's eigene Haus auseinanderfällt? (p.269).

Old attitudes die hard. Youth and progress are formally linked in the play. At the other end of the scale, therefore, Wolf offers his audience Hans and Ursel. Hans is a young worker, resettled from a town, and he and Ursel already have a relationship in the new fashion, based on mutual respect and comradeliness. The character list given by Wolf actually indicates that Ursel is older than Hans by two years, which is, in itself, a break with traditional patterns, whereby men have the authority of superior age, however slight.

It is worth noting the - albeit cursory - treatment of housework in Wolf's play, simply because the subject is so rarely touched upon in East German literature. Although Anna and Jupp, Hans and Ursel do not make an issue of their prospective domestic arrangements in their new relationships, two indications emerge of Wolf's radical views. First, the devolution of all menial chores to the female sex is set in a critical light in the scenes with Lehmkuhl and the village men. Secondly, the communal stew on the building site symbolizes the possibility of socialized cooking. Considering the vast quantity of person-hours consumed in privatized housework in the GDR *(35)*, the literary silence which surrounds the activity itself indicates that the question has not provoked the level of debate reached in Russia after 1917. And yet this apparently mundane matter is a major factor in women's emancipation. Even today, despite newly evolving attitudes, the energy expended by East German women on domestic tasks is not unrelated to their small presence in high-level positions - small, that is, given their legislated equality. The cultural image of women's lives, which includes, alongside other manifestations of ideology, their literary image, has not been challenged so fundamentally in this respect as one might have anticipated. Wolf's play is unusual, particularly for those early years, in broaching the subject, just as it is unusual in broaching other elements of the phenomenon now linguistically acknowledged in the West as 'sexism' (discrimination between individuals on the basis of their gender), a word for which there is, to date, no equivalent in East German parlance.

The general failure of theatres, critics and audiences to respond to these issues would seem to be symptomatic of a contemporary lack of interest in tackling certain female problems from an historical standpoint. Wolf's references to the sexual exploitation of women, which reveal a comprehensive acquaintance with Bebel's book, fell on stony ground. However, as a young countrywoman seizing the opportunity of socialist revolution in agriculture to realize her productive and political emancipation, Bürgermeister Anna was the founder of a new clan of dramatic protagonists.

Chapter 4

ERWIN STRITTMATTER AND HELMUT SAKOWSKI: *UNSERE BÄUERINNEN - EINE GROSSE KRAFT BEI DER SOZIALISTISCHEN UMGESTALTUNG DER LANDWIRTSCHAFT (36)*

The social grouping for whom the new system was undoubtedly to bring most changes were the women in the countryside. Formerly, they had not only been the prime victims of feudal relations on the big estates which dominated the area of the GDR geographically and politically, they had also been condemned by material hardship and conservative patriarchal ideology to backbreaking drudgery in the home, unable to discover even the small independence afforded by a factory job. Now, the rural economy was transformed in two gigantic steps. First of all, in 1945, the landowners were expropriated and the big estates were divided up amongst labourers and new settlers from the East to farm privately. A few years later came the collectivization movement, which lasted until 1961. At the same time, women were granted the same rights as men to work the land, to receive a full statutory education and to enter new, increasingly technical careers, and to participate in the structures of administrative control. The outcome was both an overall improvement in standards of living in the countryside, and a challenge to the traditionally low status of country women.

Correspondingly, there was a plethora of plays built up around the figure of a peasant woman learning to take responsibility and make decisions. The better known are Erwin Strittmatter's *Die Holländerbraut* (1960), Helmut Sakowski's *Die Entscheidung der Lene Mattke* (1959) and *Steine im Weg* (1962), and Fred Reichwald's *Das Wagnis der Maria Diehl* (1959). In all these, the political choices made by the woman protagonist are intertwined with very personal motivations, so that there is no suggestion by the author that socialism is right in itself: these women adopt a socialist stance because it is right for them in certain circumstances. But what is quite particular about the way in which political and personal behaviour are linked in these female dramatic characters is their construction around a love element, from which the whole framework of these plays is derived - the plot, the tension, and the constellation of social forces.

The literary convention which defined women in terms of their love for a man, long before the advent of socialism, was still widespread in the GDR in the fifties and early sixties, since these years provided little scope for the female function in drama to diversify. Thematically, the period was still dominated by the rejection of militarism and imperialism. Plays about the war, such as those of Hedda Zinner and Alfred Matusche, revolved around male action - with the exception of *Ravensbrücker Ballade* in its female setting. Like Rainer Kerndl in *Schatten eines Mädchens* (1961), Matusche used young women primarily to personify the ideals of peace and internationalism and to epitomize the enormous suffering of peoples oppressed by the Nazis. In *Die Dorfstraße* (1955), for example, the Polish girl Duschenka loses her eyes to the blinded German officer Ernst in a brutal surgical operation, but beyond this Duschenka plays little part. She is a symbol.

The Cold War provided considerable material for works of all genres, which combined suspense and adventure with political concern at developments in the West: the foundation of the North Atlantic Treaty Organization, nuclear tests, the banning of the West German KPD and the rehabilitation of fascists in the Federal Republic. But these works, too, reflected an overwhelmingly male world, partly because women's emancipation was not topical in this Western climate, and partly because of the conventions which favour masculine protagonists in the composition of thrillers. This trend is illustrated by writers such as Paul Herbert Freyer, Hans Lucke, Hans Pfeiffer, Slatan Dudow (alias Stephan Brodwin), Gustav von Wangenheim, Harald Hauser, Rolf Schneider and many others. There are occasionally noteworthy women in their plays, including Schneider's Frau Wulf in *Der Mann aus England* (1962), Hauser's Eleonore in *Weißes Blut* (1960), Pfeiffer's Yuki in *Laternenfest* (1957), and, inevitably, Ethel in Maximilian Scheer's documentary drama *Die Rosenbergs* (1953), but they are subsidiaries in the masculine realms of armies and political power.

On the home front, the *Zeitstück* addressed itself mainly to the world of industrial production, which was also predominantly male at that time. Thus, in the early plays of Heiner Müller, who was later to raise so many questions about women's emancipation, the patterns of characterization reflect women's absence from certain social roles. Women are found either in economic positions traditionally confined to their sex, such as secretary or canteen worker, or otherwise as somebody else's wife or girlfriend. It was the farmland that provided an early economic context in which women could be seen radically defying their traditional roles. However, even here, female protagonists continued to think and function in terms of a relationship to a man, if only by rebelling against that relationship. The 'Holländerbraut' Hanna Tainz, Maria Diehl and Lene Mattke all need to escape the tyranny imposed by loyalty to a lover or husband in order to realize their own interests - and those of the community. Even the independent Lisa Martin, in *Steine im Weg*, is obliged to come to terms with an old liaison before she can appreciate her new social position (and start a new, progressive marriage). So, although these women are portrayed as competent workers or socialist administrators, the formal structure in which they operate is still anchored in a romance (or, in the case of Lene Mattke, a strained marriage). Of course, love plots were often used in plays where the protagonists were men, not least because of the value of sentimental interest for guiding an audience's sympathies and involving it in the tension set up by amorous desires, but the direction of a hero's love is rarely so fundamental to his personality as the attachments of a heroine are to her choices and actions.

In this respect, Strittmatter's *Die Holländerbraut*, while it constitutes an attack on feudal and fascist abuses of women, does not produce a heroine who lives up to the self-assured, independent promise of the subsidiary women in his earlier play *Katzgraben*. This first drama was originally submitted by its young author to the jury of the third World Festival of Youth and Students. It was rejected, but Hans Marchwitza mentioned it to Brecht and aroused his interest. Brecht encouraged Strittmatter to rework the text with his support, and in 1953 it was performed at the *Berliner Ensemble*.

The central action concerns the class interests of three farmers, Kleinschmidt, Mittelländer and Großmann, and the provision of new amenities to their village. Although the characters who carry the plot are the men - the three farmers, especially Kleinschmidt, and party secretary Steinert - their wives are by no means shadows. Brecht was enthusiastic about Strittmatter's ability to demonstrate the newness of his society in a tangible and dialectical manner, using vivid and imaginative language. In a review article for *Sinn und Form (37)* and during rehearsals *(38)*, he illustrated his approval with Bäuerin Kleinschmidt, 'eine der schönsten Figuren der neueren deutschen Literatur' (p.398). She is both a representative of her class and sex, and yet clearly differentiated, progressive, and yet riddled with contradictions.

Her initiatives are striking. She persuades other women to order beer in the village pub like their menfolk, and she sends her daughter Elli away to study land economy, even though she desperately needs help on the farm and in the house. Strittmatter's skill in portraying how people's opinions are swayed by immediate self-interest to the point of self-contradiction is wielded on Bäuerin Mittelländer, who approves of the *Freie Deutsche Jugend* (FDJ) when it shields the maid from her husband's advances, only to pour her wrath on that organization when it protects the girl from an unpaid increase in her working week. It is the wife, in the extended version *Katzgraben 1958*, who takes the decision for her wavering husband to join the collective when the economic balance of forces has changed. Like Bäuerin Kleinschmidt, she functions very much as a verbal spur to her husband.

Throughout East German dramatic history, there has been a convention which uses female characters in a pedagogical role to influence the views of men. The reverse is rare. The trend begins with *Bürgermeister Anna* and is found again and again, in plays about collectivization, about the choice between East and West, about commitment to socialist production, and about humane relationships. Women, who have been the victims of a twofold oppression, become the visionaries because of the broader range of social and personal problems which they experience, problems related not only to productive and political life, but also to the home and the children, private relationships, and welfare services. The wider spectrum of their aspirations therefore makes them attractive to dramatists as voices enlightening the men on a number of issues. However, the convention also has its roots in historical images of women. One is the view expressed in the old adage that behind every great man there is a woman. In other words, it is the men who act in society, and the women who give encouragement and guidance. Another of these images derives from the attribution of humanitarian instincts to women. Since socialist society accepts the premise that women are as much the architects of their world as men, with the same rights and duties, the social basis for these images has to some extent been removed. Nonetheless, the images themselves persist as a cultural force.

Elli Kleinschmidt, although a minor character, fulfils this role in *Katzgraben*. Like many young women in plays about collectivization, she is in love with the wrong man. But instead of rejecting him for a more suitably progressive admirer, as her friends recommend, Elli takes Steinert's advice and sets out to change her lover. Hermann first notices the agriculturalist Elli when she returns from her town studies. To his mind, she has grown more sophisticated and attractive, whereas before she was too ordinary for him. Elli's trump card is that Hermann's one ambition is to drive tractors. (It seems from *Bürgermeister Anna, Katzgraben, Frau Flinz* and *Die Bauern* this was a popular aspiration for country lads in the early years of the GDR, and that it carried the same virile prestige that is nowadays associated by our own advertising media with sports cars and certain blends of tobacco.) If Hermann wants access to tractors, he must leave his employer Großmann and team up with the collective. Elli is thus able to entice him away from the reactionary camp.

The development of the characters in *Die Holländerbraut* is less dialectical. The forces are polarized in more absolute terms and retain their loyalties, more or less, throughout the play. However, Strittmatter continues to be adept at showing how people base their actions on immediate aims, which can fluctuate from one situation to the next, and then attempt to justify themselves in philosophical terms. This is not necessarily hypocritical, but is part of the author's explanation of historical motivations, of people's acceptance or rejection of circumstances. When Erdmann's mother revises her attitude to Hanna - now that the milkmaid has become a mayoress - she reveals herself to be devious and two-faced. Hanna, on the other hand, by twisting Malten's words and misinterpreting Gorky in order to substantiate her belief in Erdmann, simply emerges as misguidedly but sympathetically naive. Suspense in the play is geared towards her recognition that the man she loves is beyond redemption and an incorrigible enemy of the good society, and that trust is not an antidote for the abuse of power. Hanna herself is not seen progressing towards a commitment to socialism as such. In Act I, she is apolitical but a Communist's daughter. When she returns from the concentration camp after the war, in Act II, she is suddenly a mayoress, presumably on the grounds of her wartime suffering and the legend that has been attached to her past, ironically, by the villagers: to divert attention from his own culpability, the fascist lieutenant Erdmann accuses the pregnant Hanna of sleeping with a Dutch prisoner; Hanna is duly punished for her crime against the fatherland, and loses her child in the camp; in her absence, Hanna becomes a symbol of internationalism and romantic resistance to fascism. But although mayoress Hanna really is dedicated to the ideals of socialism, she is politically ingenuous and requires the watchful eye of her pragmatic counterpart 'Onkel' Malten to carry out her office.

The figure of Hanna Tainz is constructed so as to highlight her naivety and trust. It is not only the village legend that bestows on her a romantic aura: she herself is a dreamer, singing folk melodies that are rich in sentimental imagery and even superstition. Although we are informed in the first scene that Hanna was an outstandingly intelligent child, this is not a strength of her character which emerges in the play itself. She is shown much less frequently than Anna Drews exercising her mayoral functions, and even when she is, it is her human charity which is emphasized, and she displays few signs of initiative or competence. She can use logic badly when trying to escape from a lost argument, as, for example, when she unfairly woos the support of the other women by maintaining that her application for Erdmann to receive a smallholding is being rejected because of her sex. On another occasion, when the fortuitous arrival of a Soviet officer enables her to extract illegally hoarded potatoes from Klögling and Dingel, she flippantly attributes her victory to her lucky swallows, brushing aside Malten's warning to deal more severely with the enemies of the collective. When she accompanies the group seeking out spare bedding for refugees, she remains in the background, except to ask, significantly, about the bed which is actually Erdmann's. All in all, Hanna is not a good advertisement for female administrators, unlike Anna, who is shown carting bricks and mortar, studying plans and stamping documents with all the weight of naturalist properties to underline her capability. Murawski exclaims twice that Hanna is an angel, and this would appear to be her primary recommendation.

Strittmatter's mayoress, therefore, has all the qualities of an administering cherub, no head for investment, and an exceptional determination to defend a man who has subjected her to the most barbaric cruelty. Ultimately, Hanna learns from her experience to overcome her belief in Erdmann's conversion and to appreciate Gorky's real message: not that goodness is an essence of the human soul waiting to be unleashed, but that people can develop their potential for goodness only if structures of power and oppression are abolished. She comes to understand how strong the enemies of socialism still are.

To some extent, the polarization of forces compared with *Katzgraben* reflects a change in the climate of collectivization: the diplomatic (if controversial) strategy of winning over the Hermanns - the middle-ground - finally gave way in 1960 to a final onslaught on the hostile, obstructive Erdmanns. But Strittmatter's fundamental interest in *Die Holländerbraut* seems to have been the more philosophical relationship between humanitarianism and socialist power, and it was to explore this, rather than in a desire to show women in a new political capacity, that he chose his female protagonist. Hanna's faith in human nature and her compassion are, after all, traditionally held to be feminine characteristics. At the same time, Hanna's womanhood makes her vulnerable in a particularly horrendous way, for the man who seduces her is also responsible for her internment and the death of her first child. Her feelings for him, which lead her to become pregnant a second time when she should be treating him with suspicion, are thus presented as all the more striking and questionable. Nevertheless, Hanna's trust is still cast in a sympathetic light by the last line of the song with which the play ends: 'Wer liebt, der sollte mich verstehn' (p.171). The implication is that, while socialists see right and wrong in terms of social options, teaching that injustice can only be eradicated if the power to do evil is removed, a loving nature and a desire to believe in all men (and women) are still attractive and commendable qualities.

The figure of Hanna Tainz emerges strongly as a symbolical construction, and for this reason I would disagree with the analysis of *Die Holländerbraut* in *Die Geschichte der Literatur der Deutschen Demokratischen Republik* (p.380) which cites the play, alongside Sakowski's *Steine im Weg*, as a pacesetter for improved psychological differentiation in the drama of the sixties. This interpretation correctly observes that Hanna is not portrayed primarily as a representative of her class and that Strittmatter pays detailed attention to the individual development of his characters in general. But the heroine herself is not constructed as a social personality in the way that Sakowski's characters, and Strittmatter's own subsidiaries, are. Her uniqueness as a dramatic character derives to a far greater extent from her archetypal features. Hanna is not drawn from the author's observations of contemporary womanhood in a realist fashion: she is an artistic metaphor of feminine humanitarianism.

In contrast, the other characters act according to certain social laws. The property-owning men are attributed reactionary ideas about women: Klögling uses the cliché of women as naggers against Die Löffler (p.170), and Dingel and Klögling poke fun at the female administration:

> DINGEL: Du lädst uns von der Feldarbeit aufs Amt? Ja, gab's das früher, wo hier ein Mann und Bauer Bürgermeister war?
> KLÖGLING: Was gilt hier auf dem Ladungsschreiben - Gemeindesiegel oder Vogeldreck?
> DINGEL: Geht's etwa um die Hundesteuer? Mein zweiter Hund ist angemeldet, liebes Kind.
> KLÖGLING: Vielleicht ist es nicht aufnotiert bei dir. Ein bißchen durcheinander durchs Regieren - Frauenwirtschaft?
> HANNA: Stellt euch nicht dumm, Gevattern, um Kartoffeln geht's.
> BEIDE BAUERN: Jes, um Kartoffeln!
> KLÖGLING: Im Herbste ist Kartoffelernte, nicht im März, Mädel (pp.131-2).

The fascists, Erdmann and his father, are particularly exploitative in their attitude towards women, and their views are shared by Erdmann's mother, whose class identification rules out any feelings of sisterhood. Both parents approve of their son tampering with the affections of peasant girls such as

Hanna, but the girls are 'Huren' when they lose their virginity, whereas Erdmann is absolved as long as he marries into money or land. Erdmann treats Hanna as a plaything. He shows no regard for her sincere feelings, and is clearly bored when they meet on the symbolic island in the first Act. He hopes she might lose the baby by having to swim through freezing water: 'So wehrt sich die Natur gegen das Unnatürliche' (p.117). His ideas of what is natural, which he uses to justify his actions, are grotesque distortions, contrasting sharply with the selfless assistance and advice which the Dutch anti-fascist Jan van Straaten offers the stranded Hanna.

Erdmann speaks for feudal family ideology when he interprets Hanna's desire to keep the child as a manoeuvre to acquire rights over the land which he is to inherit. The hereditary system of property transfer accounts for the connexion in Erdmann's mind between children and ownership. Illegitimate children are a problem because they disrupt the concept of the family as a natural ownership unit.

But Erdmann's continued desire for Hanna after the war is not always in accordance with his class interests. Unusually, it is also explicitly sexual. He rationalizes his attempt to make her pregnant again - both to neutralize her politically and to assure his hold on her - by quoting a book he has read:

> Am Weib hat alles eine Lösung - Mutterschaft (p.150).

He is clearly thinking of Nietzsche *(39)*, recommended reading for serious Nazis such as himself:

> Alles am Weibe ist ein Rätsel, und alles am Weibe hat eine Lösung: sie heißt Schwangerschaft.

Erdmann's parents encourage this patriarchal ideology. His mother argues, rather like Jupp, 'So Weiber wollen im Sturm genommen sein' (p.146). Frau Erdmann is politically cunning and sees Hanna's conquest as the key to routing the new forces. This leads her to start justifying her son's fresh courtship with false generosity:

> Warum solln nicht auch kleine Leute hier und da was Edles haben? Der Herrgott hat die Gaben nicht immer ganz gerecht verteilt (p.146).

That amounts to her unconvincing attempt to adapt to the new social climate, at least superficially. In fact, she is a vehement spur to the (male) counter-revolutionary forces who try to sabotage the collective.

Erdmann's mother is one of a number of forceful subsidiary roles for women, who are especially well represented in Act I, when most of the men are away at war. There is a large group of village women working the land, supervised by two Nazi ladies who subsequently disappear: the vindictive Lehrersfrau and Schufnarski, whose dedication to the Nazi cause is comically and sinisterly expressed in her slogan, 'Jede Rübe für die Front!' These two lead the public ceremony to shame Hanna, instigated hypocritically by the Erdmanns with the connivance of the Baron. The Baronin and her husband make a brief but comical appearance in flight at the end of the war, and the Baronin, a provincial parody of the governor's wife in Brecht's *Der kaukasische Kreidekreis* (1948), is shown to be just as selfishly frantic to keep her valuable clothes and jewellery. On the side of the lesser peasants, Die Löffler distinguishes herself through her defiance of the Nazis during Hanna's ostracism (although none of the labouring women spit on Hanna when ordered to), and later she participates actively and argumentatively in the collective. Although Wiesel, the reactionaries' spy, tries to exploit her dissatisfaction to lure her into the enemy camp, Die Löffler proves herself to be an instinctively class-conscious member of the committee.

A quieter but equally individualized character is Die Murawski. As a compassionate and charitable figure, she is entrusted with leadership of the *Frauenausschuß*, but, rather like Hanna, she tends to be self-effacing. She is indirectly linked with Hanna through the tenderness between the mayoress and Stefan Murawski, her child, who is entranced by the 'Holländerbraut' legend. It is not until Act IV, scene i that Hanna learns of Die Murawski's past: she represents yet another case, like Hanna herself and the other examples that she quotes (p.136), of a peasant girl seduced by her wealthy employer and abandoned when pregnant:

> Ich ging in Hoffnung - von einem sogenannten Herrn . . . Und bis mein Bauch schwoll, war ich seine Sonnenrose. Ich sähe so poetisch aus, so sagte er. Das ist für Leute unsres Schlags ein Mangel. Dann war er weg (p.152).

Murawski shows her strength as a woman in a different way from the vociferous Löffler, for she decided to bring up her child to be a good person, which in her position required determination and spirit:

> Erst greinte ich, doch nach dem Weinen wurd ich wieder herb - so, wie's uns ansteht. Was hatte dieser Laff mit meinem Kind zu tun? Er gab den Anstoß, aber ich gab Säft' und Kräfte hin. Herunter mit der Sonnenrose! Ich ging von dannen. Seitdem wohn ich hier. Ich zieh mein Kind, so wie mir's richtig scheint (p.152).

Murawski's words unwittingly give Hanna the courage to break a little further away from Erdmann, even though she has not been able to obtain an illegal abortion. When she stands accused of carrying his child by the committee, she professes her independence at least with regard to parenthood:

> Es ist *mein* Kind. Dafür, daß es nicht wie der Vater wird, steh ich euch ein (p.158).

When Erdmann finally exposes himself as a counter-revolutionary, Hanna is able to denounce him without feeling bound to him through this second child.

At the time when this play was written, abortion was not permitted. However, it seems from Hanna's attempt to procure an abortion by the village wisewoman and from her quarrel with Malten that this policy did not meet with unmitigated acceptance among progressives. Malten is divided:

> MALTEN *wild:* Das Kind, das wirst du nicht bekommen!
> HANNA: Denkt die Partei so?
> MALTEN *ruhiger:* Dein Pate dachte so (p.158).

A complex and original phenomenon in this context is the village witch and abortionist, old woman Feimer. Although there is, tactfully, no suggestion that Feimer is continuing her practice under socialism, her function was certainly crucial in an age when rich and powerful men felt free to seduce poor girls without marrying them. Feimer is not a fairy-tale *Kräuterweib;* she is fully aware of her social role as an alternative medical service in a world where wealth can purchase what its own laws forbid. While she is overtly mercenary, Feimer does not emerge as immoral. The irony of Erdmann's request that she should *not* abort Hanna's child is not lost on her. Strittmatter certainly uses this character as part of his attack on the treatment of peasant women by feudal landowners, and it is also possible that he intended her to raise questions about abortion under socialism, since her conversation with Hanna is highly ambiguous. On the one hand, Feimer quotes all the best reasons why Hanna should feel ashamed to ask for a termination of her pregnancy: abortion is murder; Hanna herself has said there will be no poverty in the new society, so the child would be guaranteed its material existence; not loving the father does not mean she cannot love the child (p.155). But, on the other hand, all these arguments are alienated by Feimer's previous conversation with Erdmann, from which we know that she is being rewarded handsomely for her refusal, that she has never before had moral qualms about abortion, and that she is afraid that Hanna might report her to the authorities for her illegal practice if she complies. Nevertheless, whatever the author's opinions might be, Hanna herself, having already lost one baby, does not really want this abortion, and Feimer's arguments, whatever their motivation, contribute to her decision to raise the child:

> DIE ALTE FEIMER: Was fragt die Stute nach dem Hengst, hat sie ein Fohlen? Sie säugt es, hegt es, liebt es.
> HANNA: Bin ich ein Tier?
> DIE ALTE FEIMER: Nein, nein, du hast Vernunft, so hörte ich dich reden, und willst deshalb das Würmchen, das dir zuwächst, morden.
> HANNA *springt auf:* Hör auf! *Sie rennt hinaus* (p.155).

Hanna will follow the course taken by the admirable Murawski, joining the ranks of single mothers that were to tread the boards over subsequent decades. The abortion is avoided, and Hanna's allegorical charity and compassion remain unsullied.

Die Holländerbraut has many qualities as a play. Strittmatter combines within it a poetic atmosphere and a sense of social danger, a representation of historical forces and a respect for the individual features of subsidiary characters. From the mid-fifties, there had been repeated calls from cultural politicians and critics for an increased dimension to literary characterization. This was intended to counter the influence of a didactic mode which accompanied the mushrooming of small, often lay, cultural groups who toured workplaces and schools with short, starkly political programmes. The number of *Produktionsstücke* also multiplied, and these, too, bore many characteristics of agitprop. They drew heavily for material, as did the prose of the period, on contemporary news stories concerning the economic achievements of working people, emphasizing their historical significance rather than the personalities involved, and unsocialist attitudes and practices were quite often presented with sectarian intolerance. The *Geschichte der Literatur der Deutschen Demokratischen Republik* later established a critical distance from these works in the following terms:

> In erster Linie aber waren die künstlerischen Mängel im Zeitstück der fünfziger Jahre weltanschaulich bedingt. Durch Faktoren, die eine schöpferische Entwicklung der marxistisch-leninistischen Theorie hemmten, erschienen die Überlegenheit und die weitere Vervollkommnung des Sozialismus als eine statische Größe, was zu Konfliktarmut, geradlinig abrollender Handlung und stereotyper Charakterzeichnung führte. Tendenzen des Ökonomismus und damit die Unterschätzung des subjektiven Faktors wirkten sich gerade auf die dramatische Darstellung der Gegenwart ungünstig aus (p.371).

Drama was also shifting towards greater psychological differentiation with the eventual consolidation of socialist forces. As it became less urgent to argue for the new society against the old, so the tendency diminished for black-and-white polarizations based on class position. The theory prevalent in the period from the early sixties was that the GDR had become a socialist society with no antagonistic classes, so that any contradictions which did arise were soluble within the terms of that society. The implication was that contradictions derived from failure on the part of individuals to recognize socialism as the means to achieving their personal goals. This belief was accompanied by growing interest in the socialist citizen, the kind of personality formulated by socialist relations now that victory had been assured.

Erwin Strittmatter does not quite fit into this type of psychological writing. Although his characters are clearly differentiated, the forces of progress and reaction are relatively static, and his characters derive from pre-socialist positions which do not, in most cases, change. His major female protagonist, moreover, is a figure of somewhat metaphorical construction, who learns some bitter truths from her cautionary tale, but is not seen to develop a new relationship to society.

In this respect, the work of Helmut Sakowski, in spite of superficial similarities in plot, is quite distinct. It belongs firmly to the drama that dominated the sixties, a mode where the protagonists were shown in evolution, through doubts and conflicts, towards greater understanding of their roles as architects of socialism. The word 'understanding' is used advisedly: these characters have to come to terms with themselves, but there is hardly any debate about the course which socialism is taking, apart from admonitions that party officials and other people with responsibilities should be awake to their own faults. This is the drama of Hauser and Hammel, Kerndl and Kleineidam, and many more of the young writers who began to flock to the *Schriftstellerverband* at the turn of the decade - so much so that the 1961 conference was known as the 'Kongreß der Jungen'.

Sakowski did not confine himself to writing for the stage; he also published short stories and scripted television dramas. But in all these genres he seemed obsessed with the theme of country women, and changes in their role and personality brought about by new socio-economic patterns in agriculture. After all, as Lenin had frequently pointed out, collectivization was a crucial factor in the lives of peasant women, giving them new status and purpose. Nadezhda Krupskaya summarized this conviction in her preface to the Soviet edition of Lenin's speeches on women:

> When she takes a hand in collective-farm development, the peasant woman grows in stature, learns to govern and to fight resolutely against the kulaks, the class enemy. *(40)*

Although the peasantry was not such an overwhelming force as it had been in the Soviet revolution, the socialist transformation of rural life in German *Junkerland* offered writers striking images of change in continuation of the familiar Russian experience.

In 1959, Sakowski published a slim volume containing two short stories that were intended to suggest political and social differences between the Democratic and Federal Republics of Germany. It was called *Zwei Frauen*. The first story, *Die Entscheidung der Hanna Glauda*, was based on a newspaper report about a woman in the West seeking justice for the murder of her young son by Nazis at the end of the war. The courts do not give her satisfaction because of the connexions of the accused, so Hanna shoots him herself and is sentenced to five years in prison. The second story, *Die Entscheidung der*

Lene Mattke, concerns a peasant woman in the East, married to a good-for-nothing, who manages to win self-respect with the support of the local *Landwirtschaftliche Produktionsgenossenschaft* (LPG). Sakowski quickly adapted this story for both radio and theatre, and a comparison of the short story and stage play provides some insight into the way in which genre can affect characterization, even within the same 'realist', 'psychological' mode.

In certain respects, the illusion of reflected reality created in the theatre is more insidious that that created by the prose work. However much habit may obscure our awareness of the printed medium, it is at least relatively evident that, between the prosewriter's vision and the reader's construction, there lies a code of language, with all the complications that this entails for communication and interpretation. The theatre audience, on the other hand, confronted by flesh-and-blood human beings representing visually and orally a structure of life-like words and actions, can easily forget the artificiality of the construct. Wolf's catharsis - identification with a positive hero(ine) and tension towards the solution of his/her problems - relies on this very oblivion.

The phenomenon depends on a certain compelling dynamic: what is normally called the 'dramatic' element in a stage-work. The popularly derived meaning of the word, which is used to refer to an unusually exciting or emotionally powerful event, development or reaction, is symptomatic. Drama has been defined and described variously over the centuries, but the very nature of the stage production demands a level of concentration: of a temporal kind (three hours is about the limit to a practicable evening's entertainment, especially when the audience is expected to remain silent and seated), of a spatial kind (due to the physical parameters of the stage and the practicalities of setting), and of an economic kind (dependent on the number of actors in a company and the funds available for properties and technology).

The effects of this underlying law are visible in the stage adaptation of *Die Entscheidung der Lene Mattke*. In the story, a few paragraphs evoke a specific village with a presence and influence of its own. In the play, the village is anonymous, and its influence is represented by four characters, restructured to meet this function more aptly. Der alte Hasenpoot and Maria are built up to personify rejection and acceptance of the LPG, while the Wirtin assumes the negative characteristics attributed to Maria in the story to become a gossip, a snob and a flirt. Maria becomes more active and gives greater support to Lene. In this way, functions are rationalized, but, of course, it means that the audience receives a new, different impression of the female figures.

The plot, too, has to be collapsed, generating faster action and sharper conflict, with the resultant intensified excitement which has often been mistaken for the defining essence of drama. This process affects Lene's position in the play, giving her a weightier role. There is also a comparative centralization - comparative because so passive a figure cannot dominate events, whatever the genre - and four of the seven scenes are set in Mattke's house, since the mobility of the prose work cannot be achieved on stage.

The absence of other conventional prose devices deprives Sakowski of his original means to convey Lene's passivity and helplessness. From a colourless figure, usually referred to simply as 'die Frau', Lene becomes a physical presence in the shape of a living actor. From an uneducated, submissive woman unused to formulating and speaking her thoughts and feelings, Lene has to become articulate and confident enough to communicate her reactions to Jagosch and to argue forcefully with Mattke when her moment of decision arrives. The play thus seems to be more ambitious for Lene's development into a self-respecting, self-willed, socialist personality. The scene where Jagosch comes to Lene, not to evict her as she fears, but to offer her a job of her own in the cowshed, is an excellent illustration of the different techniques, and a similar contrast can be observed in the episode where Lene argues with Mattke that she wants to stay in the village. As a result of her new social and economic autonomy, she grows in self-knowledge and self-assurance in both the play and the book, but the level of dialogue is more expressive in the drama, which, after all, is based on intercommunication of characters, principally by means of verbal exchanges. There is no *vox ex machina* as in the short story to fill in the gaps with narrative explanations. In the story, Sakowski several times likens the submissive wife to a dog:

> Die Frau konnte nicht Worte machen wie die zungenfertige Köchin. Sie war ihm dankbar wie ein Hund, der immer getreten wurde und nun einen Menschen findet, der gut ist. Da machte sie es so, daß er nichts finden konnte an ihrer Arbeit (p.98).

It is conceivable that this could be rendered on stage, even within the nominally realist mode. Brecht, for example, used chorus, song and masks to reveal the workings of his figures. But the naturalistic, dialogue-orientated play, which has a long and deeply rooted history and has been the dominant form in the GDR, depends on artificial standards of self-expression. Conversing characters appear perfectly real in their language, although demonstrating a loquacity and eloquence which is rare offstage, particularly since speech is also the vehicle for brief expositions of unseen incidents and long-term behaviour.

As a key to unlocking Lene's private meditations in the play, Sakowski extends the function of the daughter, Lotte. In her own right, Lotte is an adolescent anxious to prove her independence and worth, and to have a wage and position. Her own rebellion against her father reinforces and provokes her mother's evolution. Lotte also counters the danger that Lene might emerge as too powerful a figure on stage, for in contrast to the daughter's ambitions and insolence the mother appears shy and accommodating.

Lene Mattke's aspirations are not earth-shattering. Like Lotte and Maria, and Lisa Martin in *Steine im Weg*, Lene is able to grow strong, not only as a result of the general liberation of farmhands from their degrading status of *Landknecht*, but also of women's opportunity to enter the social world of work with their own legal identity, independent of any husband or father. The major difference between Lene Mattke and Lisa Martin is that the earlier character still aspires to the traditional domestic role of her sex: she wants to care for her family and bring up her children in security and without poverty. The *Kindergarten* is indispensable to her participation in the collective, since, as a mother, she is responsible for the children. And the *Wohnzimmerschrank* is the hallmark, for Lene, of a stable and respectable life, a break from the poverty caused by her husband's excessive drinking long after other families are enjoying greater material comfort. Furthermore, because the cupboard is a gift from the LPG to Lene, not her husband, it is also the catalyst for her pride and independence.

Lene, in her growing self-confidence, has her opposite in the Wirtin, a woman who relies on male recognition to boost her own self-esteem. This small part fulfils a number of functions within the plot, but besides this it offers a cameo of male-orientated obsequiousness. In the story, the sympathetic ear that the Wirtin lends her customers - the grumbling Hasenpoot and the drunkard Mattke - is no more than a common trade practice. In the play, she is projected more deliberately as ideologically reactionary, not only because she encourages Hasenpoot's complaints about the LPG, but also because her encouragement of Mattke sets the seal on her own inferior status as a woman. She feels confirmed in her own value by male confidences, and she obtains these from Mattke by flirting with him, even in front of his wife, and by expressing sympathy for his tyrannical and patriarchal views, thus intensifying his anger at his wife's emancipation.

This theme of changing patterns of female self-esteem is explored further in *Steine im Weg*, which traces the fortunes of two women whose personalities have been defined by two distinct societies and their values. There is no direct conflict between Lisa Martin and Agnes Bergemann. Although both have been involved with Alfred Bergemann, both come to reject him. They never meet during the course of the play, and the contradiction is primarily between their attitudes in parallel scenes where they talk of their past, their farms, and their relationships with men. However, in historical terms, Lisa is in the ascendant and Agnes is on a decline, and this is reflected in their respective trajectories. The play was written at the time of the 'Sieg der sozialistischen Produktionsverhältnisse auf dem Lande', in other words, as the last private farmers were finally joining the more successful LPGs. In this play, bourgeois society no longer threatens as a powerful enemy; it is simply shown to survive in anachronistic ideas and practices alongside socialist relations of production. Nonetheless, even for Agnes, whose old world has broken up, the LPG offers an opportunity to escape her wrecked marriage with dignity, while the future of the individualistic Alfred Bergemann is left open: he will be able to join an LPG if he should change his mind. So, whereas *Bürgermeister Anna* and *Die Holländerbraut* contained warnings about reactionary sabotage, with Lehmkuhl farcically drawn and Erdmann a blatant villain, the emphasis in Sakowski's work is on integrating the petty bourgeoisie into socialism.

Agnes's emotional security is partly rooted in the continuity of her family traditions symbolized by the family diary, traditions which Anrees exposes and alienates from the standpoint of the long-suffering *Knecht*, and partly in her marriage and the status she derives from her husband's reputation as a cattle farmer. For a woman such as she, tied to family property by upbringing and expectation, and unused to thinking beyond the farm boundary, it is important to cling to her marriage - even though it is childless and private farming is clearly doomed - because she has nothing else on which to base her self-esteem. Rich but unattractive, Agnes was raised in the knowledge that her only chance of companionship and purpose lay in using her inheritance to capture a husband. She fell in love with Alfred, her father's farmhand, who was ambitious and hard-working, and jealously provided him with money for the maid, Lisa, to have an abortion. She also used her class position to throw the pregnant Lisa out. Agnes has no independence by which to evaluate herself, unlike Lisa, who has the satisfaction of proving her skills and worth to the community through her responsibilities in the LPG dairy. As Agnes feels Alfred and the farm slipping away from her in the face of superior collective methods, she loses her self-esteem and grows weak and ill. She finally submits graciously, handing over with the traditional family ritual to LPG chairman Paul, so as to be able to live alone and in peace with the money she still has. In this moment of decision, she exercises her power over Alfred, who had nothing when he married her, by sending him away in one last act of control:

> Die letzten Tage aber will *ich* Herr sein auf meinem Hof. Ich

will ihn allein übergeben (p.279).

Agnes's fate, to grow old alone, is that of a woman who has been entirely dependent on marriage and private property to fulfil her emotional needs, the fate of a woman whose values and life-style are intrinsically bound up with a defeated age. She cannot adapt to the new era by accepting a job in the LPG. Her symbolic illness has debilitated her too much, and such a step would mean overcoming the pride and humiliation that have passed between herself and her former social inferior, Lisa Martin, now a member of the LPG committee and an example of what Agnes is not: a self-sufficient and attractive woman.

The sterility of a relationship based on private wealth at a time when private wealth has lost its meaning is embodied in the breakdown of the Bergemann marriage. Lisa, meanwhile, is fortunate:

> Kein Mann kann mir übelnehmen, daß ich nicht feuchte Augen bekomm, wenn er mir'n Antrag macht. Jetzt prüf ich, wie einer ist, eh ich entscheide. Jetzt kann ich mir's leisten (p.252).

Although marriage is never suggested to be obsolete in the new society, a woman such as Lisa can at least have better expectations of her partner, and her demands herald a relationship of mutual consideration:

> Zuerst Vertrauen. Ein Mann müßte zu mir stehen, wie es auch kommt. Sonst soll er bleiben. Meinen Kram schmeiß ich alleine, dazu brauch ich keinen (p.256).

Agnes's father knew she would need a husband to work the farm: Lisa has her own income, status and security within a large collective. She has overcome the despair into which the Bergemanns cast her all those years ago and, having rejected in anger Bergemann's money for an abortion, she has brought up her son without a husband. This success is, however, qualified by the general opinion that the boy needs a father for discipline and male companionship. Lisa's suitor, Paul, intervenes with the necessary masculine assistance by repairing Gerhard's bicycle. Paul's case is further supported by the acknowledgement that independence does not provide immunity against loneliness. Lisa admits to fearing solitude, and marrying Paul is presented as the obvious answer. He would make a compatible partner who shares Lisa's views.

Unlike Paul, Alfred Bergemann is chauvinistic in his attitude to women, expressing similar ideas to Jupp. But while the latter was converted, so that a happy ending ensued, Alfred is rejected for his egoism and for the patriarchal reasoning which he uses to try to win back Lisa once Agnes and her farm no longer suit his purposes. He is never interested in what Lisa (and Gerhard) or Agnes might want from a relationship. He is better at furnishing reasons why his own requirements would suit them. Paul, he claims, would be a boring husband, all talk and no action, but 'eine richtige Frau will einfach genommen sein' (p.284), and Alfred and Lisa would make an ideal match:

> ALFRED: Du bist ein Weib. Bei dir weiß einer niemals genau, wie er dran ist. Mir gefällt das.
> LISA: Du kennst mich nicht.
> ALFRED: Wir sind beide aus einem Holz . . .
> LISA: Du - fährst noch in alten Gleisen (pp.284-5).

Besides, Alfred continues, the boy needs a father, and anyway Lisa belongs to him. But Alfred argues in vain. Lisa has learnt her lesson, and she has also adopted new criteria, so that Alfred has lost his desirability as a partner.

Paul, however, is not the automatic alternative, in spite of his socialist perspective. To show that building socialism is not a straightforward and unproblematical process, Sakowski creates a dilemma for him. When the Bergemanns first apply to join the LPG, Paul is torn between his desire to support Lisa, who stands to lose her job to her seducer, and his chairman's duty and instinct to consider the interests of the LPG by accepting a very tempting offer. Paul acts as he must to further the LPG - against his own ideological sympathies - and his only sin is his lack of tact towards Lisa, who breaks their engagement because he has failed her emotionally. Paul's decision is not really in question: controversial political concessions to private peasants were repeatedly made before the long-term objective of socialist collectivization was reached. What must be corrected is Lisa's personal weakness.

In constructing Lisa as both a representative of her class and also a specific individual, Sakowski shows her to have definite emotional needs which can be traced to her particular past. She still wants to repay the Bergemanns for the suffering and humiliation they once caused her. Since she is a positive, and therefore not a vindictive character, she realizes when the hour of vengeance arrives that her old wounds no longer sting so sharply. She does not want the Bergemanns to suffer, but she herself still needs to be compensated for her former rejection by a display of protective solidarity from Paul. His honest inability to put Lisa's feelings before the collective interest cause her pain and turmoil, but it is Lisa who must come to terms with her own weakness, with a little understanding from her lover. The problem is 'merely' subjective. With Lisa's change of heart, the couple can be happily reconciled.

There are no unpleasant characters in *Steine im Weg*, only characters who are projected as ideologically backward. Each personality is made comprehensible in socio-economic and psychological terms. The Bergemanns' cruelty is in the past, and Agnes actually arouses some sympathy, as her misfortune is shown to have its basis in her historical situation. Similarly, Lisa is not an exemplary achiever, and she has some minor faults which place her in a critical light. The audience is not encouraged to reject Agnes and emulate Lisa but, rather, to identify with the superior social system which has enabled Lisa to develop her own skills and personality, sustained by a broad community. In the collective, women are no longer reliant on the fortunes of a wealthy family, nor, like the forester's niece in the fairy tale told by Lisa's mother and companion, on discovering that they are of noble birth so that they can marry the count of their dreams. Their work earns them respect in their own right, as an unseen machine operator illustrates:

> Das andere erledigt das Band und Hedi Henning. Die geht mit Maschinen um, so sicher wie mit den Kerlen . . . Ein kluges Mädchen und ein bißchen Technik verkraften drei Tonnen Kartoffeln in fünf Minuten. Ist das nichts? (p.259).

Lisa, therefore, does not need to be exceptional. It is the social relations that are outstanding. Agnes was unlucky not to have such opportunities. Her negative features reflect an imprisonment.

The breakdown of the Bergemann marriage thus seems to be the inevitable outcome of an unfulfilling union, testifying to the historical failure of a society which has nothing left to offer. Optimistic identification with socialism, on the other hand, is secured by tension towards a happy ending to the romance between Paul and Lisa, which shows that even personal, emotional problems can be solved in a relationship based on mutual respect and friendship, not money and convenience. Capitalism is the key to Agnes's illness:

socialism is the key to Lisa's healthy and attractive vigour.

Chapter 5

HELMUT BAIERL: *PRINZIP DER UMKEHRUNG DER UMKEHRUNG* (41)

Whilst the naturalist theatre was refining a more individualized, psychological approach to dramatic characters, the brief but popular agitprop movement of the late fifties engendered a number of writers who turned to Brecht for their methods. They drew on the epic, 'proletarian' theatre developed by Brecht and Erwin Piscator in the twenties, using the stage and characters to illustrate economic relations; they drew on Brecht's didactic theatre to pose questions about correct attitudes; and they drew on his alienation techniques, creating a more critical distance between audience and characters than could be achieved in drama which relied on empathy. Sakowski was a little influenced by the Augsburger in his attempts to combine epic and psychological elements and to make the actions of all his figures questionable to some extent, but he stayed within the Aristotelian theatre of illusion, exploiting the persuasive potential of personal identification in a modified manner. Meanwhile, Horst Kleineidam and Horst Salomon were workers whose participation in the agitprop movement paved the way for their later careers as playwrights, even though they were to move away from Brechtian techniques. More puristic exponents included Manfred Richter, Hasso Grabner, Gerhard Fabian and Hans Pfeiffer, but Brecht's most notable disciples were Heiner Müller and Helmut Baierl.

Baierl's first stage success, *Die Feststellung*, was given five hundred and eighty performances in the two seasons from 1957 to 1959. It is another play about conditions in the countryside but, unlike the work of Wolf, Strittmatter and Sakowski, strictly didactic. The device Baierl employs - making the key characters exchange roles - is designed to stimulate insight into the social and economic reasons which motivate individual behaviour. In this sense, the play is clearly Brechtian. The audience is not supposed to respond in an unemotive manner, but anger, frustration, affirmation and hope are generated by an ideological assessment of the proceedings, rather than by means of a gripping conflict between humanitarian and exploitative forces, or any other polarization of positive and negative objectives. Baierl achieves the requisite alienation by having two characters who represent different points of view swap roles, so that the audience can see each one through the eyes of the other. The re-enacted scene actually involves three figures: the chairman of the LPG, and the peasant couple who flee when he tries to persuade them to join the collective, but later return. However, since it was almost invariably the man who negotiated the social position of such traditional rural households, the essential interaction is that between the Vorsitzender and the Bauer, and so, 'die Frau bleibt die Frau' (p.19). The wife's role as a shadow to her husband reflects a sociological phenomenon.

The gender ascribed to the other characters in the play, the village 'audience', choir and committee, is dictated by a symmetrical principle of equality, not by commitment to historical documentation. Apart from Benno, who has a special part to play as a kindred spirit to the Bauer, the collective farmers consist of one man and one woman who tend to support the Vorsitzender, and one man and one woman who tend to criticize him. The choir, whose function is to elucidate, is composed of one young man, one young woman, and one child of unspecified sex. Besides the Vorsitzender, the committee is made up of one male and one female member. In other words, a strict balance is maintained, and neither sex is identified with a particular attitude.

The outstanding character, however, is the Mechanikerin. Although she is not the fountain of all knowledge, she is the pedagogical figure who applies what she herself has learnt from the Vorsitzender to overcome his sectarian indignation at the Bauer's flight and contribute to greater mutual understanding. It is she, the woman on the committee, who urges tolerance and collective learning, and of all those present - with the exception of the town-bred Vorsitzender - it is this woman who has qualified in technological matters. The Mechanikerin therefore embodies a number of socialist aspirations for women.

These two characters, the Frau and the Mechanikerin, represent their sex in two distinct ways. The Frau is empirically typical, in the sense that she exemplifies the secondary, dependent role still played by a vast number of women in her day, especially in the countryside. The Mechanikerin is typical in the sense adopted by Engels and Brecht, in that she exemplifies an historically significant role for women which illustrates the nature of her society. Baierl, like Brecht, proved to be more interested in characters of the latter type, and he developed his two best-known protagonists, Frau Flinz and Johanna von Döbeln, in such a way that there could be no possibility of interpreting them in a documentary manner. Their stories are allegories, essentially parables about socialism, but which call for an examination of two reputedly female characteristics: motherliness and ingenuousness. Both are re-creations of Brechtian roles, but there is a fundamental difference: Frau Flinz and Johanna function in socialist society. Its contradictions, Baierl believes, are non-antagonistic. Frau Flinz does not, as a mother, have to be at odds with the state, and Johanna's refusal to compromise her principles is both a virtue and a flaw. Both plays are critical affirmations of contemporary society, not indictments, as Brecht's were.

Thus, in *Frau Flinz* (1961), the protagonist, far from being trapped in a contradictory situation, is quite simply wrong. Whereas Mutter Courage, in making a livelihood for her children, delivered them to their deaths by the same actions, Frau Flinz, who operates a survival code for her family that she has learned in an exploitative society, now has to realize that her protective behaviour runs counter to their material interests. Socialist society is fraught, not with dangers, but with solutions to the family problems: housing, employment, education, hobbies and health. Conventional motherly practices are, therefore, subverted by the play. Every step taken by Frau Flinz to protect her sons from politics impedes them initially, and then precipitates their departures and leads to qualitative progress for the very political causes of which she is suspicious. But everything turns out for the best, in spite of her resistance, and the play is different from its Brechtian forebear in one major respect: it is very funny, and the protagonist is a comic fugure.

Baierl, who began working at the *Berliner Ensemble* in 1959, wrote the part for Helene Weigel, as he recounts in his autobiographical work, *Die Köpfe oder Das noch kleinere Organon:*

> Die Prinzipalin hatte mich mit der Bemerkung engagiert: 'Schreibst mir a Rolln!', was mir so leicht erschien, daß ich unverzüglich ja gesagt hatte. Warum nicht! Und warum nicht das tun, was der Große Raucher so gern und mit so großem Erfolg getan hatte: ein Stück von einem anderen nehmen und es umdrehen. Was, wenn ich als sein Eleve mit ihm ebenso verführe? (p.13).

Weigel was, in fact, renowned for a series of Mother roles. She had played a number of parts written by her husband, starting with Pelagea Wlassowa in Brecht's adaptation of Gorky's *Matka* in 1932, following this with Teresa Carrar in *Die Gewehre der Frau Carrar* (1937) and her most celebrated role as Mutter Courage, which she played in Berlin from 1949 to 1961. In 1965, she was to play Volumnia in Brecht's adaptation of Shakespeare's *Coriolanus*. In every case, the political actions and attitudes of these mother-figures derive from their determination to further the interests of their offspring: Wlassowa overcomes her fear and joins her son's revolutionary cause; Carrar is persuaded that neutrality will not save her sons from the fascists; Mutter Courage is unable to draw the lessons from her predicament which might save her daughter's life; Volumnia's family ambitions exclude all human pity. Weigel herself commented on certain similarities between Volumnia and Frau Flinz:

> Eine Frau lebt eigentlich davon, daß sie etwas zustande bringen muß, irgendwas, ihre Familie. - Wenn Sie wollen, gibt es große Ähnlichkeiten zum Beispiel zwischen der Flinz und der Volumnia, die beide jemanden dazu bringen, was zu machen. In dem Punkt sind die beiden Frauen sich sozusagen wirklich gleich. Die Volumnia bricht ihrem Sohn doch zweimal das Genick. Und wenn ihr die Burschen nicht ausreißen würden, der Flinz, hätte sie ihnen auch das Genick gebrochen. Also, wenn Sie so wollen, das ist auch eine ziemliche Abneigung gegen bestimmte Formen der Mütterlichkeit. *(42)*

'Mütterlichkeit' as an ideal fascinated Brecht. At times he used it as a symbolical expression of the caring society, and the most obvious parallel is in *Der kaukasische Kreidekreis*. A child, so runs the message, belongs in the environment where its potential can best develop. Blood ties, like traditional laws of possession, are not necessarily the best encouragement for the individual or the community to prosper. It is the caring attitude that is most important. Brecht distinguishes between motherhood and motherliness, using the Gouverneursfrau (another Weigel role) and Grusche as examples. The Gouverneursfrau, a mother in the biological sense, is more concerned for her clothes than for her baby and forgets to take him with her in her haste to escape the enemy with as many belongings as possible. Grusche, a maid and no relative to the child, brings him up and grows to love him.

The reverse side of the coin to caring for one's progeny, at least in an exploitative society, is the callous shell that a mother figure needs as protection against the rest of the world. This is the dilemma of Shen Te in *Der gute Mensch von Sezuan* (1941) who, as Shui Ta, turns the greedy manoeuvres of her neighbours against them to earn a living for her child. The symbolic split personality illustrates a contradiction between different individual interests, and also between charity and material deprivation. Mutter Courage is caught up in a similar dilemma: for her children to live off the conditions of war, she has to risk them dying there. The ideal of motherliness cannot operate. The audience must understand Mutter Courage's motivations for living as she does, and its censure must be mitigated by insight into the socio-economic laws that govern her age, laws that the audience is invited to challenge.

This is the context in which the 'Abneigung gegenüber bestimmten Formen der Mütterlichkeit' referred to by Weigel has been created. But in *Frau Flinz* the irony has shifted. Her motherliness is turned upside-down because she fails to recognize circumstances which are, in fact, her allies. In spite of her intentions, the tactics she employs to protect her sons from society, or, as she calls it, 'die Politik', actually prevent them from achieving their objectives. Like Mutter Courage, she loses her children, but this is because they learn from her mistakes and escape her clutches to fulfil their own cherished ambitions. Ultimately, Frau Flinz is unable to flee from the politicians because they insist on making policies to suit her, however she twists and turns to resist them. They have built the foundations of a state which aims to take over the motherly function by caring for its citizens instead of exploiting them, and they keep trying to persuade Frau Flinz to take part in this process, a complete reversal of her experience under capitalism. The play is comic, as, in the final analysis, although everything Frau Flinz undertakes has the opposite to the desired effect, this is really to her advantage. The author is able to be more optimistic than Brecht because he is the advocate, not the adversary, of his society. The contradictions on which Brecht based dramatic conflicts were antagonistic, insoluble within the framework of contemporary economic relations. The contradictions illustrated by Baierl are non-antagonistic: their resolution calls for deeper understanding of the laws of socialist construction, on the part of both Frau Flinz and the Communist Weiler. Baierl elaborates, in his autobiographical account, on his humorous twist:

> Durch Umdrehung der Umdrehung (was nichts anderes als ein V-Effekt ist) kam meine Grundgeschichte zustande. Der Witwe Zins rannten ebenso wie der Madame Muth die Kinder weg, letzterer in den Krieg, ersterer (haha!) in den Frieden (pp.13-4).

As in many plays of the period, the two main characters are not enemies irreconcilable to the end. One is progressive and the other potentially so. The denouement requires the latter to identify his or her interests correctly. Drama was undergoing a phase corresponding to the current of 'Ankunftsliteratur' in the novel. This term was used by critics such as Dieter Schlenstedt and Eberhard Röhner to classify a number of novels in the sixties where the central figure finds his or her way to a socialist perspective. *(43)* The label itself is taken from the title of Brigitte Reimann's *Ankunft im Alltag*, and other notable examples are Max Walter Schulz's *Wir sind nicht Staub im Wind*, Christa Wolf's *Der geteilte Himmel*, and the second volume of Dieter Noll's *Die Abenteuer des Werner Holt*. The effect that this kind of adjustment by the protagonists was to have on dramatic conflicts meant that very often the two main characters were placed in a pedagogical relationship to one another, instead of a belligerent one. And in *Frau Flinz* the pedagogical relationship between Frau Flinz and Weiler is reciprocal.

The interaction between these two, with Frau Flinz representing the defence of private interests and Weiler representing the political party of socialism, is a model of the dialectic between, on the one hand, the people and their needs, and on the other, party policy and strategy. The party is shown as the constructive organization which formalizes mass demands, but it works against a backcloth of constantly changing needs, fluid popular consciousness and participation, and growing economic resources. This means that, while Weiler knows that his party has Frau Flinz's interests at heart in the long term, he repeatedly finds himself at odds with her over specifics. Much to the frustration of Frau Flinz, however, the demands she makes in order to thwart Weiler and hold the politicians at bay are constantly being translated into party policy, so that she is obliged to contradict herself. It is out of these contradictions in detail that socialism is seen to progress.

Frau Flinz, therefore, is not herself a changing personality: it is her circumstances and direction that alter. Even at the end of the play - which is clearly not the end of the story - she is as subversively provocative as before, and her motivation continues to be pursuit of her own selfish interest well after her sons, whose interests she rashly assumed to be similar, have left her. There is, however, no moral condemnation implied in this selfishness. In fact, Weiler at last manages to convince her that Lenin was 'der größte Egoist aller Zeiten' (p.111). She has merely learnt that the new society provides her with tools to promote her demands:

> WESTPHAL: Die Partei sagt: keine Genossenschaft. Das ist unsere Linie. Und das paßt uns oder das paßt uns nicht.
> FLAU FLINZ: Mir paßt es nicht.
> KIONKA: Das sage mal nicht so laut.
> FRAU FLINZ *laut:* Mir paßt es nicht.
> WESTPHAL: Du, bring uns nicht in Verruf, unser Dorf steht politisch gut da.
> FRAU FLINZ: Das ist mein Staat, das steht in der Zeitung, und ich sage, mir paßt es nicht.
> WESTPHAL: Du bist also gegen unseren Staat.
> FRAU FLINZ: Ja. Wenn er so ausschaut wir hier im Dorf!
> WESTPHAL: Du hast überhaupt nichts zu melden. Unsere Linie steht fest . . .
> BINKAU: Flinzen, wo willst du hin?
> FRAU FLINZ *böse:* Wo die Linie gemacht wird (p.118).

Frau Flinz's uncooperative belligerence, cultivated in protection of her brood, predisposes her to make an active and forthright socialist citizen who will participate in the formulation of policy. Frau Flinz ends the play with a leading agricultural function, like so many of her female antecedents in East German drama, but the presentation of her new role is quite different from that of Anna Drews or Hanna Tainz, and the curtain falls on an alienated anti-climax: Frau Flinz's career is reported by an impartial loudspeaker as Weiler and his old Social Democratic sparring partner gossip over a cigarette:

> WEILER: Das hätte Elstermann noch erleben müssen.
> KALUSA: Der damals den Bürgermeister gemacht hat?
> WEILER: Oberbürgermeister. Den hat es erwischt. Mitten in der Arbeit. *Sie rauchen schweigend.*
> KALUSA: Die nächsten Jahre werden nicht leichter.
> WEILER: Nein. Aber klarer.
> DER LAUTSPRECHER: Die 2. Parteikonferenz setzt ihre Beratungen fort. Als nächster spricht die Vorsitzende einer der ersten Landwirtschaftlichen Produktionsgenossenschaften, die Gastdelegierte Martha Flinz.
> KALUSA: Flinz? *Er denkt nach.* Flinz? Ist das die?
> WEILER: Ja, das ist die (pp.119-20).

This revelation is certainly a shock, and the idea of Frau Flinz adressing a party conference is indisputably funny in the light of the terseness and opposition that she has shown throughout the play. This parting shot is one of many comic examples of Baierl's ability to master the Brechtian 'V-Effekt'.

Baierl does not use conversational self-analysis to construct an emotional and moral psychology for Frau Flinz. He adopts Brecht's gestus technique, drawing the audience's attention to the consequences of her actions from a socio-economic, 'epic' perspective. The Acts and scenes carry titles which focus on the historical context, showing how each Act is set in a different phase of the transition to socialism, with different implications for the relationship between Frau Flinz and Weiler. The titles indicate either Frau Flinz's anachronistic code ('Klein, aber mein') and the illusions of capitalism ('Lasset die Kindlein zu mir kommen'), or else socialist practices and principles ('Volkskontrolle', 'Die Menschwerdung', 'Die Wahrheit ist konkret'). In some cases, of course, the scene titles relate to Weiler, who evolves in his own way from a sectarian position forged in the struggles of the twenties into a functionary of the people, a trajectory which is summarized by the incongruously self-expressive 'Beichte' (scene xiii). Frau Flinz does not reply to this monologue. To do so would contravene the manner in which she is portrayed, for her alienation as a mother-figure relies on demonstrating and ironizing her actions, not on any discourse of her own.

The very fact that Frau Flinz applies a code of practice devised in a previous era to a radically different world, with devastating results, is a clue to the author's intention. It enables him to show that behaviour patterns are influenced by social relations, and to illustrate the difference between capitalism and socialism from this angle. The desire to elucidate the laws of historical change is fundamental to the play, as Hermann Kähler summarizes:

> Baierls Komödie ist im wesentlichen nicht von einer Maxime oder Sentenz, sondern vom dargestellten Prozeß der sich ständig entwickelnden ökonomisch-gesellschaftlich-politischen Gesamtwirklichkeit her organisiert. *(44)*

The epic approach does not preclude sympathy for the dramatic characters, but the audience is made to work hard to keep apace of the many conflicts, twists of irony and realignments from which the play is composed. A critical reception is encouraged by the use of various alienation techniques. One is the opposition between intention and effect which throws apparently normal deeds into question by, literally, making them strange. Another is the multiple perspective. Frau Flinz is an attractively humorous character whose maternal motives are acceptable and who outwits Weiler wherever he reveals a political weakness, but she is also judged by her rejection of Weiler's socialist aspirations. Weiler has commendable aspirations, although his methods, at least to begin with, are sectarian. The two characters are criticisms of each other and are criticized in turn from elsewhere: Frau Flinz by the understandable rebellions of her five sons, and Weiler by his party, especially in the more enlightened form of the young comrade Käthe Raupach. All this means that the audience is constantly asked to reassess the situation and discover the reasons behind the twists.

Yet although Frau Flinz's role as a mother defending her brood from the vicissitudes of her society - albeit misguidedly - explains her motivation, this is not really a play about motherhood. Parallels are made on a symbolic and episodal level between the concerns of a mother for her children and those of a socialist society for its citizens. Above all, the play describes the socialist state and its party, which takes over the role of caregiver on behalf of people like Frau Flinz. The subversion of Frau Flinz's motherly practices is a device to illustrate the nature of the new society: the ideal concept of motherliness itself is not subverted.

What does this concept imply? It springs from a culture that identifies mothers as the exclusive natural caregivers. It is because this identification is widespread and well entrenched that Baierl and Brecht use it as an acceptable analogy for socialism. But in so doing they fail to question the social roots of the concept itself, the allocation of the caregiving role to the female parent in a number of societies where essential economic opportunity and status rest with the male, who is thus preoccupied with his role as breadwinner. At the same time, it cannot be maintained that Brecht or Baierl specifically set out to defend the idea of nuclear families or maternal responsibility. All the mother-figures quoted are single parents, which helps to preserve their allegorical function without complications. In social terms neither Brecht nor Baierl overtly sanctifies the traditional family pattern, and yet it could be argued that, insofar as they indulge in the formal exploitation of an attitude rooted within it, they may be perpetuating its ideological acceptability. In fact, in spite of the massive participation of women in the labour force and the expansion of socialized child-care, particularly in recent years, the role of mothers as prime caregivers to their children has not, as yet, been questioned to any significant degree in the GDR, and in 1965, shortly after Baierl's play was written, Ingeborg Kunze even felt pressed to warn in her inaugural thesis that 'das deutsche Denken' was 'heute noch mit Elementen des faschistischen Mutterkultes behaftet'. *(45)*

However, any danger that Baierl might incur of universalizing the archetypal mother role for the female sex is strongly counterbalanced by the young women who represent the most progressive elements in the new order. In contrast to the women in the crowd scenes, who are indicated in the text by reference to their husbands (Gampes Frau, Wagners Frau) and Anna, the wife of the capitalist Neumann, there is a whole new generation of independent women in key functions. The first is Käthe Raupach, whose more tolerant insight into the contemporary political situation clashes at first with Weiler's customary approach. Her role is very similar to that of the Mechanikerin in *Die Feststellung*. She is the older proletarian's young teacher, and voices the wisdom of the party, although there are some situations in which her intellectual understanding can benefit from Weiler's practical experience. The girl listed in the *dramatis personae* as the Vorsitzende der FDJ has a small part. She is the first socialist to befriend a Flinz son, and her little speech about Anton's commitment, complemented by a group of FDJ members singing one of Brecht's songs, contrasts sharply and ironically with the Western propaganda on the radio and the nationalistic ditties that precede her arrival in the Flinz quarters.

The staggering revelation that the MAS mechanic who mends Karl's motorcycle for him is also a young woman constitutes a forceful subversion of conventional gender roles. It is all the more unexpected because it follows immediately after Karl's argument with Betty, who embodies some archetypal 'female' vices: totally ignorant of technical matters, she bathes in the reflected glory of the men she is able to attract, and with this end in mind she dedicates her attention and abundant wealth to clothes and dances. Karl draws the conclusion that all women are, like his mother and Betty, unable to appreciate machinery: 'Kein Sinn für Technik. Das soll biologisch sein. Mit der Gehirnmasse hat das zu tun' (p.104). At this point, the unknown mechanic completes the job on the bike, removes a cloth cap - and the long hair reveals a woman. The blow to genderist assumptions is powerful. The mechanization of agriculture is thus once more represented by a female labourer, as in *Die Feststellung*. In all three cases, these progressive female figures are doubly effective: they illustrate socialist commitment to developing women's potential in technological and political spheres, and they underscore the novelty of socialist society because of the extra, alienating element of surprise afforded by ascribing these roles to women.

Baierl's later play, *Johanna von Döbeln* (1968), is quite different in that the gender constellations are rigidly traditional. There are two reasons for the polarization of Johanna and the men from the 'VEB Landmaschinenbau Rotes Banner'. The first is an allegorical recourse to the legend of Joan of Arc who, as an outstandingly ingenuous and principled maiden, entered the unquestionably male domain of medieval politics and soldiering. The second reason reflects economic reality in the GDR, where heavy industry has been an almost totally male preserve. It is not simply that ideas of women's and men's work have remained unchallenged: in many areas they have actually disappeared; but there are major exceptions, and in accordance with the traditions of the German labour movement, women are excluded from employment that is considered dangerous or very strenuous on the grounds of health (and their child-bearing potential). In the 'Rotes Banner', the only women, alluded to indirectly, are the director's secretary, one (white-collar) worker in the messengers' office, and a solitary woman doing productive work of an unusually delicate (that is, feminine) nature. The only other female figure to appear is somebody's wife, and that is the full extent of her identity. In the revised version, produced at the *Maxim-Gorki-Theater* in 1976 under the amended title *Die Abenteuer der Johanna von Döbeln*, there is no messenger Frau Weißgraber. A nurse makes a brief appearance to tend to Johanna when she falls delirious, and the importance of the flowers that Johanna takes to Lobstett is accentuated by the introduction of the flower-seller from whom Johanna is seen to purchase a bouquet in exchange for her rail-ticket home. Both of these additional occupations are female.

The protagonist, Johanna, stands for artless integrity and uncompromising humanitarianism in an environment of workaday practicalities. But the play caused Baierl many problems, and he continued rewriting it over the next few years. The basic difficulty lies in the nature of contradictions in Baierl's method, once he is no longer trying to illustrate the distinction between socialism and capitalism. Johanna's questioning and her concern for individuals are not really at odds with the aims of the 'Rotes Banner' - to build a strong people's economy that will guarantee a better life for its citizens. Hence, the symbolism is not entirely satisfactory.

At the beginning of the play, Johanna's searching openness is attractive and amusing, but by the final Act she is an obsessive nuisance. Her challenge to the 'Rotes Banner' is at first healthy, reminding the manager and officials of the purposes of their actions and the objectives of socialism by taking all their political phraseology literally. She comes to Döbeln to be turned into 'ein neuer Mensch' (p.174), drawn by the words over the gate:

> GÜNTER KLEIN: Sag mal, das Schild 'Betriebsfremden ist der Eintritt verboten' hast du übersehen?
> JOHANNA: Bitte, was für ein Schild?
> GÜNTER KLEIN: Das da: 'Betriebsfremden ist der Eintritt verboten'.
> JOHANNA: Nein, ich sehe mir alles ganz genau an, und dann richte ich mich danach, wenn wo was geschrieben steht. Als ich das Schild gelesen habe, wollte ich schon wieder umkehren. Aber dann habe ich das andere Schild gesehen und war sehr erleichtert.
> GÜNTER KLEIN: Was für ein anderes Schild?
> JOHANNA: Das darüber.
> *Günter Klein guckt zum Fenster hinaus.*
> GÜNTER KLEIN: Ich sehe kein Schild.
> JOHANNA: Doch. Das viel längere. Auch die Buchstaben sind

> mindestens fünfmal so groß.
> *Günter Klein sucht, Johanna kommt neben ihn.*
> Das da. *Sie liest.* 'Das Werk braucht jeden, jeder braucht das Werk.' (pp.169-70)

The party secretary is so anxious to discover whether Johanna is a saboteur that he cannot take either the ingenuous maiden or the factory maxim at face value. The incident is a comic example of alienation.

However, Johanna has to learn that people do sometimes choose to make sacrifices for things which they believe are more important, that life's decisions are not clear-cut, and that there is some truth to Günter's embarrassed explanation that the two signs have to be seen 'dialektisch' (p. 170). Moreover, her crusade on behalf of Paul Lobstett, the worker dismissed ten years previously, turns out to be pointless. The factory has not, after all, been unjust towards him. At the end of a long stalemate, where Baierl wrangles with the problem of making Johanna's refreshing gust of idealism appear purposeful without seeming to suggest that the 'Rotes Banner' is indifferent to human tragedies, the blame for Lobstett's dismissal is finally conceded by Lobstett to have been his own.

The last scene, in the court-room, leaves the decision open, which might, superficially, seem to be a Brechtian strategy. But in fact, Baierl is himself unable to solve the case. He has tried to blend a symbolism based on idealist absolutes, and reminiscent of Expressionism in its opposition of the human soul to the awe-inspiring 'Werk', with a materialist recognition of fluctuating economic and social priorities in everyday socialism. Johanna's ungrammatical misnomer, 'der rote Banner' (pp.171-3), is suggestive, and the more pragmatic men in the factory are obliged to exorcize Johanna's undialectical 'voice'.

This does not mean that Baierl succumbs to religious mystery. He treads a thin dividing line in his allegory between evocative parallels with the legend on the one hand and rational explanations for Johanna's mission on the other. Although she is presented as an outsider, a strange personality whose socialization is incomplete, she remains an earthly figure. Her lack of integration into the ways of the world is accounted for by her rural background and the fact that she is an orphan. As a grandfather substitute to whom she can relate in fantasy, she has selected a foreigner who died before she was born, Iwan Wladimirowitsch Mitschurin, a biologist who wore the Lenin Order and the Red Banner of Labour. This Communist pioneer is her 'voice'. Forthright, honest instincts underlie her secular variety of saintliness. For example, she is able to identify Jochen as the director despite attempts to deceive her because she notices that everyone present is watching his reactions. Baierl uses this allegorical incident to create an awareness of incipient attitudes of subalternity, but Johanna's insight is itself not miraculous: it is an exaggerated form of ingenuous wisdom.

Baierl's problems with the play were discussed at the 1973 *Brecht-Woche*, at a seminar where a number of dramatists, along with Ernst Schumacher, were evaluating the relevance of Brecht's methods for East German theatre in the seventies. Baierl confessed his difficulties, and was taken to task by Heiner Müller:

> BAIERL: Ich war vor Jahren in Vorbereitung eines Stückes, *Johanna von Döbeln*, in einem Bestbetrieb, und ich habe da immer geguckt, wo eigentlich Konflikte sind. Ich ging programmgemäß davon aus, daß Kollisionen und Konflikte, also Widersprüche, bei uns nicht-antagonistischen Charakter

> haben, und sosehr ich guckte, sosehr hinderte mich diese Brille, die Schwierigkeiten selbst zu finden und zu gestalten. Denn tatsächlich waren einerseits viele, die meisten Arbeiter damit beschäftigt, indem sie durch ihre Arbeit den Betrieb täglich, stündlich verbesserten, die Konflikte überhaupt aus der Welt zu schaffen, andererseits war es vielleicht ein wenig abstrakt, diese Verhinderung der Konflikte selbst als Konflikt zu begreifen. Aber es mußte doch welche geben, sicher nicht auf der Straße, wie manche Leute in früherer Zeit ständig behaupteten, aber doch vorhanden in der Wirklichkeit, wenn auch schwer entdeckbar.
>
> MÜLLER: Das ist sehr theoretisch.
>
> BAIERL: Ja, klar, vorerst . . .
>
> MÜLLER: Ihr seid doch da in den Betrieb gegangen als Schizophrene, einerseits mit der Absicht, Konflikte zu finden, weil ihr die braucht für die Theatralisierung der Geschichte, andererseits mit dem politischen Vorsatz, keine zu finden.
>
> BAIERL: Das eine ist richtig, das zweite eine Unterstellung, und im übrigen war ich nur allein dort . . .
>
> MÜLLER: Das ist doch ein Dilemma des Stücks. *(46)*

The implications of this dilemma for the Johanna figure are that she combines the status of a legendary ideal - unsullied maidenhood and child-like honesty - with a worldly immaturity which is revealed in her dealings with men of sincerity and experience: Günter Klein, the imaginative party secretary with his Marxist learning and affectionate humour; Jochen Krämer, the director who carries the burden of turning the 'Rotes Banner' into a first-class enterprise for its workers and whose motives for dismissing Lobstett prove to be unimpeachable; and Kabulla, the trade union chairman, a confident and dependable proletarian. Paul Lobstett himself ultimately adopts a teacher's role towards Johanna when he tells her that her interest in his past was misguided, and even the caricature of a bureaucratic judge makes her seem like a guilty schoolgirl when he reveals the identity of her 'grandfather'. The parable misfires under the non-antagonistic conditions. The witty, lively, impressive figure loses her own conviction, and the little girl in the final scene confuses the audience with her own confusion. In the revised version, Baierl tries to reduce the significance of the allegory by abandoning the symbolic suit of armour in which Johanna recited her prologue and introducing an incident where Johanna falls ill and raves deliriously about martyrdom, but the new prologue is still obliged to admit that the play suffers dramatically from the lack of a proper antagonist.

I have not discovered any contribution to the discussion of this play which takes note of its use of a woman as a social conscience, even though the tradition is evident. The programme published for the play's revival in 1976 places a heavy emphasis, instead, on the questioning role of youth, a theme that was very topical that year, with the IXth SED Congress considering ways of giving more responsibility to young people.

By this time, the play was being interpreted in an historical light. It treated problems of the sixties that were felt to have been overcome. More attention was being paid under the country's new leadership to the quality of the working environment, and more money was being channelled into the social wage, whereas previously the objective of building a strong economic base had overridden many other, often personal, considerations. Nonetheless, Johanna still had a purpose: to kindle vigilance so that individual needs and feelings were not again submerged (if they ever had been) under immediate economic pressures.

There is, however, a gulf between these historical nuances concerning a play which examines moral dilemmas and a play in the epic mode such as *Frau Flinz*. Of course, the moral issues in *Johanna von Döbeln* are historical in that they are specific to a certain country and period, but the playwright's method has shifted, so that he lends more substance to the attitudes and psychological idiosyncracies of his various characters - representative as they may be of different contemporary shades of feeling. During the Brecht seminar of 1973, Baierl described the changes in his relationship to Brecht over his career. He was drawing less directly on Brecht's techniques, but preserving what he called the 'faktisches Substrat' (p.209), Brecht's two basic concepts of 'Haltung' and 'Historisieren':

> Während die 'Haltungen' den tiefgehenden Individualbereich umfassen, bedeutet 'Historisieren', das Ganze des Kunstwerks in geschichtliche Relativität zu tauchen, also nicht nur im historischen Stück historisch zu sein, sondern und gerade im Gegenwartsstück. Und diese beiden Begriffe müssen sich scheiden. Es ist nie gut, wenn ausschließlich der historische Gesichtspunkt vorkommt und das Persönliche, Individuelle, also die konkreten Haltungen zu kurz. Das gilt auch umgekehrt.
>
> Es wurde in der Vergangenheit, auch von mir selbst, oft zu großer Wert gelegt auf Dinge, die vom historischen, vom sozialen Gestus getragen wurden, und zu wenig wert auf das Finden individueller Haltungen (p.209).

In *Johanna von Döbeln*, the responses of the individuals to a problem of human relationships are certainly of paramount interest, whereas in *Frau Flinz* greater attention was paid to the operation of socio-economic structures. But Baierl does not simply concentrate more on 'Haltungen': he also becomes more compellingly involved with them, rather than showing them to a 'Rauchertheater' by taking advantage of the alienation effects he mastered in earlier plays. On the historical level, *Frau Flinz* traces history by covering a broader span of time and space, while *Johanna von Döbeln* focusses on a nucleus of characters in a brief episode. The fact that this play is conceived historically is evidenced by the differences between Johanna and, on the one hand, Joan of Arc, and, on the other, Brecht's heroine in *Die heilige Johanna der Schlachthöfe* (1930). Unlike exploitative Chicago, Döbeln is a human town, possessing the means to resolve its own conflicts. Johanna von Nächterstett may be an outsider in the 'Rotes Banner', but they are complementary, the idealistic and pragmatical sides to socialism which can learn from and reinforce one another. Brecht's Johanna is driven to the conclusion that Mauler is evil and that justice, since it is not being provided by God, can only be obtained with force. The play's dramatic polarizations reflect this context.

In drawing away from the epic and didactic style of his earlier work, Baierl was following the more general theoretical trend away from argumentation for socialism - 'aufklärerische Anliegen' for 'aufklärerische Zeiten' *(47)* - to concentrate more on socialist personality. Ethical attitudes replaced historical laws as a formal foundation.

Even so, one aspect of socialist behaviour patterns which actually receives less attention in the later play, in spite of ample opportunity, is the nature of relations between the two sexes. We have already observed how restricted the representation of women is in *Johanna von Döbeln*, reflecting gender-orientated employment in the GDR. Johanna herself complies with this categorization: her typing and shorthand quickly qualify her to take over the vacant post of director's secretary. This division of labour is not an issue. Neither is the teasing innuendo of the young workmen to whom she sells the works newspaper. Their flirtation has to be appreciated in terms of its function within the major problematic: Johanna is worried because everybody in the 'Rotes Banner' seems so happy, oblivious of the wrong done to Lobstett. The flirtatious jokes are therefore designed to stress how cheerful the workmen are. The ideology underlying their humour is not in question, and although Johanna does not find it funny, the men simply assume the right to make light-hearted advances. They judge women in terms of appearance, and Johanna, unlike Frau Weißgraber, offers 'materieller Anreiz' (p.187). The fact that Johanna fails to see the humour in their remarks does not constitute a critique, since it could be explained by her maidenly lack of interest in men and her preoccupation with Lobstett. She is thus in no position to parry this additional example of male initiative in a man's world.

In *Johanna von Döbeln*, Baierl is lured into the trap of attempting to apportion blame for a case of bitterness that has arisen in socialism. In the model antithesis which he sets up between artless ideals and pragmatic expedience, there is nowhere for the blame to fit. In the two earlier plays, blame was ackowledged to be a far more dialectical affair: characters reacted against each other, and the outcome was the complex stuff on which socialism is made. *Die Feststellung* had shown that socialism is only acceptable to individuals when they can relate it to their own lives, and *Frau Flinz* had shown how a socialist structure enables people's requirements to be realized as social policies. *Johanna von Döbeln* does not show how socialism functions: it enters the realms of abstract ethics - and fails. But all these plays have one factor in common which distinguishes them from the works of the previous authors, and that is that characters are not divided for purposes of dramatic conflict into a camp representing and a camp opposing socialism. There are some characters who have a more penetrating insight and political awareness, and some of these are women, but Baierl's 'heroines' do not acquire their central role by virtue of a conscious decision to escape their two-fold oppression. Their symbolism, where they are symbolic, derives from older conventions of femininity, the Mother and the Maiden, which Baierl explores to make allegorical observations about the mechanisms of contemporary society.

Chapter 6

HARALD HAUSER, CLAUS HAMMEL AND RAINER KERNDL: *DIE EIGENVERANTWORTUNG DES MENSCHEN FÜR DIE ENTWICKLUNG SEINER PERSÖNLICHKEIT* *(48)*

By the early sixties, the programme drawn up by the SED in 1946 for achieving basic socialist productive relations had been carried out, and the VIth Party Congress in 1963 therefore passed a new one, this time for developing socialism. The ideological battle over fundamentals was dying down, and a decade and a half of socialist schooling meant that people committed to the perspective of the SED were now entering their professions. The objective of education and leisure was now primarily to proceed with cultivating the 'allseitig und harmonisch entwickelte, körperlich und geistig hochgebildete Persönlichkeit eines jeden Menschen'. *(49)* After the literature of the fifties had been so concerned with economic matters, and with promoting the world of work to its more respectable, influential status as a subject, writers began to turn to life outside the farm and factory gates as an extension, rather than an alternative, to the contemporary concept of socialist personality. Playwrights had established the central importance of work and socio-economic relations at the point of production for personal development, and this was vital to projecting working women for a public so accustomed to the ideological implications of the *Hausfrau* image. Now, it was recalled that Marx and Lenin had described how, in creating new social relations, the working classes would be able to create a whole new life-style affecting every sphere of human interaction with a specific moral profile:

> Die Persönlichkeit in der sozialistischen Gesellschaft wird vor allem durch die *aktive und bewußte Tätigkeit* für die Erhaltung des Friedens und den Aufbau der sozialistischen und kommunistischen Gesellschaft, durch die Aneignung der marxistisch-leninistischen Weltanschauung, durch das Streben nach allseitiger Bildung und hohem fachlichen Wissen und Können und durch die Aneignung und Verwirklichung der Grundsätze der sozialistischen Moral sowie durch eine optimistische Lebensauffassung, schöpferische Selbständigkeit und Aufgeschlossenheit gegenüber dem Neuen charakterisiert. *(50)*

As a result, even though the theatres in the early sixties were caught up in the aftermath and assessment of the sealed German border, the theme of choice for East or West was presented less frequently as a subject of economic class war and increasingly as the choice for or against personal fulfilment. As the decade drew onwards, and the GDR became more prosperous, this question of individual potential became interwoven with attacks on selfish complacency and petty-bourgeois manifestations of *Spießbürgerlichkeit*. Love and marriage came under particular scrutiny, since a person's attitude in domestic and intimate affairs was considered symptomatic of his or her overall social *Einstellung*.

Parallel to this general cultural development, the sixties had witnessed a debate about the status of women in contemporary society, and exhortations for greater female participation in the mechanisms of political and professsional responsibility. Much discussion followed a communiqué issued by the Central Committee of the SED in 1961: *Die Frau - Der Frieden und der Sozialismus*, that was mentioned frequently in political speeches over the next few years. Concrete steps were taken to encourage women to improve their qualifications, in conjunction with the scientific-technical revolution, under a wide scheme known as 'Frauenförderung'. This topic was to provide material for the playwrights Rolf Gozell and Siegfried Pfaff towards the end of the sixties, while the broader issues of gender roles received varied treatment from the pens of Peter Hacks, Joachim Knauth, Volker Braun and Heiner Müller, as well as many lesser known writers.

In the meantime, the major form to evolve through the sixties was the *Konversationsstück*. For many critics, this term came to be somewhat pejorative. It was considered a weakness to write a play that was a 'mere' conversation piece. Some playwrights defied this prejudice to write plays that were little more than exchanges of views in a small and static setting; others combined discussion of this nature with a more dynamic plot. Nevertheless, as a generic term the word has its uses, and it is employed here without evaluative sense. Dramatists were looking for new structures. The battlefronts of internal class war were receding, there was a climate of basic consensus, socialism had been consolidated and the direction the country was moving in was felt to be more or less settled. Non-antagonistic contradictions were the order of the day. For playwrights who had written in the struggle between socialism and capitalism, even younger ones such as Baierl, these new conditions posed problems for the conventional dramatic approach with its protagonist and antagonist, as the failure of *Johanna von Döbeln* testified. The *Konversationsstück* posited the principles of self-analysis, of taking responsibility for one's faults and resolving to grow as a person and become a more considerate member of the community. It did this by exposing one or more characters to the criticisms of an interlocutor.

In considering the structure and evolution of this method, I shall be examining the female characters of three authors, Harald Hauser, Claus Hammel and Rainer Kerndl, in relation to two common themes: the choice for or against socialist Germany, and the role of housewife as a restriction on personality development. Since generic nouns are useful approximations but no more, a comparison of their plays should further serve to draw attention to distinguishing features.

On the whole, the *Konversationsstück* was the work of a fresh generation of writers. Harald Hauser was an older recruit, and the formal contradictions of class conflict emerge more strongly in his plays than in those of his younger colleagues. He belonged to the generation that had experienced Hitler as adults. He spent his exile in France, where he fought in the Resistance and worked on the underground newspaper of the German opposition, *Volk und Vaterland*. Returning to Berlin in the late forties, he came under the influence of Friedrich Wolf, and as a playwright he subscribed largely to Wolf's Aristotelian methods. The theme which preoccupied Hauser throughout his dramatic career was Western anti-communism and sabotage, and it was from this angle that he approached the subject-matter of *Barbara* (1963).

The plot for *Barbara* is borrowed in many respects from an earlier work, *Am Ende der Nacht* (1953), which had been performed at almost every theatre in the country between 1955 and 1963, a total of 39 productions and almost a thousand performances. The original play was conceived as a thriller, set against a crisis at work and with a strong love element. The absorbing relationships between the three characters are inspired by a backcloth of sabotage and blackmail at the height of the Cold War. Harassed by threatening letters about his collaboration with the Nazis, the engineer Jenssen secretly plans to leave for a post in India with his fiancée, the laboratory technician Eva. Jenssen is frightened that his superior, the Russian Strogow, is a former prisoner-of-war who would have cause to despise him, and he also fears that Eva is falling in love with this man because of her greater enthusiasm for socialist developments. When Eva learns of his plans, she is horrified that he wants to abandon his work just when a fault in the generator threatens to stop production and cause damage. The denouement, collapsed into a single night, sets the tension for probing dialogue, as Eva and Jenssen question themselves and each other, with Strogow functioning as the wise and witty Communist mentor.

Eva is primarily defined as a character by the love interest she provides, and although she works in the laboratory, allusions to her technical activities are brief, whereas the men are constantly called to the engineering challenge which faces them. This play, in its turn, is similar to Karl Grünberg's *Golden fließt der Stahl* (1950), where another laboratory assistant called Eva, representing progress, exposes an act of sabotage, thereby rehabilitating the man she loves. Again, her profile is romantic rather than professional, and neither play breaks fundamentally with the convention according to which men dominate the professional action in thrillers. Hauser's Eva is not constructed, initially, as a woman of confidence, initiative or political sophistication. Yet it is her task to convince Jenssen of the error of his decision, or at least to clear the way for Strogow to do so.

Hauser's trio represent a more general comment on the future of the GDR itself. Under the guidance of Soviet allies, with the experience of history behind them, Germans can build a socialist society of their own. On the one hand, they are unable to do this without help, symbolized here not only by Strogow's intervention in the personal life of Eva and Jenssen, but also by the gift of the Soviet stock company to its German workers. (These transfers reached a peak in 1952-3.) On the other hand, they must be the agents of their own history, learning as they build. Eva, who is of working-class, Social-Democratic parentage, represents the vanguard of the German people, identifying socialism as her cause on the simplest level. Jenssen's origins are petty-bourgeois and collaborationist. He must be taught by Eva to overcome the past.

Because the play is dependent on the 'ability' of the figures to articulate feelings and ethics, Eva is obliged to undergo a rapid transformation in the middle act in order to persuade Jenssen to stay: she must move from hesitancy and confusion, by way of pertinent questions and defence of Strogow's administration, to powerful reason and, ultimately, anger. Eva, whose relationship to Jenssen is personal, unlike Strogow's, is essential to the conversion because Jenssen's political fears, suspicions and prejudices spring from feelings rooted in his private life: his family background, his nationalism, the war and his love of Eva. This function of bridging the divide between the private and the professional/political falls, by means of her romantic role, to the woman.

The function is taken over by Barbara in the later play, but with a difference. Barbara is an engineer and a party member who intervenes when Uwe, a colleague whom she loves, sabotages the plant where they work with the intention of fleeing across the border with his delinquent daughter, Karin. However, it is the night of 13th August, 1961, and Uwe's plans are disrupted by the sealing of the Berlin border. Barbara convinces Uwe and Karin that they should stay and make a fresh start in their hitherto negative and resentful lives.

The distinction between Eva and Barbara can be explained by ten years of East German history. In the sixties, it is the SED which plays the key role in directing and building socialism, independently of outsiders. Barbara is, therefore, a well-versed German Communist. Secondly, the industrial status of women has changed. Barbara is a doctor of engineering, like Uwe. Such women were rare in 1953, but in 1963 Barbara is 'typical' as the reflection of a trend initiated and encouraged by the party.

Hauser's method in *Barbara* is also new. The plot has, of course, been adapted to rest on the construction of the Berlin wall. While the theme of anti-imperialism was not a new one for Hauser, by this time the concept of socialist patriotism had, in the face of a seemingly irreversible division, replaced aspirations for a united Germany. Literature in general was expressing a great deal of interest in identification with the GDR and rejection of the temptations proferred by the Federal Republic, which had long used West Berlin as a base for propaganda exercises and economic interference. *(51)*

However, more had changed than the shell. Hauser posed his argument in a different way, using certain techniques to destroy the fourth wall, thereby 'allowing' the characters to present their own case to the audience. The historical contradictions between advocates and opponents of socialism no longer determined Hauser's approach, and the two main figures, both Germans, one a Communist and one a cynic whose bitterness could be understood in terms of disappointments arising out of East German history itself, were not polarized in such a clear-cut manner. The guiding imbalance of *Am Ende der Nacht* between the pleasant mentor-figure and the impetuous fugitive had to be replaced, enabling the audience to acquire some leeway in shifting its sympathies. Even so, there is no real doubt about who is right. Barbara's consistent morality and socialist commitment are superior to Uwe's aloof desire to solve his problems by flight. And Karin's predicament, while she has an obvious grievance in her unjustified penal conviction, is presented as the rectifiable result of an erroneous assessment by short-sighted outsiders. The standard literary history describes Barbara with approval:

> Hohes Verantwortungsbewußtsein, geschichtliche Einsicht und persönlicher Einsatz formen diese lebensvolle Frauengestalt zu einer sozialistischen Persönlichkeit. *(52)*

Nevertheless, the disequilibrium was still unsatisfactory, and in a later version of the play, *Barbara: 3 Biographien in 2 Akten* (1968), Hauser cut much of Barbara's moralizing and added a framework which placed her in a more vulnerable and ambivalent light: seven years later, she herself wants to escape, this time from an unfulfilling marriage to Uwe, and it is Karin who refuses to let her run away. The daughter has developed from a teenage rebel with dreams of Riviera casinos into a celebrated veterinary surgeon, which both gives her greater dramatic status, and also testifies to the opportunities the GDR can provide for willing youth and for women. This adaptation took place, it would seem, because the earlier Barbara was too good to be true and needed a dose of dramatic flaw.

On superficial inspection, Hauser appears to use a Brechtian principle in *Barbara*, that of the gestus. In the first version, the end of the play is revealed at the beginning by the framework of a theatre within a theatre. The three characters come out of the audience to tell their story by *showing* their behaviour on that fateful night. This gives the impression of a study of the three figures, reinforced by the black-out and spotlight as each one narrates his or her story, interspersed with acted dialogue. The effect, however, is far from Brechtian. The lyrical language conveying psychological moods evokes a powerful emotional response. The suspense element is still present, and the same darkness which isolates the characters simultaneously provides a further thrilling magnetism. The romantic factor is also crucial in drawing tension and empathy for Uwe's political choice.

Although Barbara emerges as an exemplary Communist, committed to people and anxious to guide and help, her actual motivation for becoming involved with Uwe and trying to win his confidence is her love. Her pedagogic function is made dramatically exciting by a romance, so that the link is forged between the individuals on stage and the historical backcloth. Barbara insists that there is no contradiction between her identity as a woman in love and her identity as a party functionary: again, it falls to the woman to bridge the false divide. For Uwe, the idea of a party member loving a social cynic is the 'Quadratur des Kreises' (p.21). As an exemplary comrade, however, Barbara believes in the power of reason. She differs from the 'Partisanin' in the film they have seen (the reference is to *Der Einundvierzigste*) because she loves enough to want to persuade, whereas the Partisanin kills her lover. The qualities that distinguish her in personal relationships are those that make her a good Communist: commitment, integrity, human understanding and faith in the ability of right to prevail. In fact, there is a difference between Barbara and her party not explicitly elaborated: she gives Uwe the opportunity to try to cross the border, but the party has taken action to seal the frontier, thus preventing Uwe from leaving - even if the motive is to prevent outsiders from getting in, as Barbara suggests. In this version, Uwe freely decides to stay. In the later version, he tries to escape, but fails.

It is Barbara's task to explain the party's action. She relates their love directly to its historical context, as the tanks roll past to the accompaniment of what was reputedly Lenin's favourite classical piece, Beethoven's 'Appassionata':

> UWE: Beethoven! Im feindlichen Rasseln der Panzer! Pervers! Schön bist du! *Schließt sie in die Arme.* Wo sind wir? Wo sind Musik, Schönheit, Liebe . . .? Alles unwirklich! Alles! Außer den Panzern.
> BARBARA: Alles wirklich: Schönheit, Liebe. Und die Panzer.
> UWE: Die Panzer zermalmen unsere Liebe.
> BARBARA: Sie schützen sie (p.43).

The pattern of identification between a woman and love and progress is already a familiar one. What is new is the identification of the woman with the tougher aspects of class war and anti-imperialism. It occurred in plays set in times of war and resistance, but hardly in years of superficial peace. Hauser's message, here, is that an act of coercion may be necessary in the interests of peace, and the figure Barbara signifies a harmony between rational understanding of this iron law of history and emotional acceptance of it.

Barbara's professional profile, like Eva's, is unconvincing. Both Barbara and Uwe are qualified engineers, but only Uwe is defined as an engineer by his language. His soliloquies betray a preoccupation with his work and his act of sabotage, whereas Barbara's parallel monologues are devoted to the man she loves. In spite of a formal recognition of female equality, then, Hauser still uses gender-based conventions in constructing these figures. It is thus through Uwe that the economic stage is set. As a politically neutral intellectual of bourgeois origins, whose advice is overruled by a careerist, he resents the implications of the *Plan Neue Technik,* which called upon ordinary workers to use their creative powers to improve workplace technology. The electrical power system he aims to disrupt symbolizes the audacious technological progress of socialism.

That Barbara is also competent in her work is learnt only indirectly, through Uwe's anecdote about the barge she salvaged:

> Als Sie den betrunkenen Schlepperkapitän an Land hievten und seinen Kahn vor die Rampe bugsierten: wie ein erfahrener Flußschiffer. Mit Präzision und Charme. Ich wunderte mich, daß Ihnen die schwarzen Kerle gehorchten, ohne zu maulen (p.16).

This tells us that Barbara has the authoritative manner befitting a pedagogue. It is this manner which she adopts for Karin. The girl needs and admires firmness, and Uwe has not provided it because he has used his daughter as an excuse to despise his environment, instead of coming to terms with it and fighting for what is right. The reason for his cynicism is explained by the past. Impetuous and idealistic in his political allegiances, he was betrayed by both Hitler and Stalin. As a man, he was made a killer by the war. Barbara, meanwhile, as a young girl, protected a resistance fighter with her silence. Uwe calls her a 'kommunistische Jungfrau' (p.34). Again, it is the historically passive woman who stands for peace, trust and goodness, invoking the symbols of Christian holiness. The man, Uwe, had to be sullied by action. His coldness isolates him and prevents him from confronting adversity. Barbara is the very opposite. She possesses the psychological insight so often attributed to women, enabling her to pierce souls, analyze weaknesses and offer guidance. This is essential to her role as mentor. Barbara has assimilated Strogow's function and combined it with Eva's. The Soviet citizen, as the *deus ex machina*, a comparative outsider with the power of experience behind him, has made way for the German still learning from her mistakes and enmeshed by her own feelings. Barbara is concerned for Uwe as a potential Communist and a potential husband.

Five years later, in the new version, Hauser envisages the subsequent marriage of Barbara and Uwe, introducing some critical observations about patriarchal attitudes in the husband which pursue a theme touched upon by Eva in 1953. Uwe's love, like Jenssen's, is protective and possessive, and stifles a woman's personality. Barbara in 1968 has given up her job for their young child and is unhappy at growing out of touch with her profession. Uwe, absorbed by a demanding and challenging position, discusses his work not with her, but with a (female) colleague. He 'helps' Barbara with her diploma by solving problems for, not with her. In short, he shows no respect for her scientific training, and showers her instead with flowers and gifts, as if she were a goddess on a pedestal, not a woman of intellect.

The connexion between this framework and the retelling of the 1961 episode is tenuous: Karin, now a woman who has achieved great things in her own right, advises Barbara not to be escapist, and asks Barbara and Uwe to reconstruct the night when Barbara herself tried to prevent the fugitives from refusing to face problems. The idea that occasional self-assessment strengthens a marriage foreshadows works by Hammel and Kerndl, but in this case, Karin's suggestion that the couple can learn about themselves by re-enacting the past is not followed up sufficiently to justify the exercise. However, by introducing a further level of theatre so that we are suddenly, at the end, confronted with actors acting actors acting the characters re-enacting themselves, Hauser playfully rejects the construction of either a happy or a sad ending. The actors refuse to play such hackneyed climaxes, leaving the audience to discuss the implications of the experiment. The open-ended play was becoming a familiar means of inviting audience discussion by this period. Baierl's *Johanna von Döbeln* was written in the same year, and other dramatists were to follow suit, especially when writing for the *Kammertheater*. All the same, it must be recognized that Hauser had loaded the dice slightly by setting a mood to encourage the audience to want the marriage to succeed. The idea was to invite criticism of selfish forms of behaviour with a view to (self-)correction, not to state the case for divorce. Rudi Strahl's *In Sachen Adam und Eva,* first performed the following year, was a more successful attempt at the same thing.

The later version of *Barbara* is the final play, and the most purely conversational, of a trio that were in some ways the same work. The first two plays are also thrillers, like most of Hauser's earlier writing, but the conversational form was embryonic in *Am Ende der Nacht,* with its middle act of confession and ethical argumentation. In the first *Barbara,* the suspense and adventure are still there, but the non-antagonistic confrontation of values and beliefs is predominant in the absence of an anonymous class enemy. Although the memories of the three characters are presented in parallel, creating a multiple perspective, a kind of dialogue emerges, blending sporadically into actual conversations. This is theatre of conversion, of *Ankunft. Barbara: 3 Biographien in 2 Akten* lacks even that element of opposition. It is theatre of self-examination, of *Bewährung,* the literary current concerned with the ability of protagonists to preserve their socialist values in the more settled days of 'der entwickelte Sozialismus'. The pedagogue Barbara is challenged to remember her own lessons, and to find the will to reapply them. The conventional function of the female teacher had changed to reflect developments in history, and the position of women in particular.

It is over the device of the pedagogue that the drama of Claus Hammel departs most markedly from the fashion. The social mentors in his plays are male characters, who offer a sobering hand of guidance to their female counterparts. Sabine, in *Um neun an der Achterbahn* (1964), is silly and immature in putting her boyfriend, the party secretary Moritz, to the test, and Jette, in *Morgen kommt der Schornsteinfeger* (1967), behaves like a headstrong little girl in rejecting the experience of her old sweep Ratunde. But neither of these young women can be dismissed for their foolish behaviour. Hammel is clearly aware that this might have been a danger, as disclaimers in the text indicate:

> SABINE: Bist du nicht, wie man sein soll? Tüchtig, geradeaus, linientreu? Und ich: albern, unreif, überheblich. Du der Mann - ich eine dumme Gans (p.163),

> JETTE: Offenbar hat er übersehn, daß ich älter geworden bin . . . Er nennt mich einen albernen Backfisch (p.301).

Both are motivated by concerns which are important to them in discovering their own identity, and both are capable of responsible development.

Hammel was anxious that his characters should not be played as stereotypes, and he constantly warned producers, actors and the public against clichés. He has always become very involved with his characters in the process of writing them, altering the original formal conception of his plays again and again once the characters start to assume compulsive personalities of their own, as he described to Irene Böhme in an interview:

> Und nun geschieht es natürlich, daß diese Geschöpfe, da sie einmal da sind, mit den Plänen nicht nur ihres Schöpfers, sondern auch denen der anderen Geschöpfe, die auch da sind - absichtsvoll da sind -, und mit diesen Geschöpfen selbst zusammenstoßen: mit deren Plänen, Anschauungen, Gesinnungen, Irrtümern, Eigentümlichkeiten (den 'Macken'), Zielen usw. *(53)*

Interesting formal experiments with jigsaw models - the idea of a fairy tale about a girl who believes her happiness comes entirely from herself and who is then stripped piece by piece of those parts of her which are not self-generating *(Morgen kommt der Schornsteinfeger)*, or the attempt to translate the complexities of socio-technological progress into the story of a village's transformation into a city *(Rom oder Die zweite Erschaffung der Welt*, 1976) - are pushed into the background as Hammel grapples with the more enthralling material provided by the characters. Hammel acknowledges an affinity with Naturalism in his endeavours to portray normal individuals with relatively quotidian preoccupations. He writes a kind of *milieu* drama, avoiding too many gripping events on stage and preferring to report action within the dominant conversational style. In both *Um neun an der Achterbahn* and *Morgen kommt der Schornsteinfeger* he uses the device of the dinner or housewarming party, where guests sharpen their wits on each other, revealing attitudes and comparing philosophies. Dialogues on matters of ethics and outlook, leading to personal decisions, are a major component of his plays. His concern to protect the individuality of his characters is intended to awaken sympathy and deter hasty condemnation. His figures have choices, but these are made against a background which conditions them and determines these choices. Hammel insists that proper attention to the personal details of a role will induce understanding of the many subtle ways in which the environment moulds people. In a letter to Rüdiger Bernhardt, Hammel maintains that the everyday touches which producers so often avoid are what the audience want, and need, to help them bridge the gap between themselves and the characters they are asked to judge. *(54)*

There are many examples of this in *Um neun an der Achterbahn*, where the central character leaves her foster-parents in Berlin in a fit of pique against her boyfriend, to accompany her own mother, a stranger, to Hanover. Sabine's game of buying oranges one at a time to irritate shopkeepers indicates the nature of capitalist economic relationships and their effect on sales behaviour, and it also reveals Sabine's response as an outsider from a different society. When a neighbour discloses that *Astoria* are Willi's favourite cigarettes, he is describing the GDR's dependence on foreign goods, but also highlighting Willi's pride in refusing them from Toni, Sabine's arrogant Western mother.

This play, too, began as something quite different - an attempt to compare living communities of people at a time when the GDR was building a consciousness of its own distinctive identity. Hammel was then drawn into the problems of his maturing heroine, which became the primary subject of the work, and the context became less obtrusive, although it was still decisive, as Hammel's 'Nachwort' makes clear:

> Ich glaube, die Geschichte ist sehr einfach und übersichtlich erzählt: Ein junges Mädchen wird erwachsen. Die Umstände sind zum Teil ungewöhnlich insofern, als nur wenige Mädchen weniger Länder auf der Erde solche Bedingungen zum Erwachsenwerden haben wie Sabine. Es ist kein Fehler, wenn das Publikum nach der Vorstellung findet, die Geschichte gehe doch eigentlich über die Geschichte eines jungen Mädchens hinaus, sie habe einen doppelten Boden. Den hat sie nun tatsächlich. Aber doppelte Böden werden beispielsweise in Schmugglerkoffern nicht angebracht, damit sie, was sie bergen, auch gleich effektvoll darbieten, eher im Gegenteil - nicht wahr? So bitte ich dringend, mit Friedrich Dürrenmatt, den Vordergrund, den ich gebe, richtig zu spielen; der Hintergrund wird sich von selbst einstellen (p.183).

The result is a mixture of individual, chance factors and social, typical factors influencing Sabine to return to Berlin. To see the play as positing purely an opposition of East and West German society within the microcosm of Sabine's world would be as one-sided a misreading as to miss Hammel's political premise, but clearly a theatre company can do much to reinforce or banish the impression that Sabine's choice is simply for socialism. As she points out to Moritz in relation to her pregnancy and her disillusionment with her selfish Western boyfriend, Michael:

> Das passiert seit tausend Jahren und hätt mir auch hier passieren können. Vielleicht nicht von dir, aber sonst. Mach mir also keine Rechnung daraus, daß mir das nur dort passieren konnte; denn es stimmt nicht (p.167).

But the 'fact' is that it *was* in the West that Sabine's personal tragedies happened, including the death of her stepfather, of whom she was so fond in spite of political differences. These misfortunes carry their own dramatic consequences - for the plot and for audience sympathies.

A breakdown of the factors in Sabine's ultimate decision reveals three categories of motive. There are 'chance' factors: it is in the West that Michael lets her down and Rudolf dies; it is in the East that she was brought up, in the East that she has friends and familiar surroundings to run to for comfort. Then there are many factors which are conditioned by differences in society: in the East, Sabine has her own job, whilst in the West she is bored. Sabine's mother is entirely a creature of her environment - her material problems before her remarriage and the degrading life she led prevented her from offering Sabine a home, or so she insists; her distorted vision of the GDR makes her analysis of Sabine's needs inaccurate; her social hypocrisy is a result of business concerns. Michael's particular form of anti-establishment rebellion, combined with his readiness to use his father's money, is also the product of a middle-class Western upbringing. There is, however, a third category of factors which are not necessarily socially typical: Moritz offers Sabine a more stimulating relationship because Michael has no social aspirations to fight for, and that is partly because the opposition in the play is between working-class conditions in the GDR and middle-class conditions in the Federal Republic. The behaviour of the Hanover circle typifies one economic class - albeit the dominant one - in a society that is in contradiction. Sabine's choice, then, is determined by all these particularities.

Hammel achieves something which Hauser could only postulate in *Barbara* - a tangled web of private and political, 'contingent' and 'necessary' motivations. The epic element is considerably reduced and obscured. Unlike Barbara, who always knows what is right, the pedagogue Moritz experiences a tussle between the temptation to use party machinery to keep Sabine near him, as she demands, and his political integrity and indignation at Sabine's immaturity.

Hammel's inspiration for the play was an actual case of a young girl whose 'real' (biological) mother appeared from the West to claim her. This offered Hammel an opportunity to exploit his much-favoured device: the outsider observing an alien world. The blend of realism to emerge has two aims. One is a social comparison, and the other an explanation of people in terms of their environment, as Hammel pleaded in his 'Nachwort':

> 'Die Menschen da drüben haben die Nase auch mitten im Gesicht.' So sollten sie auch gespielt werden: mit der Nase mitten im Gesicht, als normale Menschen eben . . . Aber selbst bei strengster 'Objektivität' ergäben sich die . . . gewissen Unterschiede zwischen Nase und Nase. Die Menschen dort leben

> in anderen Verhältnissen, nicht nur an sich, sondern auch zueinander (p.184).

The way that Sabine responds to both her environments is above all determined by her experience as a young woman.

Hammel inscribes the familiar message of *Der kaukasische Kreidekreis* beneath the play's title: 'die Kinder den Mütterlichen, damit sie gedeihen' (p.89). Hammel explores this theme on three levels. Sabine has to choose between two societies, but also between two mothers, and subsequently she has to choose an environment where she can become a mother herself. Hammel has almost always found a domestic vehicle for his political material: Jette is concerned with her identity as a wife, Jenny Treibel (*Frau Jenny Treibel*, 1963) and Mercadet (*Le Faiseur*, 1970) with matchmaking for their brood, and Viktoria, in *Rom*, with reuniting her family. Sabine, as a daughter and prospective mother, permits the playwright to approach his theme from various angles.

Sabine seeks status from her reputation as a casual conqueror of men's hearts. She ascribes a colleague's antagonism disdainfully to 'Torschlußpanik' (p.92). Being attractive to men is a measure of success. But Sabine's true feelings are quite different, and when she meets Moritz the act is difficult to maintain. The invitation to Hanover is meaningless to her compared with her desperate attempt to obtain a public declaration of love from a man who represents the supreme status symbol: the party. It is only her adolescent resentment at losing the challenge that sends her to Hanover.

There, Sabine's life is governed by her role as daughter of a wealthy house. She has nothing to do but accompany the maid on shopping trips, an intimacy which Toni dislikes. Toni's dinner parties are partly intended to introduce Sabine to advantageous marriage candidates, and Sabine rebels by being obnoxious and threatening to mention shocking subjects, such as contraception and abortion, as a counter to Toni's compliant table talk.

Sabine is thus confronted with a new kind of dependence on men. When she signs a petition in town, the repercussions at home show how her identity is subsumed to that of the Schneider household. Michael is diverting, but he has other concerns, including his studies, and the picture Sergius paints of a marriage of convenience would leave her in the role of a legally kept woman. This dependence is confirmed when Sabine reveals her pregnancy. She faces a choice between an illegal, hypocritical abortion, or else marriage to preserve respectability in a circle where appearances breed business.

In the GDR, single parenthood is a viable possibility. If Sabine is to make her own decisions about her life and her child, it must be there. The different attitudes of the two communities are voiced by Sabine's mothers. Toni puts respectability first, but Sabine will not sacrifice her personal integrity meaninglessly and rejects marriage as a solution. Clara, her foster mother, although she has expressed conventional attitudes about somebody else's illegitimate child (to show that old ideas die hard), defends Sabine's right to bring up a child on her own.

Sabine is thus able to avoid the spectre of abortion in the East German context. At the time, abortion was still illegal on both sides of the border. The only point which Hammel tries to make, therefore, is that the medical profession in the West (Michael) adopts double standards because of prejudices inherent in the commercial family system. Sabine is not shocked by the idea of abortion itself. It had, after all, long been a left-wing demand, even though demographic considerations and deference to certain bodies of opinion delayed its introduction until 1972. She is perturbed by the unwillingness of her boyfriend and mother to consult her about her feelings. The contrast between Michael and Moritz is thus complete without Moritz expressing any opinions about abortion: Michael finds it hard to accept Sabine's individuality, whereas Moritz encourages her to make her own choices.

Moritz helps Sabine to grow up, and the GDR provides the material conditions for her personal development, so that Sabine learns how not to live in the reflected glory of her male conquests and escapes assimilation into patriarchal family structures. But although audience interest has been aroused from the first scene by the romantic potential of Sabine's relationship with Moritz, the curtain falls before a final happy embrace. Sabine's decision to stay is not the end of her story, but a prerequisite for her to accept her responsibilities to herself and her child.

Jette Columbus, in *Morgen kommt der Schornsteinfeger*, does not have the problem of identifying the material basis for her happiness. She takes socialism entirely for granted as something good and necessary, but complete: the fight is over, the war and the class struggle have been won, and now the younger generation can relax and enjoy the fruits of prosperity sown by their elders. Or so Jette believes. The sweep Ratunde, her father-figure, tries to convince her that life is not so simple.

Hammel explores the housewife function to represent Jette's retreat from social activity. She believes that happiness is there for the taking and does not have to be worked for by individuals and communities. The role of housewife itself is not under attack as a form of self-indulgent laziness. There are several references to the work that must be done in the home. However, Hammel does draw attention to the isolation and monotony of domestic routine. Jette's lack of social intercourse, caused by giving up her job and moving to a new flat, will deprive her of the personal nourishment she needs to feed her marriage to Jule.

Jette visualizes the future in her new home idealistically and with a touch of superstition. She is the child that was born on the Sabbath Day (p.325), a lucky person, whose life is charmed by her special relationship with the neighbourhood sweep. (She was an orphan and he became her fairy godfather.) In German folklore, too, sweeps bring luck. But chimneys are obsolete, and Jette is moving to a centrally-heated *Neubauwohnung*. Ratunde is therefore sceptical about her plans to spend her time on an abstract indulgence which she calls 'erwachsen sein' (p.331). Life, argues Ratunde, needs content, and the individual has to make the content for him/herself. Jette's search for a magical recipe is pointless. Jule's good salary is not a reason for her to leave her job, with the opportunities this affords for self-fulfilment, contact and participation in the community.

The housewarming party in Act IV is a warning about the options which might tempt Jette if she relinquishes her own sense of identity: an obsession with furniture, larger cars, and name-dropping. Jette becomes increasingly aware that her role as a housewife is inserting her into a new patriarchal structure. Having rejected Ratunde's advice as paternalistic, she has substituted him with a husband whom she admires to the point of self-negation:

> Ich hab ihn nicht mehr soviel gefragt wie früher. Schließlich bin ich verheiratet, und Jule ist auch nicht der Dümmste (p.302).

She married Jule to enjoy his reflected glory:

> Er gefiel mir. Er ist was. Ich kann mich mit ihm sehen lassen (p.332).

But Jette discovers that she does not like running around at Jule's beck and call. She eventually decides that he has no insight into her worries and no respect for her feelings. Nor does he share his thoughts with her. Act V is the culmination of these fears: a plea for regular analysis of their relationship.

Hammel does not present Jule's choice in terms of either paid employment or a housewife's duties. Domestic chores will have to be done in either case, and there is still clear division of labour in the Columbus household, since Jule is something of a 'Pascha' (p.312). A job is a beginning because it brings acknowledgement, however routine:

> Dann hab ich nämlich Kollegen und kann beweisen, daß ich ein maßgeblicher gesellschaftlicher Faktor bin (p.363).

This is a basis for personal development, but people often exist outside the factory gates, too, and work is not the sole purpose of life. The terms of debate have moved on from Sakowski's world. For Lene Mattke and Lisa Martin, joining the ranks of the employed was a means of finding an identity and fostering one's own creativity. They countered prejudices, particularly strong on the land, about the status of women. Hammel's characters, including Jette, ask a new question about the broader implications of self-fulfilment and individual aspirations, especially in domestic relationships. Lene Mattke's kitchen dresser symbolized her self-esteem and her worth to the community: Jette has more material comforts than Lene might have dreamed of, but she learns that she does not want to be a *Möbelmensch* like Barbara Engel. By exploiting the situation of the 'little woman' as an extension, servant and refuge for her important husband, Hammel draws attention to the individual's need for affirmation in respect of his or her own life. In so doing, he also paints an effective portrait of a respected man, with a position and a party card, who has unenlightened attitudes towards his wife. It is not an issue which Hammel elaborates very far. Jule is a likeable person, and once Jette articulates her objections, he adapts.

Hammel has referred to a need for a 'prophylaktische Dramaturgie', as distinct from the more traditional cathartic or 'therapeutische Dramaturgie'. *(55)* In the late sixties, political complacency and economic prosperity gave rise to a brand of technocratic *Spießbürgerlichkeit*, and consumerism acquired some force. Young people found it difficult to identify with an ethos of struggle when it seemed that everything was running smoothly without demanding much of their participation. In the West, where the Social Democrats were gaining support, annexationist threats were obscured, and Western propaganda broadcasts concentrated on the more seductive ideology of the *Konvergenztheorie*. Hammel's plays are fundamentally debates which seek to involve the audience in multi-sided argumentation about socialist values. *Morgen kommt der Schornsteinfeger* relies heavily on the technique of counterposing attitudes through characters who are not to be presented as stereotypes, with the aim of inciting the audience to agree or disagree with certain sentiments. Hammel saw his object in this play as an alarum to vigilance:

> Zur Wachsamkeit gegen die Beruhigung, daß es keine Feinde mehr um uns und in uns selbst, in jedem einzelnen gäbe, seit wir Betreiber und Nutznießer der Gesellschaft des entwickelten Sozialismus sind. Diese Feinde - nennen wir sie ruhig so - schlafen nie. Sie heißen: Genügsamkeit, Trägheit, Überheblichkeit, Bildungsstillstand, Versöhnlertum, Mangel an Selbstkritik, Undiszipliniertheit usw. Einer, ein besonders gefährlicher, heißt: Entideologisierung. *(56)*

Hammel's purposes are very similar to those of Rainer Kerndl, who saw it as his task to kindle the fires of critical self-awareness, especially among the socialist 'middle-classes' - intellectuals, professionals and functionaries - whence he draws most of his characters:

> Mich interessiert die Gegenwart und wie sie sich reflektiert in den Menschen. Alarmieren will sie angesichts satter Gewohnheiten, genügsamer Selbstzufriedenheit, feiger Furcht, den Widerspruch auch in sich selbst zu erkennen und zu benennen. *(57)*

Like Hammel, Kerndl acknowledges his distance from Brechtian theatre. His characters are predominantly concerned with self-analysis, often after being spurred into scrutiny of their past and present lives by a catalysing event or arrival. As with Hammel, the cause of self-examination is frequently an outsider, who obliges the protagonist(s) to defend a position. After writing two plays suited for *Kammertheater* - *Ich bin einem Mädchen begegnet* (1968) and *Wann kommt Ehrlicher?* (1971) - Kerndl was accused by more straitlaced critics of indulging his characters in an excessively intimate form of psychological dialogue. Both of these plays take place at night, in a flat and a bedroom respectively, and for casts of two and five. Some of the antagonism shown by these critics towards such private settings is attributable to the fact that the plays touch fleetingly upon the game of extra-marital sexual seduction - an innovation in the puritanical history of East German drama.

Kerndl defended this intimacy from a formal point of view:

> Die ganze Welt (kann) durchaus in der Begegnung von nur zwei Menschen stattfinden. Und ich weiß eben auch, und das ließe sich belegen, daß in Stücken mit vierzig Leuten nicht einmal die Kreisstadt stattgefunden hat. *(58)*

He also expressed reservations about the idea that there was a category of personal problems which did not offer significant material for *Gegenwartsdramatik:*

> Mir ist gelegentlich in letzter Zeit untergekommen . . . daß schon wieder sehr allgemeine Warnungen erhoben wurden gegen Stücke - ich war natürlich nicht ganz unbetroffen -, die angeblich zu sehr sich zurückziehen auf den privaten und psychologischen Bereich und daß sich damit doch eigentlich für unsere Gesellschaft nicht das Wesentliche gesagt werden könne. Da werden, wie ich meine, durchaus mögliche Wege der zeitgenössischen, der sozialistischen Dramatik eingeschränkt auf eine unüberlegte, verallgemeinernde Weise. *(59)*

Although criticism of this kind still found a voice, even in the early seventies, the premises of socialist realism had undergone some reappraisal in the previous decade. Glib labels such as 'Formalismus', 'Dekadenz' and 'Modernismus' were replaced by more sophisticated aesthetic analysis, as writers and theoreticians elaborated new tools. A climate which enabled more diverse exploration of people's lives in the young Republic encouraged them to discard the mechanistic anthropomorphizations of socio-economic conflict that the academic Hans Koch attacked in 1965:

> Das Individuelle erscheint nur 'statthaft' als das sinnlich konkrete Erscheinen einer gesellschaftswissenschaftlichen Abstraktion. 'Die Arbeiterklasse ist ... und also muß die literarische Gestalt des Schlossers X ... !' 'Die Mittelbauern in der DDR sind ... und deshalb hat gefälligst auch die

> literarische Gestalt des Mittelbauern Y ... !' 'Sind die Komplementare in unserer Republik nicht ... und darf demzufolge der Komplementar Z in dem Drama auch nicht?!' Durch eine solche Argumentation droht die Gefahr, die Rolle der Kunst als originale Form der Erkenntnis und Aneignung der Welt zu entwerten. Ihr wird dann die Knechtsaufgabe einer bloßen bildhaften Illustration wissenschaftlich durchleuchteter historisch-klassenmäßiger Gesetze und Erkenntnisse zuteil. Gerade hier liegt eine der tiefsten theoretischen Wurzeln des Schematismus in der ästhetischen Theorie wie auch in der künstlerischen Darstellung selbst. Ein solcher Schematismus widerspricht direkt der materialistischen Dialektik, die unserer Geschichtsauffassung, wie unserer Politik innewohnt. *(60)*

The methodological problems of conflating international historical processes with individual development have led Rainer Kerndl to various experiments. These have ranged from the epic, episodal *Die seltsame Reise des Alois Fingerlein* (1967) to the confined and intimate *Ich bin einem Mädchen begegnet* and from the forum of personal and political conflict in *Seine Kinder* (1963) and *Plädoyer für die Suchenden* (1966) to stylized subjective responses to the Middle East crisis in *Nacht mit Kompromissen* (1973). The plea which underlies and unites all these plays, however, is for the individual to come to terms with his or her faults, even if they lie buried in the past. Far from permitting his figures the luxury of navel contemplation, Kerndl suggests that this moral analysis is a foundation for honest, community-minded activity.

Referring to his first play, *Schatten eines Mädchens* (1961), Kerndl was explicit about the need for 'das Fertigwerden mit der faschistischen Vergangenheit und die notwendige Einsicht, daß etwas Neues nicht auf schlecht zugeschütteten Unterhöhlungen, sondern nur auf festem Boden entstehen kann'. *(61)* The characters are largely representatives of national generalities: Dieter, the Nazi; his father, an unprotesting instrument of fascism; Ulrich, the German who befriends Poles; his mother, the unwitting home front; and Halina, the personification of resistance, *the* Pole. The romance between Ulrich and Halina is symbolic only. Halina has no individualized features. In the Polish production in Olsztyn, the first German play in the town's history, the symbol was easily adapted to suit the Polish palate by the implication that Halina did not really love Ulrich, but only used him to hide weapons, thus becoming an unambiguous testimony to Polish heroism. Ulrich's later memories of her, re-enacted on a blacked-out stage (a technique used in several of Kerndl's plays to evoke the past), are an emotional springboard for audience condemnation of Dieter.

Subsequently, Kerndl meandered away from such abstractions, and his figures became more individualized. He was faced with a problem, epitomized in the fate of Beerendonk, the writer's fictional hero in *Ich bin einem Mädchen begegnet,* due to the demise of the individual protagonist as an exemplary crusader for social justice. Social advance was now a collective task, to which many characters contributed, all with their own personal flaws. Moreover, if each individual would analyze his or her own faults, he or she could take a more enlightened and considerate part in the democratic process. After all, as a character in *Der vierzehnte Sommer* (1977, unpublished) summed it up, 'wie einer mit dem liebsten Menschen umgeht, so geht er auch mit der Gesellschaft um'. *(62)*

In *Seine Kinder* Kerndl again used the family as a framework. The contrived Sorge family, based on adoptions at a time of upheaval after the war, reflects social and racial bonds in the German community, recalling *Nathan der Weise*. The family ties between Sorge, Rolf, Judith and Alfred also permit concise treatment of political material. Their background - Judith's Jewish parentage and Rolf's Nazi parentage, and Sorge's loss of his own son Alfred - is portrayed in flashbacks which provide historical and international dimensions to a brief episode in a small town. The dual roles of Sorge (father and *Landrat*), Rolf (son, foster-brother/companion and *Kreisbaudirektor*), Judith (daughter, foster-sister/companion and doctor) and Alfred (estranged son and Westerner), allow discussions of duties and commitments to shift from the domestic sphere into the broader community and back again, and to overlap.

Judith plays a marginal part in the political crisis at Hohengereuth, but she performs a conciliatory function with regard to the Western visitor. Her correspondence and then her affair with Alfred bring the father and son back together. This catalyses assessment, especially by Sorge, of their personal relationship, and the rights and wrongs of the past. Alfred, a self-professed Marxist with idealist notions, is furthermore an arbiter of social progress in the GDR who puts this society to the test. He is disappointed by the reality he finds, and Judith assumes the task of making him understand the complexities involved.

She is not, however, shown very much in her pedagogical role. It is said that Judith has explained things to Alfred, and we are told that she has spent three days taking him round the neighbourhood. The scenes showing them together are romantic rather than polemical. Judith, although she has firm opinions about Rolf's building schemes, does not participate in the stormy debate at the village meeting. This is *her* failing - remaining aloof from the decision-making, being submerged in her private life. Alfred's questions provoke her into realizing this, but ultimately it is left to Sorge, the most far-sighted and experienced character, to tinge Alfred's disillusionment with a dose of constructive realism in front of the audience, and to win him back as a son and a socialist.

Judith is primarily a prop for characters with a clearer profile of their own. She has some kinship with Halina, since she represents Jewry protected by the anti-fascist Sorge at a time when he was sacrificing his own marriage and child for his beliefs. She also impels the confrontation between Rolf and Sorge - at home and as public functionaries - by questioning Rolf's professional conduct. By drawing attention to his self-imposed isolation from her in the flat where they live together, she indicates that he is losing touch with communicative, democratic principles. But Judith has little substance of her own. Her professional interest in Hohengereuth prevents her from being entirely identified by her romantic involvements, but she is the opposite of her father in so far as these involvements sway her political behaviour rather than being swayed by them. Her estrangement from Rolf and her affair with Alfred draw her away from the debate in Hohengereuth in pursuit of her own happiness. Her remark that to live for others - in her caring 'woman's' work as a doctor - is not enough in life was to be echoed by the girl in *Ich bin einem Mädchen begegnet*, who makes the same discovery in another altruistic 'female' vocation, nursing.

In Kerndl's next play, *Plädoyer für die Suchenden*, which relies on a similar conflation of personal and political crises as a forum for verbal debate, the woman Inge shows the same proclivity as Judith for being guided in her politics by episodes of the heart, except that Inge has a detailed, central professional profile, too. Since the play which followed, *Die seltsame Reise des Alois Fingerlein*, offered only minor female roles, with a limited function as factors in Alois's development, it was not until *Ich bin einem Mädchen begegnet* that Kerndl produced a well-delineated woman of some dramatic stature.

The girl, Sie, emerges as a figure with many idiosyncrasies. The play is not built on actions and conflicts of political import, so that the two characters are less determined by plot functions. Their confrontation is not directly antagonistic. They are exposed to each other for discussion and criticism in a single place over a few nocturnal hours. Their conversation touches upon many issues, but Kerndl's pervasive theme of individual responsibility pulls the threads together. The circumstances of their meeting generate feelings of opposition: the writer, Er, indignant at the embarrassing night-time intrusion of Sie, a stranger with a suitcase, into his flat; Sie, on an impetuous quest for recognition and fulfilment in the city, irritated by his claims to superior understanding of the world and the discrepancy between his writing and his private life. But in relating their grievances to each other they also find some support and guidance, so that Er can conclude:

> Ich glaube, daß man in jedem Menschen, mit dem man mal was zu tun hatte, ein Stückchen von sich selber zurückläßt. Und wenn man sich da nicht mehr drum kümmert, verliert man sich selber (p.290).

Again, the conversation is a vehicle for non-antagonistic drama. The girl is the worker, in terms of class, but she has as much right and wrong on her side as the socialist intellectual, the writer. His work is to find literary expression for the moral problems facing his society. She finds that his own practice does not concord with his moral postulations. Furthermore, some of his devices are outdated, as the working class does not consist of heroes and dogmatic stooges. The girl, too, reveals inconsistencies and tells half-truths, which the writer exposes. Her practical insight is blended with escapism, her self-interest with consideration for other people. The contradictions of class have been superseded by contradictions within the individual, played out through interactions between people.

Er and Sie are only partially determined as figures by their gender, and even when their male and female characteristics surface they are ironized or reversed by Kerndl's excursion into gentle comedy. The girl at first creates the impression of straightforward young enthusiasm bursting into the bachelor domain of cynical worldliness, but her inflated image of her adventure is soon punctured by the writer with a sarcastic reference to *Johanna von Döbeln* (p.258).

The very first point that Kerndl establishes about the girl is that she is the more practical of the two. The incident where she rescues the writer from his bathroom flood with a suitcase of useful tools depends for its comic effect on reversing the cultural norm. However, her superior technical status is not later revoked. Kerndl goes on to fill in her background as a works electrician, thus making her knowledge seem possible and natural in contemporary society.

Further assumptions about gender are attacked by a number of amusing idioms which the girl uses. Of her colleagues, she observes:

> Wenn ich drauf warten wollt, bis die mir meine Perspektive optimieren, könnt ich noch als Oma mit'm Werkzeugkasten rumlatschen (p.281),

and:

> Die Lucie ist nämlich gar kein schlechter Kerl (p.262).

She accepts an elegant garment from the writer's wardrobe with the proviso:

> Wenn das Kleid herrenlos ist (p.278).

Nevertheless, as Er realizes, Sie is also anxious to take advantage of her femininity in her search for acknowledgement. In mocking her desire to appear attractive to men, he succeeds in deflecting challenges which he himself finds uncomfortable. For example, she rejects cosy consumerism:

> SIE: Ich seh's doch alle Tage.
> ER: Ist alles immer so, wie's aussieht?
> SIE: Schließlich hab ich Augen im Kopf.
> ER: Hübsche Augen, zweifellos. *Er steht auf.* Haben Sie Hunger? (p.263),

and she criticizes his betrayal of the character Beerendonk:

> SIE: Den Beerendonk dürfen Sie nicht versauen. Sie gehen noch mal zu diesem Theatermenschen. Gleich morgen. Sie müssen hingehen, begreifen Sie das nicht?
> ER: Wozu, mein Kind? Sie sind übrigens ganz verklärt in Ihrer heiligen Entrüstung. Direkt überirdisch schön sind Sie da. Wußten Sie das? Entrüsten Sie Sich öfter, mein Engel; es dient Ihrem Image (p.270).

The girl records similar patronizing comments from her fellow-workers:

> Was stehst du dir aus, Mädchen, bist doch viel zu schön für Theorie (p.261).

Her report of their refusal to let her study has the effect, at this point, of placing such discrimination in a critical light, but when we subsequently learn that the girl has been spinning yarns to explain her very ordinary achievements, we are at a loss to know whether this prejudice was her own wishful invention or whether it had some basis in fact.

The girl's boasts are ambiguous throughout the play. She wants to be different from her friends, to accomplish more than marriage and motherhood, but her ambitions generate emotional contradictions, and she is still extremely dependent on displays of esteem from other people, whatever their nature. She is indignant at having been approached on the street by a man making suggestive advances - still a feature of city life in the GDR and one which rarely receives a mention in literature or in the media, although Irmtraud Morgner succeeded in provoking some debate on the matter with scenes from her montage novel *Leben und Abenteuer der Trobadora Beatriz nach Zeugnissen ihrer Spielfrau Laura*, published in 1974. At the same time, however, the girl is, in a certain sense, proud to have attracted these advances. Since she cares about her appeal to men, her behaviour with the writer is also coquettish. When he makes a pass at her, he believes she provoked him deliberately. Her angry rejection reveals that she is not so self-possessed as she seems, and that she is actually quite insecure about the impression she makes on other people. The writer, too, has mixed feelings about expectations of relationships between men and women, and he remarks with both regretful disbelief and proud amusement that a girl has spent the night in his flat, 'aber es hat nichts stattgefunden' (p.290).

Apart from broaching the subject of sexual behaviour, Kerndl's play delves earnestly into an aspect of family law that began to attract public attention as the divorce rate accelerated: the status of fatherhood. As in many other societies, mothers are commonly considered to be essential to a child's welfare. It is usually mothers who stay at home with newborn or sick children, and it is usually mothers who receive custody of the children in a dissolved marriage. The idea that mothers belong naturally with their children is not as rigid within the East German legal code as in our own, and psychologists who argue against the suitability of creches for babies under a year talk advisedly of the child's need for a 'Bezugsperson'. However, politicians persist in defining women as 'Arbeiterinnen und Mütter' without adopting parallel terminology for men, and the imagery of loving, protective motherhood (as opposed to parenthood) that is reflected in the frequent Mother-symbolism of literature and art appears to have been extended into socialized child-care, where it is almost impossible for men to train as nursery workers (a backlash to the exclusion of women from certain dangerous or strenuous jobs). Considerable discussion of the mother's automatic superiority as a parent was provoked by Eberhard Panitz in 1975 with his story *Absage an Viktoria*, but such challenges have been rare, or else paradoxically limited to female orbits such as the magazine *Für Dich*. *(63)*

That Kerndl had some argument with this assumption can already be detected in *Seine Kinder*. Sorge loses his own son, first to a Nazi stepfather and then to the West, because the mother, too weak to fight the regime, has prior rights. The stage direction (p.62) demands that Sorge should be bitter about this. The writer in *Ich bin einem Mädchen begegnet* also questions maternal privilege, although there is no attempt to compare him with his former wife as a suitable parent. His cynical remarks seem to conceal some ruefulness that his relationship with his son is confined to a financial transaction. The faultless logic of his argument, that it is not blood ties, but living together that makes a bond between parent and child, is negated by the wistful presence on stage of a teddy bear, bought as a present and never given. In both plays, the father-figure acknowledges that circumstances have dictated realities, but both are plagued by doubts. The writer's torn feelings about fatherhood amount to one more of the personal, emotional contradictions which form the basis of Kerndl's *Konversationsstück*.

Wann kommt Ehrlicher? is contained in the same way by unity of time and place, reinforced by the intimacy of night and a bedroom setting. It attracted similar criticisms as its predecessor, and Irene Böhme complained:

> Die Figuren ziehen sich immer stärker auf sich selbst zurück. Es werden die Fenster und Türen geschlossen, man schaut in die Wohnstube oder neuerlich auf Schlafstätten und kann dann stiller Zeuge einer seelischen Entblätterung werden. *(64)*

Böhme, in fact, overlooks the significance of the doors and windows in these two plays. The arrival of the girl through the flat door in *Ich bin einem Mädchen begegnet* heralds a challenge to the writer's ethical laxity, and a counter-challenge to her own. The window in *Wann kommt Ehrlicher?*, which is imagined to be between auditorium and stage, is used frequently by the characters and is a constant excuse for reminders about the effects of Kurt's non-communicative arrogance on the townspeople who work for his factory. True, these devices are employed strictly within the illusory conventions of Aristotelian theatre, with its fourth wall. Even memories are no longer recalled in flashback scenes on a darkened stage, but through narration. However, critics like Böhme overlooked Kerndl's approach to social problems, which was to see them reflected in a domestic unit. Kurt's vices as a husband echo his vices as a director. His failure to respect Ev's feelings and opinions, and his self-righteousness at home, are parallel to his failure to consult the workforce and his absolute faith in the correctness of his grandiose plans for the future as a works director. He even decorates the flat with his diagrams, which he does not explain to Ev, in preference to the Manet and other paintings which hung there before. The brief appearance of the workers Paul and Arthur is part of an attempt to emphasize the relevance of Kurt's professional conduct to his relationship with Ev. The play was written at a time when methods of economic leadership and the importance of democratic involvement in planning were at the forefront of political discussion. These issues penetrate Kurt's household.

At the same time, the play charts a stage in the breakdown of a marriage. It may or may not be an irrevocable breakdown. The final lines of the text give cause for optimism, and this is the cue that Zipes takes in his reading of the play *(65)*, but the productions in Potsdam and Karl-Marx-Stadt were unable to salvage the wreckage of Ev's rebellion, spurred on by a friend from the couple's youth, Su. Ev and Kurt are bound by nothing more than common memories of the time when they were in love twelve years previously. Kurt's admission that he fears Paul and Arthur, a result of his guilty refusal to consult the workforce, and his sudden attempts to take an interest in the children and the shopping suggest a willingness to reform. A tardy, encouraging phone-call from Ehrlicher, whose invitation to dinner has caused so many stirrings and worries, gives Kurt a chance to move constructively, but Ev has already realized that the marriage she was so anxious to defend from an outside temptation is no more than a habit. Su's wild, romantic imaginings, even though they prove to have been inventions, have given her a taste for something else. Her questions are not entirely answered when the curtain falls.

Plays about marriage breakdowns are rareties. *Wann kommt Ehrlicher?* pursues a theme raised by Jette in *Morgen kommt der Schornsteinfeger:* the need to revitalize marriage sporadically by analyzing and assessing. But while Jette's idea pre-empts disaster, Ev is catapulted into doubt after years of resignation by figures from the past. Her resignation is established visually at the beginning of the play as Ev, applying her make-up in front of the mirror (a symbol of her role as an attractive wife), listens to Kurt's complaints, quibbles and accusations in relative silence, conveying the impression that she has heard it all before and has renounced any attempt at reaction or communication. Meanwhile, Kurt establishes himself as one of the most blatantly chauvinist husbands in the East German dramatic repertoire. He refuses to explain his argument with Ehrlicher, an old schoolfriend who arrived unexpectedly at the factory to investigate its position, and, it emerges, never tells her anything about his work. When she asks, ironically, what opinion she is to hold of the argument, he tells her obliviously to stay out of it (p.301). He, on the other hand, is not interested in her (woman's) job as a teacher (p.304) and repeatedly underestimates it (p.298, p.302). He gave her no encouragement to take up research, so that she renounced an attractive opportunity (p.304). He despises housework and expects her to do it, and at the same time he is critical of the results (pp.299-301). He only likes her to work so that they can acquire consumer symbols more rapidly and because it suits his image as a socialist director to have a working wife (p.302). He is completely complacent about her fidelity, sulks if criticized, considers it a service that he is faithful to her, and praises her only for being an attractive woman (p.304), which makes her feel like a prize possession. He accepts no criticism from her of his professional genius, and attributes her questions about Ehrlicher's reservations not to political insight, but to a past emotional attachment. Ehrlicher, the Godot who never arrives, thus exercises two catalysing functions: he represents high-level displeasure with Kurt's management, and he stirs up nostalgia and jealousy in a stagnant marriage. It is Kurt's self-importance which is held responsible for the marital breakdown. Ev is the wronged party.

Into this bursts Su, who enjoys provoking people and destroying complacency. Her romantic vision of self-contained success, travel and constant new relationships and enterprises appeals to Ev, who feels captive, and elicits her admission of attraction to another man some years before. Su also exposes Kurt for his duplicity as a director. But the idealist notions she has culled from books and pictures are overdone and set Kurt on the political offensive. He rediscovers his beliefs and integrity in condemning Su's fantasies. This provides him with his first common ground with Ev and with a basis for a constructive turnabout.

Henceforward it is Su, the challenger, who emerges as the most dejected failure. Her views on the *condition féminine*, on the iniquity of marriage, the tyranny of men and the bliss of sexual freedom, while they make a certain impression on the level-headed Ev, are too absolute. They are born of the despair that she herself has fallen into as a wife and nothing but a wife. She does not have the tenacity to develop an identity of her own, but compensates for her lack of self-fulfilment by dreaming extraordinary adventures, mostly of other people's creation. She is a more extreme version of Sie: contemptuous of the power men have over their wives, but desperate to be sexually attractive. Her extravagances hide insecurity.

By contrast, Ev, who represents balance and common sense in opposition to the hysterical Su and the patriarchal Kurt, is pressed to defend the general principle of married partnership, allowing for rejection of marriage when it is a stale habit. Like Barbara and Jette before her, she is not content with the role of the little woman. She wants to be socially active. Her involvement with the parent-teacher association has been hampered by Kurt's martyred reluctance to collect the children or help with the shopping. She wants recognition for her own work and for her own political development. Her expectations of her husband are therefore higher than they would have been in previous ages, and this reflects what experts hold to be a major cause of the high divorce rate and of the fact that two thirds of applications are filed by women. She also has a professional and intellectual objective which can only be achieved if her marriage is supportive, showing how the personal problems of married women are directly linked to their economic and political record outside the home. Ev's position and her arguments are intended to foster the principles of socialist marriage, a union based on mutual respect for the all-round development of two individuals.

Chapter 7

SIEGFRIED PFAFF AND ROLF GOZELL: *FRAUENFÖRDERUNG*

The communiqué *Die Frau - Der Frieden und der Sozialismus* called for increased state and social support for women, both to enable them to combine their domestic duties with the demands made by their jobs and political commitments, and to encourage them to aim for greater skills and responsibilities. The SED echoed Marx's critique of liberal bourgeois thinking by recognizing that equality could not be achieved purely by the legal declaration of rights. Social, material and ideological disadvantages would have to be countered if women were to climb the professional and political scales as freely as men.

In fact, however, the SED itself also limited the arena for female equality by referring in the same breath to women as workers and as housewives/mothers. Since it does not define a corresponding dual role for men, it is difficult to ascertain whether the SED has simply taken a pragmatic view of the additional burdens on women, legislating for their 'double shift' in the belief that it will eventually become obsolete in the wake of other changes, or whether the party actually accepts, either implicitly or for economic reasons, the gender-based assumptions of its own culture concerning parental and domestic labour. The practice and ideology of political organizations in the GDR have been riddled with contradictions in this matter, and although considerable *state* support has been introduced over the years to help women wanting to study, to offer incentive and encouragement for their social development, and to alleviate some of the housework and child-care which still tends to fall to women, challenges to *gender*-orientated roles in the domestic sphere have been sporadic and unsystematic, so that there has been less active pressure on husbands to reform than in the celebrated case of revolutionary Cuba.

The complex issues involved in *Frauenförderung* were highlighted by two plays in particular: Siegfried Pfaff's *Regina B. - Ein Tag in ihrem Leben* (1968) and Rolf Gozell's *Der Aufstieg der Edith Eiserbeck* (1970). Pfaff's play reflects that political trend which envisages the community intervening to relieve individual women of their traditional cares. Regina B. is a single parent, so that a wife/husband confrontation about responsibility for the children is never broached. Although the worker Regina is initially motivated to take a part-time degree in engineering in the hope of preventing a break-up with her better educated boyfriend, Krüger, her attitudes to both the man and the course change rapidly within the significant day in her life to which the title refers. Some of Regina's friends still believe that a good marriage, guaranteeing clothes and other material items, must be the true aspiration of any woman. Regina's neighbour Gertrud worries that Regina's children are very attached to Krüger and would be unhappy if he left them. Gertrud's husband, on the other hand, remarks that Krüger is selfish towards Regina, that he never helps her at home and that he restricts her political and vocational development. Regina B., after her day of contemplations and arguments, rejects the opportunity to 'catch' a father for her children and is poised to embark on a more ambitious, independent career of her own.

She cannot achieve this alone, however. Pfaff illustrates the social network of which his character is a part in order to show that the qualifications of one woman are of interest to the whole community, and to contend that the community should therefore accept its responsibility to assist her.

Regina's intentions arouse both approval and condemnation among her superiors, who are loath to lose her on day release in the short term, whilst needing more qualified engineers for the future. Regina must have the good will and support of others if her studies are to be at all practicable. The positive characters, whose effect lies in their moral appeal to the audience, are those who acknowledge Regina's aspirations and, whatever their own commitments, try to help: the neighbours who look after the children, for example, and the busy director who offers Regina a regular lift.

In Gozell's play, by contrast, the role of the husband is crucial. In a sense, Gozell translates the mother-symbolism of *Der kaukasische Kreidekreis* - mothers as a nurturing force enabling growth and development - into a husband-function. The plot concerns a woman who is leaving her husband and her job with another man, ostensibly because she is being condemned for adultery by her employer. As the characters re-enact her arrival at the factory in search of a job, and her progress there, it emerges that her presence has disrupted cadre policy. The director is initially reluctant to employ her because she is unskilled. He gives her a chance, providing that she learns the most skilled job in the factory within a month. She learns too quickly, and her organizational ability and rationalization schemes make her unpopular with the workforce. Once she has learnt her job, there is no suitable post for her, so that she must either leave, work in the canteen, or accept delegation to an advanced training course. As a wife and mother, she cannot accept the commitment of a course, but there is a unanimous decision to delegate her for the sake of the enterprise. Edith is now opposed to her own promotion and attempts to escape. At this point, the director attempts to appease her: he does not want to lose valuable labour, and anyway the party has impressed upon him the disastrous implications of his failure to be more supportive. In chronological terms, this is where the re-enactment and argument begins.

Although the play embraces related issues, such as the prejudice encountered by women at work and the contradictory economic consequences of training the workforce, it is the triangle situation which provides the work with its formal shape. After Parthey has presented the characters in the Prologue, the first scene depicts Edith leaving home with Pelzer, while her husband Alban quibbles about the belongings she is taking. This theme is quickly and repeatedly linked with the workplace situation: the director Nurtech intervenes to prevent Edith's departure, because Parthey (the party secretary) has impressed upon him the socio-economic consequences of her case:

> Der Fall der Kollegin Eiserbeck wird als abschreckendes Beispiel gelten. Qualifizier dich, und du fliegst (p.3).

But the planned adultery remains determinant. Nurtech himself makes it so by lending a moralistic rationale to his economically motivated cadre policy: he has turned feeling against Edith because her skills have upset his technocratic harmony in the factory, disguising his aggression in condemnations of her 'immoral' affair with workmate Pelzer.

The two strands are interwoven in two ways. The first device is the alternation of scenes representing the present (the scene outside the Eiserbeck flat where Nurtech now tries to cajole Edith into staying and the members of her brigade discuss the issues) and the past (where the characters re-enact Edith's arrival and her progress at the highly technical control panel). The panel is represented by the painted side of the furniture-waggon, visible from the beginning of the performance. It is one of two props, both of which draw attention to the play as theatre: Battel's guitar, the other, is brought on by a stage-hand.

The second connexion is made by the conflation of roles: Edith's husband is also her foreman, and her lover was the colleague who trained her. Alban's attitudes to Edith's work change with the wind. He himself is a skilled craftsman, but has no insight into the human problems of his team. Edith's success is a threat to his position as her husband and as her superior, and his comments about her are negative because they are defined by self-interest. His reaction to her proposed promotion is typical:

> Also von mir aus. Ja. Zwei Meister in der Familie sind besser als einer. Heutzutage kann die Frau nicht hinter ihrem Mann zurückstehen. Unter einer Bedingung. Der Haushalt muß weiterlaufen. Der Mensch braucht sein geregeltes Leben (p.66).

In this case, 'der Mensch' means Alban, who is not averse to extra income so long as he does not have to wash up. Gozell's method is devised to draw attention to the material interest that can motivate people's decisions, and to spotlight hypocritical phrasemongering by juxtaposing grandiose sentiments and selfish intent. Alban represents patriarchal husbands who inhibit their wives' advance. Pelzer, on the other hand, is portrayed in a progressive partnership of mutual benefit with Edith. In scene 10 he teaches her his job at the control panel while she teaches him to wash floors. By scene 12 we are presented with an exemplary relationship in which Pelzer and Edith have redivided their labour to share both the cleaning and the skilled work. Their partnership is also creative: Edith has had an idea for rationalizing labour, and Pelzer applies his experience to elaborating the details.

In scene 13, Pinkmarie, the cleaner representing unskilled female labour which stands to benefit from Edith's 'Aufstieg', whose function comes closest to that of the voice of progress and reason, overturns the moral premise which underlies the condemnation of adultery:

> *Auf Pelzer:* Der macht aus ihr was. Nehmt doch himmeleinbär als Maßstab einen gesellschaftlichen, schon findet ihr es in Ordnung. Wer ist durch eine Mißheirat verurteilt, sein Leben zu vertrauern? Jeder hat nur eins. *Auf Pelzer:* Das ist ein wertvoller Mensch (p.71).

If Edith stays with Alban, her career will stagnate: if she goes with Pelzer, he will offer support while she trains as a supervisor. The husband is crucial to the woman's enhancement.

Of course, the husband is not the only factor in *Der Aufstieg der Edith Eiserbeck*, nor is community support the only factor in *Regina B. - Ein Tag in ihrem Leben*. Both authors have an historical materialist understanding of social progress, and both plays illustrate the social matrix in which moral decisions are moulded. Both depict the economic and ideological contradictions at play in the changing status and opportunity of working women. But Pfaff and Gozell chose to highlight different aspects of this process, and their dramatic methods are correspondingly dissimilar, as were the fates of their two works.

Pfaff first wrote his play for radio. In adapting it for the stage he applied the same skill in conveying considerable information about the lives and personalities of his characters colourfully and concisely through their conversation. If they sometimes talk at length about trivia - be it fashion, cars or the price of apples - this is indicative of their preoccupations. Whereas Gozell introduces his characters in a formal Prologue, Pfaff's opening scene shows a cross-section of workers gossiping as they queue for the morning bus. In this way he sets the scene and provides background information for the 'day' which ensues. Pfaff concentrates on naturalistic detail, especially in speech, to create psychologically motivated characters who demand sympathy, or at least analysis, from the lay psychologist (the spectator). Where minor roles are concerned, he often takes a short-cut to characterization by using names which suggest their function: the Heymes are the kind, homely neighbours who look after Regina's children; the personnel officer who likes to understand people is called Klarmann and the psychologist is called Klopfer; Krafft is a politically active worker, and Mehlmacher is the interfering works reporter whose clichés almost deter Regina from her project. Gozell, too, adopts a symbolic nomenclature, but one which reinforces the comic reduction of his characters, who are presented without the emotional humanity which is so essential to the dramatic form and message of Pfaff's play. The figures are alienated by their names: Nurtech, the technocratic director; Parthey, who passes on directives from the SED; Alban, who is stupid; and Wurzelpeter, who drinks. The other workers, Blonder and Schwarzer, have strictly utilitarian names to distinguish them.

Edith Eiserbeck herself is not a heroine with whom one can identify, because she is not a soul who can be read, unlike Regina B., whose psychological consistency is a feature of naturalist characterization. By exploring the personality projected as Regina's, the audience considers questions about the social desirability of women improving their qualifications, posed by the author in terms of moral values as well as communal gain. Pfaff indicates his own attitude to progress through the trajectory which Regina makes over her formally tidy day. She grows in awareness and is what East German critics call an 'entwicklungsträchtige Persönlichkeit'. A decision originally taken partly out of defiance after the foreman had betrayed his lack of confidence in women, and partly as a tactic to keep Krüger, confronts Regina squarely with her position as a single parent, and with her own individual potential. In her self-assessment, she realizes the serious implications of her action. This unity of time and character is not applied to Gozell's figures. The shifts of interest which affect relations between the characters are ironized by rapid verbal self-justifications, and characters contradict themselves easily. By twisting the sequence of scenes, Gozell juxtaposes conflicting stances, using the 'present' to alienate the 'past'. Because he highlights the socio-economic contradictions which arise when new qualifications create an imbalance in the workforce, and the speed with which individual objectives can change, psychological motivation is less significant. Edith, for example, initially accepts the traditional role of housewife:

> Die Familie standesgemäß zu versorgen, ist Aufgabe des Mannes (p.17);

but then, ostensibly because of her impatience with the ineffectual Alban, she suddenly demands a job, defending her right to work against the unwilling Nurtech using phrases culled from newspapers:

> So kann man mit Kollegen aus der nichtarbeitenden Bevölkerung nicht umgehen. Wie geschrieben steht: Nicht selten aber begegnet man seelenlosem, bürokratischem Verhalten. Es wird noch zu sehr kommandiert, abgewiesen, rechthaberisch aufgetreten und bevormundet (p.32);

> Die Partei würde sich höheren Orts sehr wundern, wenn sie wüßte, wie Sie mein Recht auf Arbeit verwirklichen. Habe vielleicht ich gesagt, der entscheidende Bereich, in dem sich der neue Mensch entwickelt, ist die Arbeit unter den sozialistischen Produktions-

> verhältnissen? Er ist betrebt, ein wissender Mensch, eine allseitig gebildete Persönlichkeit zu werden, bewußt das Leben zu gestalten und an der Entwicklung unserer sozialistischen Demokratie schöpferisch teilzunehmen? (p.32);

> Was mich hergebracht hat, ist die Gleichberechtigung der Frau und ihr Anspruch auf Teilnahme am gesellschaftlichen Leben (p.33).

It is, in fact, not unusual for these characters to use language that is untypical of the people they represent socially, language which corresponds rather to a choral function, interpreting the proceedings for the audience, and supplying a humorous element at the same time because of its blatant incongruity. The cleaner, Pinkmarie, for example, challenges:

> Wagt einer zu behaupten, daß gesellschaftliche Veränderungen sich in der privaten Sphäre nicht niederschlagen? (p.77),

and the worker Schwarzer observes:

> Die Moral ist eine spezifische Form des gesellschaftlichen Bewußtseins (p.74).

In other words, the characters themselves give a transparent sociological account of their own dramatic function: the illustration of the social dialectic.

Since Gozell's aim is to make the objectives of his characters crystal clear in this manner, Edith emerges as a somewhat gruff and self-confident figure, precisely because she always speaks her intentions and vaunts her own skills. She thus makes a more straightforward and determined impact in her central role than the modest and cautious Regina. In constructing characters with psychological depth, Pfaff also respects the probability that they do not always tell each other the complete truth, whether because they are too polite, too prudent, or too dishonest. There are a number of factors which prevent Regina from creating a fuss about her wish to study. Not least among these are her reluctance to impose on the generosity of others, her unwillingness to talk openly about her relationship with Krüger, and her doubts about her own abilities. Regina, therefore, is considerably more reserved than Edith. Indeed, she explains to her director, Erfurth, that it is still unacceptable for a woman to appear too assertive:

> Der Albrecht wurde auch mal laut, wenn er zum Beispiel durch die Halle ging und es lief nicht. Niemand nahm das übel. Aber eine Frau wäre dann ein Mannweib. - Ich wundere mich überhaupt nicht, daß so wenig Frauen die erste Geige spielen bei uns im Werk und überhaupt, bis in die Regierung . . . Man verlangt zuviel. Sie sollen dasselbe leisten und bei ihren Leuten erreichen wie die Männer. Aber mit Charme! Wenn ich von unserm Meister Charme verlange, schmeißt er mich raus (p.67).

Regina's comments about the quality of charm in women are certainly pertinent to the social image of the 'schöne Geschlecht' in the GDR. Writers of literature and propaganda alike have often felt the need to reassure readers that even emancipated women preserve this virtue, historically associated with the decorative role of the female. Wolf uses the epithet for his Bürgermeister Anna (page 27 above). Kerndl uses it to describe Johanna von Döbeln in the review pages of *Neues Deutschland* (24 June 1976). Hauser's Uwe uses it in *Barbara* to demonstrate that the heroine does not lose her femininity by adopting an authoritative tone with hardened sailors (page 63 above).

The *Panorama* booklet *Women and Socialism* stresses the womanliness of factory 'foreman' Gerda Hagen in the same way:

> Her charm is combined with maternal feelings, self-confidence, and with the knowledge that she is not a nobody, has something to offer and is respected for that fact (p.21).

Charm is an attribute that Edith Eiserbeck does not possess. However, the impossibility of identifying with Edith as a character is created by more than a lack of such psychological nuances. She is further alienated by the comical representation of what seems to be an absurd contradiction between her easy command of the most difficult job on the shop floor and the gravity with which she refers to her domestic chores. The East German convention has been to project household duties as demanding but stultifying. Gozell overturns this image and portrays the skills of the housewife as a source of great economic potential. The apparent contradiction between, on the one hand, Edith's pride in trivial preoccupations -

> Ich kann Quarktorte backen. Ohne Boden (p.30) -

and, on the other, her technological prowess is resolved by the redirection of her organizational efficiency. There are several metaphors for this. Edith applies ergonomics to the tea-break:

> Sie halten mir die Teller. *Zu Wurzelpeter:* Sie reichen zu. *Zu Schwarzer:* Und Sie verteilen (p.46),

and to manning levels:

> Zum Beispiel, daß ich sonntags auf zwei Flammen vier Gerichte koche. Das geht. Hier kocht man den Eintopf auf fünf Flammen (p.57).

Gozell's unusual approach amounts to a reassessment of the value of women's work and thus of their acquired abilities. Pinkmarie elaborates the argument. By mimicking the men, she illustrates how they arbitrarily determine what is prestigious labour and only ascribe value to what they do themselves:

> *Zu Blonder:* Das ist Männerarbeit. Aber Wassereimer kann ich wuchten! *Zu Schwarzer:* Davon verstehst du nichts. Was verstehst senn du selber? Mein ewiges Aufgabengebiet sind dreckige Fußböden (p.38).

Pinkmarie is Edith's most tenacious defendant, because she sees that her own prospects are affected by Edith's success.

This does not mean to say that Pinkmarie emerges in so damning a light as Nurtech and Alban. Certainly, her behaviour is based on identification of her own interests, but Gozell does have a scale of values. Nurtech and Alban are hypocritical and spineless. They never make an unselfish gesture. Nurtech, for example, cannot understand the reasons which force Edith to refuse delegation to a study course:

> Man kann sich vorkommen wie der Weihnachtsmann. Neuen Typus. Sack voll Gaben und keiner will sie (p.66).

Self-righteous because he has offered a woman the chance to improve her lot, he cannot recognize that her domestic burden must prevent her from accepting. His gesture is empty, and in any case motivated by his ambition to claim the credit for directing the first factory to train a female supervisor. Alban is no better. The one reaction to Edith's affair which he never shows is a lover's jealousy. His readiness to forgive and forget is motivated by his inability to find a replacement cook. Alban is a grumbler and Nurtech a technocrat: neither has any interest in building socialism.

The workers who condemn Edith's 'immorality' are shown to have a relatively understandable motive for resenting her, since they stand to lose their present jobs as a result of her rationalization plan. They come to realize through the self-criticism demanded by Pelzer, Parthey and Pinkmarie that their aggression was misguided. Their willingness to devalue Edith's metamorphosis as a tale of sin and lust derives from their own unhealthy desire for titillating gossip. They are not against the idea of a woman acquiring skills, but their openness to malicious insinuations based on obsolete morality becomes a restraining force on Edith's emancipation.

Pinkmarie and Pelzer, who offer Edith support and act in the spirit of *Frauenförderung*, are the two most likeable of her associates. It is Pinkmarie who makes the most moral appeal of the play by challenging Edith not to shirk her responsibilities. Edith, tired of the resentment she meets from all quarters and unable to persevere with her old job, wants to leave for a factory where more support is given to the workforce. Her comments to Parthey are escapist:

> Paul, du hast gesagt, der Sozialismus kann aus jedem alles machen. *Auf Nurtech:* Diese Art von Sozialismus macht mich fertig . . . Wir fliehen nicht vor dem Sozialismus. Der ist Gott sei Dank überall. Wir bauen den Sozialismus woanders auf (p.9).

Pelzer also makes a moral appeal, to both characters and audience, by asking them to reassess the events. Gozell uses the re-enactment device, like Hauser, to address questions of socialist criteria to the audience. He is more successful in establishing a critical distance, through his comic reductions, but an ethical slant is still obvious.

If the characters can be evaluated against a scale of support for the concept of *Frauenförderung*, then Pinkmarie, who (unrealistically) offers Edith her flat to make her stay, and Pelzer, who declares his commitment to Edith's qualification, are the most positive figures in the play. Edith herself reaches a point where she is opposed to her own advance because it is too much of a struggle. Pinkmarie and Pelzer have the commendable task of spurring her on. Pelzer makes an inspiring speech in scene 2, when the audience is trying to grasp the situation in outline, in which he condemns Alban and Nurtech:

> Wie hier mit Menschen umgegangen wird, dazu stehe ich nicht. Ihr habt die Moral von Kaffeetanten. Keinem von euch beiden leuchtet ein, daß hier eine ihre Fesseln zerrissen hat. Daß diese Entwicklung nicht unterbrochen wird, dafür sorge ich (p.10).

Nevertheless, not even he escapes alienation. When Pelzer is called upon to protest his sincerity, he is struck by lightning. Fortunately he is unscathed but he is compromised as a knight in shining armour.

Even so, Gozell's play finishes light-heartedly with a fully-fledged happy ending. Battel sings a romantic song to his guitar, and Edith and Pelzer are obliged by their workmates to embrace on the street. The ending is facetious, since the audience is well aware of the artificiality of this spectacle. Gozell's approach to social questions is, in fact, far from idealistic, but his brand of optimism emerges from his critical humour. The play is intended to provoke a radical appraisal of socialist progress. Moral postulations are inadequate, for it is foolish to rely solely on the good will of individuals to achieve equal rights for women. As Battel points out:

> Die Bedürfnisse des Menschen müssen befriedigt sein. Anders ist der Sozialismus nicht aufzubauen (p.81).

Siegfried Pfaff concludes in quite the opposite manner. Regina's day, having been constructed on the basis of unity of time and character to create the illusion of reality, is left open-ended. After Krüger's departure, she also rejects the drunken advances of Hans, and is thus left without the support of a husband or boyfriend. Pfaff does not suggest, like Sakowski, that Regina's family can only be complete if she finds a father for her illegitimate children. Regina's single parenthood is not presented as an oddity that fails to conform to a desirable norm. Neither of Regina's suitors are helpful companions, and Pfaff implies that she is better without them. He uses Regina's status as an unmarried mother to intensify her internal conflict by emphasizing the burden that study would place on her life. But, unlike Edith, Regina is not swayed by immediate personal advantage in deciding her course of action. She understands the full social implications of taking her degree course. She knows it would be hard, but believes it is important enough to herself and to her community. In this way, she is presented as a more moral heroine than Edith. Even so, her choice is not yet made. The function of Roland's accident at school on this very day is to exaggerate her awareness of her children's needs. Gertrud, however, does not condemn Regina as a bad mother for leaving the children with her after school. Gertrud, in her day, would have seized Regina's opportunity, and the children, she argues, can benefit from an educated mother in a scientific age. Regina is left in the evening with a moral choice to make, and, in leaving her undecided, Pfaff is inviting his audience to make a moral choice to encourage any Reginas that they might know themselves.

Pfaff's play brought him success and acclaim. The *Geschichte der Literatur der Deutschen Demokratischen Republik* accepted it as a document of reality:

> Das Stück lebt von einer Fülle sehr treffsicher erfaßter Details aus dem Lebens- und Arbeitsalltag. Mit wenigen Strichen entwirft der Autor Situationen, Schicksale und Realitätsbezüge. Der Wirklichkeitsaufriß reicht vom Leben der 'einfachen' Arbeiterin Regina bis hin zu den Klassenkämpfen der Gegenwart. Der Bühnenerfolg des Stückes erklärt sich vor allem daraus, daß die Probleme, mit denen die Frau trotz Gleichberechtigung konfrontiert wird, lebensnah behandelt sind (p.684).

Gozell, meanwhile, is not even mentioned in the weighty tome.

The unpopularity or incomprehension that met Gozell's play cannot be attributed to its contravention of aesthetic values alone. The way in which dramatic figures are constructed and related to one another is not simply a formal matter. It corresponds to a method of social analysis and an ideological approach to human behaviour. Pfaff's characterization induces identification with particular, positive personalities, fostering the comforting thought that there are considerate people in the socialist community prepared to work for progressive ideals. Gozell's method, however, was reductive in a manner similar to that of the didactic theatre, isolating the influence of immediate personal interest on social behaviour, and, at the same time, illustrating the ease with which such interest can be disguised by moral rectitude. Gozell thus defied naturalist convention by suspending the humanitarian aims of his characters.

In a culture steeped in naturalist assumptions about characterization, and especially at a time when the theatre was dominated by a moralizing, conversational style, far removed from epic considerations, this dramatic form was threatening. Rather than being accepted as a comment about a specific aspect of the intricate social dialectic, it was interpreted as a negative and cynical summary of human nature.

The limited appeal of drama which breaks with the naturalist code, from *didaktisches Lehrtheater* in the fifties to Heiner Müller's *Die Hamletmaschine* and the work of Stefan Schütz in the seventies - cannot be explained solely by the censorship or censure of politicians anxious to project the claim of socialist society to humanitarian values. Such drama also offends that broad section of the public who have learned, at school, through the media, and in the theatres themselves, to look for moral qualities in fictional characers. An analysis of the history of reception in the GDR cannot fall within the scope of this investigation, but we may observe that dramatic methods which rely on alienation, and which are reductive in an unfamiliar and thus noticeable way, are frequently condemned by spectators at East German theatres as one-sided and pessimistic.

Rolf Gozell was to find an advocate in his colleague, Heiner Müller, who has always maintained that the public must develop a new relationship to the stage in order to play a more creative role, not only within the spectacle, but as agents and critics of society. Müller placed the demise of Gozell as a writer in a wider context of conservative limitations which restrict the evolution of East German drama as a tool of political analysis. He takes as his starting-point an incident when a member of the audience criticized *Der Lohndrücker* because the author (Müller) does not 'reveal' whether a former SA bully is allowed to join the SED:

> Die 'Zuschaukunst' hat mit der Schauspielkunst nicht Schritt gehalten. Es versteht sich, daß sie nur an neuen Inhalten entwickelt werden kann. Das gilt, auf wenig längere Sicht, für die Schauspielkunst genau so. Die Kritik orientiert Publikum und Produzenten auf den Erfolg, ohne die Kriterien des Erfolgs neu zu bestimmen. Sie behauptet das Primat des Ästhetischen vor dem Sozialen, des Gefälligen vor dem Konstruktiven, der Routine vor dem Experiment, . . . des Besonderen vor dem Nachahmbaren. Sozialistisches Theater, sozialistische Kunst überhaupt, ist nicht ohne ein Element des Didaktischen . . .
>
> Die fachliche Qualifikation der Dramaturgien steht ihrer politischen nach, genauer: ihre politische Qualifikation ist nicht auf der Höhe ihrer Aufgaben. Der Blick für die technologische Seite der Kunstproduktion ist nicht ausgebildet, nicht die Sensibilität für das Besondere (Konkrete) eines Materials und eines Autors, das in gegebene Formen nicht ohne Wirklichkeits- (Wirkungs-) Verlust eingebracht werden kann, nicht die Fähigkeit, solche Widerstände produktiv zu machen. (Rolf Gozell zum Beispiel, den seine Sprache, das nicht Lernbare, als große Begabung ausweist, ist durch eine Dramaturgie, gegen die sein Material sich sperrt, mit AUFSTIEG DER EDITH EISERBECK auf das Abstellgleis rangiert worden.)
>
> Die Institutionen, die den kollektiven Lernprozeß zu organisieren hätten, die Formulierung von Ergebnissen, die Aufhebung von Erfahrungen in Produktion, verbrauchen ihre besten Kräfte für die Herstellung eines oberflächlichen Konsensus, der den Meinungsstreit

beendet, bevor er begonnen hat, konträre Standpunkte nivelliert, bevor sie formuliert sind . . . Unsre Ästhetik aus den Bedürfnissen unsrer Gesellschaft ableitend, sollten wir nicht vergessen, daß deren erste Bedürfnis die Kritik der Bedürfnisse ist.

. . . Brechts These, daß die Gesellschaft aus der Vorführung asozialer Verhaltensmuster den größten Nutzen ziehen kann, mag utopisch sein, solange Theater sich aus der Teilung in Spieler und Zuschauer konstituiert, aber das Positive kann nicht mehr einfach über die Identifikation mit einem Helden transportiert, die Funktion des Publikums nicht mehr an die Institutionen delegiert werden. Was Brecht über die Umformung des Schöpferischen durch die Arbeitsteilung sagt: Der Schöpfungsakt ist ein kollektiver Schöpfungsprozeß geworden, ein Kontinuum dialektischer Art, gilt, heute mehr als 1948, auch für die Rezeption. *(66)*

Chapter 8

RUDI STRAHL: *DIE SOZIALISTISCHE EHE*

Popularity has never been a problem for Rudi Strahl, who began his successful career as a comedy writer in 1969. Strahl's plays raise a number of questions about relationships between men and women in contemporary society. They do not, however, attempt to challenge dominant cultural assumptions concerning masculine and feminine behaviour. Neither do they examine the social origins of romantic and marital partnerships, although couples, quarrelling and drawing together, are the foundation stones of Strahl's work.

The themes of love and marriage provide the framework for his skilful farce and repartee. Conjugal partnership is the starting-point for social activity; it is also the major preoccupation of most of Strahl's characters, who are allocated to his plays with a sexual symmetry that begs for matchmaking. Indeed, Strahl's stock denouement is inconceivable without the implication of at least one plighting of troth. The importance of the marriage institution within East German society is reflected in the comments of officialdom. The widow in *Der Todestag* (1974), dreaming a conversation with her dead husband - fantasy which expresses how torn she feels between loyalty to his memory and the proposals of new suitors - repeats the advice of her personnel manager:

> In aller Behutsamkeit, aber immerhin . . . Ausgehend von Karl Marx - siehe 'die Familie als kleinste Zelle des Staates' -, endend bei der Feststellung, daß das Betriebsklima unter meiner Witwenschaft leidet (p.184);

and the Richter presiding *In Sachen Adam und Eva* (1969) solemnly warns the young couple:

> Ihr wollt also heiraten. Das ist schön, meine Freunde, denn erst die Ehe erhebt ein Individuum zum kollektiven menschlichen Wesen. Und ihr sollt also heiraten, denn unsere Gesellschaft fördert jeden Schritt vom Ich zum Wir. *Mit erhobener Stimme* Aber ihr sollt nicht heiraten, um eines Tages wieder zu Individuen herabzusinken! (p.9).

Although Strahl presents the personnel manager and the Richter as ridiculous characters, it is the pompous form, and not the content of their beliefs, that is the object of mirth. The commitment to monogamy as the desirable basis for human existence is entirely within the spirit of Strahl's work.

Rudi Strahl's comedies rely heavily on stereotyped characters: married men whose attentions are easily distracted by a mini-skirt; young Romeos with their minds on the next football match; girls who idolize their boyfriends; women jealously mustering or attacking female competition; intellectuals fighting their amorous inclinations. Inevitably, some of the traditional stereotypes have been updated. The setting is a society where professional relationships are based on equality of the sexes. Dr Angelika Unglaube, for example, the pretty young woman sent to investigate allegations of witchcraft against a dashing party secretary in a Mecklenburg village, is a humourless student of the scientific society, anxiously guarding the sober reputation of her party - until Matthes persuades her to spend a night (alone) in his hayloft, where the sweet aroma penetrates her prudish exterior to release her romantic instincts. Angelika's position and education are a novelty in the comedy of manners, but she remains the proper young virgin in need of a healthy seduction that has amused audiences from ancient Rome until today. Dr Unglaube is a symptom of cultural contradictions in an age of change, when women frequent universities as the peers of men (and even came to outweigh them numerically in the late seventies on the basis of common entrance standards), but when the prejudice of patriarchal society is still forceful enough to make the 'career woman' seem funnier than the overworked businessman.

The speed and wit of his dialogue have been major elements in the success of Strahl's ventures into theatre, but he has also understood how to direct the conventions of comedy at two deeply entrenched emotions on the part of his audience: first, delight in recognizing familiar foibles in the characters (a pleasure which is largely dependent on conservative images and not normally conducive to accepting novelties in human behaviour patterns); and, secondly, the desire to see couples happily united. Angelika, therefore, yields to her better nature, once she has established that Lydia is married to Paul and not attached to Matthes, and *Ein irrer Duft von frischem Heu* (1975) duly ends with a double romance. *In Sachen Adam und Eva* may, on the surface, be open-ended, as it is left to the audience to decide whether Adam and Eva should be married at once or else go away to reflect for a few months on their compatibility, but the couple reiterate their intention to wed in spite of the seeds of doubt that the court has tried to sow. In any case, the stage directions indicate that, should the audience seem indecisive during the vote, the characters must try to elicit an affirmative response. Hansi and Hela are united, and the Anwalt makes advances to the Gegenanwältin. In *Wie die ersten Menschen* (1972), a mate is found for all three women as well as the she-ape, and only the old man renounces his flirtations for his inventions. Although love is primarily for characters with youthful good looks in Strahl's fantastic world, the elderly also have their opportunity in *Keine Leute, keine Leute* (1973) - even if a little fun is made of the attempts by Charly and Mona to conceal their true age from one another. In the end they are united, along with the warring karate experts Huschke and Leila, and even the multi-purpose subsidiary characters, 'der Mann' and 'die Frau'. Lady Steeplespoon, unfortunately, loses her old sea-dog Bollo (who never enters on stage) to the other happy end, the recruitment of staff for the hotel, but Charly, ever the gentleman, finds her a warm embrace from another quarter:

> LADY S. *laut:* Und wer küßt *mir?*
> CHARLY: Da muß sich jeder freilich selber kümmern . . . *Zum Publikum: Sie* tuns, nicht wahr? - So wollen wir den Abend rasch beschließen, denn morgen, Freunde, geht es wieder rund! (p.170).

Strahl is quite unabashed about these happy endings. They are deliberately obvious, and are sometimes accompanied by an address to the audience to underscore the spectacle. The audience is made aware that it is being robustly entertained, and Strahl is, indeed, a master of rollicking comedy. Nevertheless, while he draws on many of the components of farcical tradition, his works certainly cannot be dismissed as farces which, by definition, set out to be no more than 'stuffing' - pure amusement. These, by contrast, are *Gegenwartsstücke,* comedies of socialist manners. Each one broaches subjects of gravity, despite the facetiousness. *Ein irrer Duft von frischem Heu,* for example, concerns the image of the SED in rural Mecklenburg, steeped in superstition even after the industrialization of agriculture, and draws material from relations between the party and the Church. *Keine Leute, keine Leute,* as that familiar lamentation suggests, examines the effects of understaffing on a collective and takes a humorous look at shortcomings which hotel staff are obliged to tolerate in their guests.

In his first play, *In Sachen Adam und Eva,* Strahl used comedy to involve his audience in a serious social issue: the advisability of marriage for a couple who have not known each other for long. (For the purposes of comedy, their acquaintance is reduced to three weeks.) In the years preceding this production, there were a quarter as many divorces as there were marriages, and the particularly high divorce rate amongst young couples was causing concern, as it still does. Many people, especially those playing some part in the broad education of young socialist citizens, felt that marriages were being solemnized too hastily, before the partners had matured sufficiently to know their own minds or to accept the necessary responsibilities to their spouse, and this is the implication in the case of Adam and Eva. The audience is not inspired to discuss the desirability of marriage as an institution, for the parameters of debate are set by Strahl from the beginning.

The auditorium is the public gallery of a courtroom, and the Protokollant opens the play by invoking the appropriate respect:

> *sich jäh dem Publikum zuwendend:* Damit Sie Bescheid wissen: Geraucht wird hier nicht! Auch nicht, daß Sie plötzlich anfangen zu singen oder rumzuknutschen! *Versöhnlicher:* Höchstens, wenn Sie weinen müssen - das dürfen Sie. Oder lachen - bitte . . . *Wieder eindringlicher:* Aber daß Sie auch aufstehen, wenn das Gericht reinkommt! (p.7).

Strahl imposes the same restrictions on his audience as a court of law does on a jury, which is there, not to judge the law, but to indicate whether a person is guilty or innocent within the stipulated terms of that law. The young couple are cross-examined, and the Richter demands a Yes or No:

> Sie alle, meine Damen und Herren, kennen die Risiken und Chancen des Ehelebens. Auch haben Sie täglich Entscheidungen zu treffen, die für andere Menschen nicht minder wichtig sind wie unsere hier für Adam und Eva. Darum sollen *Sie* auch hier entscheiden . . . und in freier Abstimmung die Frage beantworten, ob Adam und Eva heiraten sollen oder nicht! (p.49).

An alternative, less formal partnership is not envisaged. The potential failures in this marriage are demonstrated to the audience, and the question is: are there sufficient bonds to wed these two people for better or for worse?

The parameters set here by Strahl reflect the evolution of East German socialist morality. In our own society, challenges to the traditional status of women have often been accompanied by challenges to the marriage institution itself. Social scientists and pedagogues in the GDR, on the other hand, accept long-term commitment to a monogamous relationship as the basic expression of companionship and sexuality in socialism. It is acknowledged that love, the only valid justification for marriage, can be transitory, so that divorce will always occur to some extent, but the experts prefer to emphasize the positive changes that socialism brings about in the nature of marriage - allowing for lags in the cultural superstructure - once women are no longer economically dependent on their husbands, sharing equal rights, a similar education, and wide-ranging access to other channels of self-fulfilment. There is a curriculum for sex education in schools, as for other subjects, which is both thorough and partisan. Its moral objective is to impress on young people the seriousness and sense of responsibility with which they should embark on any physical relationship, which must be seen as complementary to other forms of emotional attachment. It does not frown altogether on the extra-marital expression of sexuality, which the social system is, in fact, quite able to absorb: couples can apply jointly for a flat without being married, for example, and contraception is available on demand to all women over the age of sixteen. But the school syllabus, echoed in little handbooks of socialist morality such as Anita Grandke's *Junge Leute in der Ehe* and Ursula Hafranke's *Arbeitskollektiv und Familie*, suggests that marriage will be the ultimate aim:

> (Die Geschlechtserziehung) umfaßt im weitesten Sinne die Erziehung der Heranwachsenden zu sittlich wertvoller Partnerschaft in Freundschaft, Liebe, Ehe und Familie, die Erziehung unserer Mädchen und Jungen zur gegenseitigen Achtung, zum Verständnis für die Probleme und Besonderheiten des anderen Geschlechts, zur Verantwortung für den Partner, das Kind und die Gesellschaft, zum Kampf gegen die bürgerliche Scheinmoral und alle Erscheinungen der Konvergenztheorie in diesem Bereich. *(67)*

These are the criteria to be applied to Adam and Eva. Is their relationship based on mutual respect and understanding? And what are the negative influences which might prejudice their life together? The pattern that emerges reflects many of the problems that often beset young couples, but in a greatly exaggerated manner: the prospect of Adam's national service separating them for eighteen months (and a wet winter on the island of Rügen would put the fidelity of any young husband to the test); and the prospect, then still a likely one for many newly-weds, of having to live with parents (and sharing two rooms with Eva's stock-in-trade mother-in-law would strain even the tenderest romance).

The idiosyncracies of personality that form the basis for their partnership, including those which might become grounds for conflict, are compounded into familiar, comic stereotypes of young male and young female behaviour. Adam is a model of virility. He is older than Eva by the conventional year befitting the partner with authority. He takes the initiative, comforting Eva when she cries, explaining officialdom to her, and acting as the gallant hero on the Heringsdorf campsite where they meet by removing Eva's splinter, ferrying Hela to hospital, and rescuing other campers in the storm. Eva, less self-assured, looks to her man to confirm her testimony in his more confident tones:

> Nicht, Adi?
> Genau (p.13),

> Ist es doch, nicht, Adi?
> Klar (p.22).

The only matter in which Eva is more insistent is the wedding ceremony, a 'typical' female anxiety. Their trades are conventional: Adam is a motor mechanic, Eva an apprentice paediatric nurse. Adam drives his motor cycle fast and is a fanatical football player; Eva prefers the theatre, so that there are already conflicts of interest. Eva wears fashionable mini-skirts which her mother-in-law thinks are too short. Where women are decorative, men, the reverse side of the same coin, pursue them, and Adam is sufficiently responsive to a low-cut blouse to succumb, with the help of his lonely military posting and a little alcohol, to the charms of another woman, another seductress called Eva.

During the trial, the crime of adultery is attributed potentially to Adam. Again, it is the assumption of a patriarchal culture that this is a male prerogative. Women, however innocently, adorn themselves to entice, but men are the initiators of relationships. The pattern is repeated and elaborated in *Wie die ersten Menschen*, and echoed in Leila's mock seduction in *Keine Leute, keine Leute*. Eva, too, is guilty of disloyalty of a kind, but hers is less reprehensible. In suddenly abandoning Hansi for Adam, she has been hurtful and capricious, but she has not broken a marriage vow. Moreover, the two infidelities differ in another respect. The feeling that Eva transferred from Hansi to Adam was a 'female' one: admiration. The feeling that Adam experiences for the other Eva is primarily physical, or 'male'. Adam is also seeking consolation, which women in patriarchal culture are expected to offer their life-weary menfolk. Even in breaking faith, Adam and Eva are defined by their gender.

These classic stereotypes are reflected by other male/female counterparts in this geometrically balanced play. Hansi is as obsessed about the trumpet as Adam is about football. (The masculine fanaticism devoted to hobbies is a motif met again in *Wie die ersten Menschen*.) Hela adulates his dedication and supports him in his pastime.

The assistant magistrates represent a further dichotomy based on gender roles which derive from obsolete social distinctions. In spite of a society which offers equal opportunity for personal development, the woman symbolizes cheerful compassion, and the man stern reason:

> Beisitzer des Verfahrens sind Frau Fröhlich und Herr Streng;
> sie werden das Gericht mit Herz und Verstand beraten (p.11).

The more sinister aspects of simple faith in marriage are incarnated by counsels for the defence and prosecution. The Anwalt, a bachelor, enthusiastically presses for the wedding to take place. He is ignorant of the pitfalls and, like his namesake, the Archangel Michael, ready to forgive any signs of immaturity or weakness in his clients. The Gegenanwältin is a woman whose marriage was a failure and a disillusionment, and she is determined to protect Eva from the same fate, for women are seen as victims when adultery is assumed to be a male vice. It is for reasons of pessimistic solidarity that she exposes Adam's infidelity with her charade of seduction. Like her own namesake, Gabriel in the Garden of Eden, she is the guardian of morals, quick to sense any suggestion that Adam and Eva may have embarked prematurely on an erotic entanglement. Such a step would, after all, be an indication of their lack of responsibility, and would affect the court against their case. However, even the Gegenanwältin overcomes her suspicion of men, in the interests of dramatic symmetry and Strahl's light-hearted conviction that all his female characters are amenable to romance, when the Anwalt invites her to come camping in Heringsdorf. With the Richter hurrying away, as a note of irony reveals, to his own third divorce, only the widowed Protokollant is left partnerless to clear the court.

As his choice of title illustrates, Strahl sets up models of recognizable masculinity and femininity as the butt of critical humour. In no sense does he undermine conventional images of male and female practice. The characters are funny, but acceptable. Their idiosyncracies are amusing because they are exaggerated, and because they are taken so seriously by the characters themselves. Strahl appeals to the capacity of his audience to identify the familiar, irritating traits of their own partners and to look upon them with some affection and understanding, while at the same time taking a measured view of personal excesses. Strahl's method, using comedy of manners, operates on the audience in a similar way to Kerndl's journalistic *Kammerspiele* and Hammel's 'prophylaktische Dramaturgie', turning criticism of the characters into self-criticism, urging a greater sense of considerate responsibility. The implicit advice that Strahl is offering to married couples and those intending to marry is: respect your partner, learn to compromise, to communicate, and to share your lives. These are moral postulates which place the onus on the 'masculine' male and the 'feminine' female to fit as harmoniously as possible into the accepted social framework for their coexistence. Strahl does not present masculinity and femininity as changeable phenomena, either by exposing the historical mechanisms which govern moral codes in the manner of epic theatre, or by posing exemplary alternatives in the style of Wolf or Sakowski. It is only in *Wie die ersten Menschen* that Strahl introduces an element of speculation about the history of patriarchy, but even there, in the final analysis, the use of comic anachronisms only seems to eternalize the stereotypes taken from modern culture.

The play, set in primitive times when people lived in caves (and the older ones still in trees), is populated with conventional figures: the men, obsessed with their hobbies and ignoring their womenfolk, prevented by their wives and daughters from pursuing a newcomer in a primeval mini-skirt; and a teenage girl with a frustrated infatuation for a jargonistic student of historical materialism. The action revolves around a struggle for power between the sexes. The struggle is not supposed to be historically accurate. Strahl's comedy is intended to ridicule the behaviour of modern married couples, and men in particular. He is suggesting that it is unworthy of a twentieth-century, socialist marriage for men to continue resisting their share of household chores, to indulge selfishly in leisure interests, to ignore their wives, and to flirt with other women. Women are satirized primarily as naggers, but with the attenuating factor that their scolding is evidently justifiable.

The battle of the sexes is placed superficially in an historical context by the peace-loving Junge, whose pedantic observations on the evolution of matriarchy and patriarchy are themselves a caricature of sociology. The Junge's reminders can be no more than superficial since, although he stresses the dependence of the superstructure on the economic base, Strahl's comic device of anachronism actually reverses the Marxist link between personality and the division of labour. The women have assumed power over the men *because* the men are lazy, irresponsible dreamers, shirking their duties and applying themselves to meaningless inventions and abstract notions. The women, on the other hand, are practical, level-headed and efficient and have a proper sense of priorities, which is the *reason* for their control over the organization of domestic labour (which in those times was all significant labour). Most of this they carry out themselves, while the men have to be coaxed, bullied, and ultimately enslaved with ball and chain.

The implications are idealist. The social practice which Strahl portrays, albeit humorously, derives from subsequent cultural assumptions about the distinctive natures of the sexes. Because the men are lazy, and because the women thwart their instinct to seduce unattached females, they become resentful, and one of them invents war. By creating armies and states, the men provide themselves with a structure through which they can hold power and indulge their military and political fanaticism, singing jingoistic songs and making demagogic speeches.

The Junge rejects this form of rebellion and advocates equality of the sexes, but he finds other pretexts for avoiding productive work. He invents art, painting a totally unrecognizable mammoth (which he justifies as Symbolism) and strumming 'Yeah, yeah, yeah' to a guitar. He rationalizes this division of labour by paying tribute to sexual differences:

> Die Basis ist das Fundament des Überbaus, somit rechtfertigt der Überbau die Existenz der Basis. Ist doch ganz einfach. *Mit erhobener Stimme:* Und wäre vielleicht sogar eine Möglichkeit, endlich die Gleichberechtigung zu realisieren! Euer praktischer Sinn und unsere schöpferische Phantasie . . . (p.100).

Strahl, of course, does not deliberately claim that men are incorrigibly lazy, selfish and fanatical. His comedy is intended to provoke argument about contemporary division of labour in the household, and his primitive setting makes well-entrenched habits seem not only funny, but absurd. Unfortunately, his anachronistic presentation has the effect of obscuring the origins of modern stereotypes, and failing to question them. Again, the audience laughs at this illustration of human foibles, and Strahl's plea is for reform and tolerance, but not for a radical challenge to assumptions about the socialization of the sexes. Had Strahl confined himself, like Roland Ender, to modest domestic situations planted firmly in the present, the absence of historical relativity may have seemed less blatant. Ender, another writer of farce, took the stock-in-trade situation of the inexperienced husband left to cope disastrously with household tasks, and the result, *Frauen sind Männersache* (1977) was a clear moral appeal to men to carry their share of the domestic burden. Strahl delves whimsically into the broader ramifications of patriarchal attitudes, but, while his work is certainly more imaginative and richer in humour and wit, it tends to a polarization of male and female personality from which there seems to be no escape.

There is a capricious suggestion in Strahl's play that the belligerent, anti-social escapades which dominate history were only imposed on humanity because men, impractical beings that they are, were able to conquer power. The Frau tries to educate them in the closing lines:

> Lernt erst mal arbeiten - alle! Los, vor den Karren mit euch! Schafft damit Baumstämme herbei; jetzt wird erst mal ein Haus gebaut . . . Sonst habt ihr eines Tages *wirklich* das Fliegen erfunden und das Wohnungsproblem noch immer nicht gelöst . . . Aber dann hätten wir auch auf den Bäumen bleiben können! (p.112).

Women are more admirable creatures, as an earlier debate demonstrates:

> DER JUNGE: Warum sind sie uns anscheinend überlegen?
> DER MANN: Wegens Geschlechtliche.
> DER JUNGE: Nein: Weil sich bei ihnen Gefühl und Verstand zu höherer menschlicher Harmonie verbinden! (p.62).

Whilst these sentiments are clearly meant as an ironical reminder of the nonsense that has been composed over the centuries to justify sexual discrimination, Strahl engages here in a discussion that was to develop over the seventies in what is loosely termed *Frauenliteratur*. It was a discussion about the potential that women's emancipation had unleashed for human development. Writers such as Christa Wolf, Irmtraud Morgner, Gerti Tetzner, Brigitte Reimann and Maxie Wander were wondering whether men would be able to break away from the psychology that had conditioned their priorities as principal agents of history, and whether women had any claims to a superior humanity which they might teach men.

Chapter 9

PETER HACKS: *DIE FRAU, GOTTLOB, IST ANDERS*

By the end of the sixties, adapting themes from antiquity was becoming an increasingly popular method of approaching contemporary questions. The fall of matriarchy, the myths of Greek culture surrounding its demise, and the works of Greek and Roman playwrights on this subject were used as material by a number of authors. The *Geschichte der Literatur der Deutschen Demokratischen Republik* acknowledges this new source of interest:

> Von aktuellem Interesse für das sozialistische Publikum war auch die Darstellung des Verhältnisses der Geschlechter. Fast alle antiken Tragödien, auch manche der aristophanischen Komödien reflektieren die welthistorische Ablösung des Matriarchats. Die römischen Stücke und die Shakespeares oder die - in der sozialistischen Dramatik allerdings kaum rezipierten - spanischen beklagen die Unterdrückung der Frau oder gehen davon aus; einige zeigen Frauen, die meist mit List um ihr Recht kämpfen und ihre Position behaupten oder erobern ('Wie es euch gefällt', 'Amphitryon'). Für die Zeitgenossen der sozialistischen Revolution, die erst die Gleichberechtigung der Frau erkämpft haben und sie Schritt für Schritt festigen, können diese Stoffe überaus wichtig sein (pp.652-3).

The classics are then praised for their mastery of dramatic techniques: action, poetic language, suspense and comedy. They are not only enlightening, but also entertaining and uplifting. Furthermore, the myths and dramas of antiquity, corresponding as they do to the transition from primitive community to early class society, are still able to express human aspirations unsullied by sectional strife.

This warm welcome for excursions into the world of myth could not have been extended twenty years earlier. Enormous changes had occurred in the field of aesthetics since Ilse Langner's proto-feminist plays, *Iphigenie kehrt heim* (1939, published 1948) and *Klytämnestra* (1934-47, published 1949), were condemned to the dust of library shelves.

In the early years of the Republic, classical myths on stage were regarded with some suspicion. They were used widely by Western existentialist and modernist writers, who drew on them to project an anguished image of human activity alien to socialist commitment, and the pages of *Theater der Zeit* in the late forties and early fifties carry an abundance of criticism of dramatists such as Giraudoux, Anouilh and Sartre. In time, however, East German writers and theoreticians developed their own critique of the classical tradition, and by the early sixties two well-established playwrights, Peter Hacks and Heiner Müller, hitherto associated with Brechtian and didactic theatre, had begun to rework Greek myths. Both were concerned to stimulate subjective appropriation by individuals of their new historic potential. Their methods and their own political and philosophical rationalizations of these methods were, nonetheless, quite distinct.

When Peter Hacks settled in the GDR from Bavaria in 1955, he was already writing historical dramas, set in periods of social transformation, which aimed both at illustrating the laws of historical development and at satirizing some respected figures of the past. He continued to write these plays, but his move confronted him with a different political environment and a different role as an artist. At the turn of the decade, he wrote two plays using contemporary material, *Die Sorgen und die Macht* (1959) and *Moritz Tassow* (1961). At the time, these plays suffered attacks from numerous cultural politicians because they bore the suggestion that certain human aspirations were thwarted by socialist society. Since optimism was the spirit of the day, this was interpreted as a failure by the author to indicate his socialist commitment consistently. Hacks, however, was working on a cultural theory of his own, which he began to publish in various magazines from 1960. The essence of his approach lay in the view that the need for agitational, educational theatre had been superseded with the achievement of a basic socialist framework for advance. What Hacks called 'post-revolutionäre Dramaturgie' required artists to turn their creativity to expressing poetic aspirations which would inspire a quest for new emotional and sensory experiences. Drawing on the classical theories of Schiller and Schlegel, Hacks affirmed mankind's need to poeticize the world - a need that had been frustrated by alienation in class society, and that could now afford to reassert itself. This view was compounded with the belief that the only state of perfection is the act of striving for perfection, which must, of course, imply a state of imperfection. The gulf between the ideal and the pursuit of the ideal, already apparent in Hacks's two *Gegenwartsstücke*, also determined his interest in the Greek myths that he went on to interpret for the modern stage.

The emotional and sensory awareness that Hacks has sought to stimulate embraces erotic experience. Sensual motivations and frustrations are already attributed to Max Fidorra and Hede Stoll and to Moritz Tassow in the *Gegenwartsstücke*, and popular bawdy elements are a recurring feature of Hacks's work. In his exposition of a theory of classical socialist drama, Hacks is quite explicit. Its sole aim, he comments, should be:

> das Mündigwerden des Menschen, d.i. die Erlangung seines Rechtes auf Verwirklichung seiner sämtlichen Möglichkeiten, des Rechtes zu sehen, zu hören, zu denken, zu wollen, die Tugend und den Beischlaf zu üben. *(68)*

In fact, Hacks uses the erotic act in a number of plays as an analogy for the pursuit of perfection. The functions of men and women in these plays are defined by the conventional antithesis: man as the socially active being, emotionally hardened, and woman as the sheltered vessel of love. The exception to this pattern is *Adam und Eva* (1972), where the dichotomy between the sexes is overshadowed by the dichotomy between humans (imperfect, frantically seeking perfection) and gods (perfect, and unable to enjoy the pursuit of any goal).

Hacks's *Amphitryon* (1967) tells the story of Alkmene's seduction by the god Jupiter in the guise of her husband Amphitryon. It differs from the usual tale - and from the adaptation by Armin Stolper written in the same year - in one fundamental detail: Alkmene agrees to the seduction in the knowledge that her lover is Jupiter in disguise. She does this in order to experience for once a perfect act of love, because her earthly husband is so exhausted and distracted by his social involvement in wars and business that he is unable to bring any enthusiasm to the marriage bed. Amphitryon observes that life is too demanding for a man to devote himself properly to all its aspects and stresses the irony that only a god is capable of being a complete man. For Jupiter, meanwhile, the problem is that real love can only be experienced in the fraught world of mankind. Jupiter has an indefatigable source of energy and creativity, but nothing to which he can apply it. The comparison, however, is between males, terrestrial and godly. Alkmene, the woman, although she is a conscious mistress of her fate in this version of the legend, remains the *object* in the search for love. Eva and Hans Kaufmann, who analyze Hacks's portrayal of male/female relationships, note parallels elsewhere in his work for this attitude to love:

> (Es) ist nicht zu verkennen, daß in dem männlichen und weiblichen Prinzip, wo es sich bei Hacks darstellt, die traditionelle, historisch fixierte Stellung von Mann und Frau reproduziert wird und unangetastet bleibt. Alkmene vergleicht sich selbst mit einem Musikinstrument, das vom Künstler, dem zur Liebe fähigen Mann, gehandhabt werden will. Der Mann erscheint als ein durch sein gesellschaftliches Sein geprägtes Wesen in seiner menschlichen Unzulänglichkeit. Die Frau gibt als die zur Liebe Fähige den Maßstab ab, zu dem der Mann zuerst emporreifen muß; sie ist und bleibt eben darum ein geschichtsloses Wesen, zu nichts als zur Liebe gut. Selbstparodistisch kehrt diese Figurenkonstellation in den *Briefen* wieder, mit denen Hacks seinen neuen Gedichtband einleitet. Er schildert sich als konventionell schmachtenden Ritter und Sänger, der seiner Dame zu Füßen liegt und ihr, die für nichts als Schmeicheleien ein Ohr hat, seine Poetik erläutert. Unfreiwillig erweckt Hacks damit den fürchterlichen Verdacht, er stelle sich die Leserinnen seiner Gedichte so vor wie dieses Rokoko-Gänschen seiner *Briefe. (69)*

This antithesis is repeated with even greater clarity in *Omphale* (1969). Hacks took as his material the legend of Hercules, sent by Apollo to serve the Lydian queen Omphale in woman's clothes. The original reasons for this strange behaviour are obscure, but the tale was later taken up by Moralists to illustrate male strength most shamefully humiliated by this female garb. For the subsidiary characters in *Omphale*, Herakles's decision to assume the dress and role of Queen Omphale seems degrading and inexplicable. But these characters are conditioned by their society, and have no insight into the tragedy of both Herakles and Omphale, who are paragons of their respective genders and also restricted by them. Omphale, the epitomy of beauty, grace, sensitivity and love, yearns to perform heroic deeds. Herakles, the fearless lion-slayer and saviour of peoples, seeks the tranquility of love. In theory at least, they represent equally important aspects of human potential. Omphale's virtues are as valuable to Herakles as his are to her. Society holds male heroism in greater esteem, and the lovers are obliged to abandon their false roles because of the pressing need for Herakles to rescue Pimplea from Lityerses, the poison-breathed monster whom only Herakles can defeat. To balance this act of heroism, since she cannot emulate it, Omphale simultaneously achieves a superlative feat of female endeavour by giving birth, in intense pain, to three sons of Herakles, who hold the key to the country's future. For Hacks, both masculine and feminine attributes are essential elements of the complete human personality, which both Omphale and Herakles strive to become. But no individual can realize all this potential at once. The dilemma is that social and biological pressures oblige the man and woman to remain as they are, fragmented by the restrictions of their sex. Both anima and animus are frustrated.

This polarization is not upheld simply by the characterization of Herakles and Omphale, and the symbols which they exchange: lion's skin and club for clothes, jewelry and cosmetics. It permeates the pattern of action and language throughout the play. It is part of Hacks's conception of classical drama that the formal elements - plot, tragedy and comedy, structure and language - should be handled with skill and craftsmanship which themselves inspire pleasure. In fact, he subsequently adapted *Omphale* as an opera without having to alter the original text radically. The blank verse in which the play was written - except where free verse serves as a deliberate prosaic contrast to lyrical expression - is full of musical rhythms, assonance and geometrical patterns.

The play falls into three phases. The first concerns the meeting of Omphale and Herakles, the second their attempt to reverse roles and unite in love, ending when Herakles succumbs to Lityerses's challenge, and the third shows hero and heroine renouncing their experiment to accomplish the great deeds for which their sex has destined them.

The functions of the protagonists must, by the nature of their dilemma, be unequal. True, the play takes its name from the woman, but it is Herakles who provides the dynamic for the plot. Omphale represents his ideal. His social involvement, which restrains him from this ideal, generates the pressure on their experiment and the reactions of the satellite characters. Omphale cannot create action because activity is not a part of her female essence. As queen of Lydia, she can only suffer with the afflictions of her people, and as a woman her quality is to love. Even in this she is confined by passivity. The woman loves the man, but to give physical expression to this love she is dependent on the lust of the man to take possession of her. At the same time, as a woman, she must be repelled by the lovelessness of male lust, a distinction which the male is unable to grasp. Such paradoxes as these provide Hacks with the opportunity for an enthusiastic exploration of antithesis. The scene in which they reverse roles contains abundant examples of interwoven contradictions which have the effect of emphasizing the incompatibility of ideal and reality. Compounded with the antithesis between lust and love is the paradox that waiting for what is desired is more desirable than the desired itself. This is a common maxim in Hacks's work, and in this case he uses the analogy of an erotic encounter. The general revelry of negations is intensified by the fact that Omphale is playing at being Herakles, while Herakles is playing at being Omphale, so that the whole scene seems to be played out in a mirror, with the polarized roles rigidly defined. Herakles waits with longing for Omphale to return from the hunt, willing her to arrive quickly, but greets her arrival with disappointment:

HERAKLES: So plötzlich?
OMPHALE: Kann plötzlich kommen, was erwartet ist?
HERAKLES: Ja, das war schön, das Warten.
OMPHALE: Schön ist auch
Erwartetwerden (p.388).

Herakles now rejects Omphale's hasty advances:

HERAKLES: Faß mich nicht an.
OMPHALE: Gäb es, was ich nicht darf?
HERAKLES: Soeben noch, als deine Hand den Arm
Beiläufig und ganz ungewollt mir streifte,
Da fühlt ich mich von Zärtlichkeit durchschauert.
Doch fest nicht lieb ichs und nicht absichtsvoll.
OMPHALE: Wenn du mich fortschickst, gut, so geh ich denn.
HERAKLES: Nicht fortgehn. Nein, nicht küssen.
OMPHALE: Das nicht und das nicht?
Was mach ich?
HERAKLES: Mußt du stets was machen? Setz

Dich zu mir nieder in entfernter Nähe
Und sprich von Liebe mir und nicht von Lust (p.389).

The argument is now reflected in antithetical and paradoxical stichomythia:

OMPHALE: Was trennst du da?
HERAKLES: Was erst zusammen soll.
OMPHALE: Bei mir sind Lust und Liebe eine Sache.
HERAKLES: Ein Wort, weil Liebe dir nur Lust bedeutet.
OMPHALE: Willst du Lust lieblos, Liebe lustlos schelten?
HERAKLES: Nein. Mach mich fühlend, und ich bin begehrlich.
OMPHALE: Wenn du begehrtest, fühltest du schon was (pp.389-90).

Further on, the strange interaction between desire and imperfection, joy and pain is carried by oxymoron:

OMPHALE: Wie wenig willst du.
HERAKLES: Alles.
OMPHALE: Also nichts.
Nichts will, wer aufs Vollkommne sich versteift (p.390);

OMPHALE: Weinst du?
HERAKLES: Vor Glück.
OMPHALE: Vor Glück?
HERAKLES: Ja, ich bewein
Die Zeit, da ich nicht glücklich war und sein werd,
Die ohne Liebe fortgetane Zeit
Vor dem Geborensein und nach dem Sterben
Und zwischen denen die, an der wir schuld sind.
Ach, Glück, ans Unglück stets erinnerst du.
OMPHALE: Weine doch nicht.
HERAKLES: Du tröstest mich, wie dumm.
Sag ich nicht dauernd, daß ich glücklich bin? (p.391).

These opposite poles, the straightforward man of action and the complicated woman of emotion, attract. The unity to which they aspire is impossible because their opposition is absolute and exclusive. The desire to complement the self by identification with the opposite causes both joy and the pain of frustration. That pain itself is projected by Hacks as an enviable state, because it is indicative of a restless, ambitious soul, and he applies the best of his lyrical craft to its expression.

The love between Omphale and Herakles is unique. Running alongside it is the love between Daphnis and Pimplea, which is also lyrically endowed, but which lacks the bitter-sweet resistance to its own limitations. Daphnis, too, is a conventional male, courageously determined to rescue his beloved from the monster Lityerses, but without the supreme skill of Herakles. Pimplea, the helpless damsel, waits and longs for her lover to save her. They are unperturbed by the definitions imposed upon their personalities by these restricted functions, and their love is therefore expressed without jarring exchanges, in verse which flows more smoothly and tenderly to show that Daphnis and Pimplea accept one another as complements, not challenges, to their own selves. Hacks introduces the couple in the 'Landstraße' scene, presenting Daphnis on the road in search of his lost maiden, and Pimplea, captive in Lityerses's cave, waiting for him. Hacks exploits chiasmus to reflect their harmonious relationship:

DAPHNIS: Pimplea.
PIMPLEA: Daphnis.

DAPHNIS: Du mein Traumgesicht.
Zag nicht, ich komme.
PIMPLEA: Komm, ich zage nicht . . .
Daphnis.
DAPHNIS: Pimplea.
PIMPLEA: Du mein Traumgesicht,
Ich zag nicht, komm.
DAPHNIS: Ich komme, zage nicht (p.378).

During the climax at the end of the play, when Herakles and Omphale fulfil their historic male and female missions, Daphnis and Pimplea express the admiration of an ordinary man and woman witnessing the epitome of masculinity and femininity. These are the roles to which they themselves unquestioningly aspire. They thus combine the empathy of similars with the wonder of lesser beings, so that their commentary is a condonement of male heroism and female childbearing, roles which Herakles and Omphale have sought to reverse:

PIMPLEA: Dort Omphale. Sie liegt in schweren Wehen.
DAPHNIS: Dort Herakles. Kämpfend, unfern dem Sieg.
PIMPLEA: Ihr schönes Antlitz ist von Zähren häßlich.
Den schmalen Leib in Krämpfen wirft, durch keine
Lage erleichtert, vor und rückwärts sie.
DAPHNIS: Wie wenn die Pflugschar eines pflügenden
Gottes auf einen Fels des Himmels stößt,
Mit grellem Klang, und weiß entfährt der Blitz
Dem aufgerührten Feldstaub, so, in solchem
Gewitter grausenvoll begegnet sich
Des Helden Keule mit des Untiers Schädel.
PIMPLEA: Daß ich sie sehn darf in dem höchsten Glück.
DAPHNIS: Daß ich ihn sehn darf in dem höchsten Glück (pp.409-10).

If Daphnis and Pimplea serve to illustrate unambitious, gender-based roles humbly performed, Malis and Iphikles represent the mediocrity of unspectacular men and women, narrowly conditioned by conventions which they cannot even begin to match. They are spitefully intolerant of Herakles's attempt to assume the garb and personality of Omphale, and, with all the prejudice of the unimaginative, consider it a shameful act. Both are poor specimens of their sex, but Iphikles emerges as a more effective character, because there is greater dramatic substance to a cowardly man of action than to an unsustaining object of male seduction. Malis is easily overshadowed by Omphale, and her only compensation for defeat in love is the glory promised to her son. Herakles may have forced his attentions on the servant first, but he cannot remember her on the following day, and becomes obsessed with the more beautiful and graceful queen. Malis's miraculous experience in giving birth to Alkaios on the morning following his conception, and watching him grow to adolescence on the first day of his life, pales to insignificance when Omphale delivers three powerful sons who can speak from the womb. Beyond this function as an inferior reflection of Omphale, Malis is a useful character for reporting developments and bearing messages. Iphikles is more satirically drawn. A spineless weakling himself, he seeks to bathe in Herakles's glory, boasting responsibility for the Herculean Labours. Far from taming monsters, however, he submits to the evil will of Lityerses, which does not prevent him, after Herakles's victory, from accepting the thanks of Daphnis in place of his modest brother (albeit in ignoble prose).

Within the context of their society, under pressure from all these subsidiary figures, Omphale and Herakles must remain opposites. They are obliged to comply with male and female imperatives. Nevertheless, there are two keys to a possible resolution of the antithesis in certain respects. The first is the suggestion, in the final scene, that class may lose its significance: Omphale may be greater than Malis, but the servant's issue, it is predicted, will eventually be kings themselves. Since Omphale derives much of her exclusive superiority from her majestic charms, this revelation heralds a new era of opportunity and dignity for those not of royal birth. The play then finishes with a symbolic gesture by Herakles, who plants his club so that it grows into an olive tree. This signifies his relinquishment of the heroic role, which he experiences as an oppression, and intimates that an age of peace will free men from the need to dedicate themselves to bold deeds. In a peaceful, classless society, the restrictive essence of masculinity and femininity, or, rather, the conflicting aims of social commitment and personal tenderness, may be moderated. In one sense, however, a woman can never escape her gender, as Omphale ultimately concedes:

> *legt das Löwenfell ab*
> Nicht die du jüngst verließest triffst du noch.
> Du findest Mutter mich und aus der Freiheit,
> Dem vorgegebnen Weibsein zu entrinnen,
> In meinem Leib, durch Schmerz, zurückgeworfen (p.411).

Omphale and Herakles are concisely defined by their symbolism. They are not intended to be psychological profiles of a man and a woman. By using mythical entities, Hacks was able to meet the demands of Hegelian drama for simplicity of theme. In *Omphale*, this theme is the relativity of *human* potential in societies where there is strife. In *Adam und Eva*, the first example in East German theatre of a Biblical story, Hacks explores the paradox of aspiration from a different and equally selective angle. Adam and Eva are also mythical figures:

> Grundsätzlich unerlaubt ist, mythischen Charakteren mittels neuzeitlicher Psychologie aufzuhelfen. Sie müssen sich, auch in moderner Darstellung, vornehmlich aus ihren Handlungen erklären *(70)*,

but the Bible is contradictory material, precisely because of its abstractions:

> Vielmehr steckt die Schwierigkeit des Stoffes im Fehlen von Gesellschaftlichen. Die auftretenden Charaktere sind kaum soziabel. Gott ist offensichtlich ein Eigenbrödler, die Engel leiden an einer für den Dramatiker verhängnisvollen Reinheit, und Adam und Eva verkörpern, vor dem Sündenfall, das pure Gattungswesen; sie sind unvereinzelt, was für die Kunst nicht viel weniger besagt als unvorhanden. Immerhin und allenfalls: Geschlechtswesen sind sie. Mulier aliter facta; die Frau, gottlob, ist anders. *(71)*

Thus, along with the usual problems facing those who have adapted Genesis - the paradox of omniscience and omnipotence, the puzzle of sin committed in innocence, and the implications of the Manichean heresy - Hacks is confronted with the problem of making distinctions between the man and the woman without a social background against which he might place them in some kind of relief. The characteristics which he attributes to them are conventional. Eva, like the Belinde to whom Hacks addresses his letters, has an ear for flattery. Adam courageously copies her crime out of loyalty, because he cannot bear the prospect of losing her. The novelty of Hacks's interpretation is that, by knowing selfish thoughts and the pain of erotic desires, Adam and Eva are making themselves the envy of God, who finds harmony extremely boring. The scandalous sexual behaviour of Adam and Eva, which shocks Gabriel and amazes even Satanael, arouses God's anthropological curiosity. To create real perfection, he had to create knowledge of imperfection and a desire to achieve an ideal forever lost. Once more, the erotic act so vividly described to God by Gabriel and Satanael (after it has been coyly concealed from the audience) is an analogy for all human striving. Adam und Eva, instead of appearing before God in shame, are defiant and happy. They appear together, man and woman, representing mankind, although they are sufficiently governed by gender roles for Adam to assume the role of spokesman.

From using symbolical figures such as these, Hacks has more recently turned his attention to historical characters again. His interest is no longer overtly in the social laws under which they operate, as it had been in his historical dramas. In 1964, when he was expounding his theory of classical socialist aesthetics, Hacks postulated the view that audiences in the GDR had already absorbed the lessons of epic theatre:

> Alle guten Leute hier haben in einer Periode des episch-soziologischen Theaters gelernt, gesellschaftliche Vorgänge auf der Bühne darzustellen, und können jetzt darüber hinausgehen. Jetzt können sie große Geschichten von Leuten erzählen, ohne die Tatsache zu vernachlässigen, daß diese Leute in einer Gesellschaft angesiedelt sind. *(72)*

Hacks became increasingly involved with individuals, to the extent that Klaus Schuhmann criticized him for setting up a polarization between individual and society which unnecessarily negated the dramatic conventions which he was taking for granted. *(73)* At the same time, however, the shift in emphasis which can be observed through *Rosie träumt* (1974) to *Ein Gespräch im Hause Stein über den abwesenden Herrn von Goethe* (1974) is not simply towards greater concentration on individuality, but also towards a more detailed respect for the specific social nature of the emotions. Both these plays are encounters with particular women, one legendary and one historical, and in both Hacks continues to use the phenomenon of love as a formal basis.

Rosie träumt is a love story which continues the antithesis in Hacks's work between reality and ideal. In his own commentary of the play, originally written for the programme which accompanied the first production, at the *Maxim-Gorki-Theater*, Hacks described some of the devices which dramatists have used in order to turn a love story into a vehicle for 'eine Absicht von Wert'. *(74)* There was the 'Vormundfabel', which has now lost its social basis, in which a father (representing a belief) tried to marry his daughter to a man who shared his sympathies, whereas the daughter was in love with another man (representing an opposing belief). In an age when fathers cannot so dictate to their daughters, a similar purpose is fulfilled by the device of the eternal triangle, and by stories in which the protagonist's duty to a cherished cause is at odds with her (or his) romantic inclinations. Hacks mentions *Der Einundvierzigste*, the film which Barbara and Uwe discuss in Hauser's play, as an example:

> In solchen Stücken brechen das Bedürfnis, sich liebend als Individuum zu verwirklichen, und das, sich denkend und handelnd in der Welt zu verwirklichen, feindlich auseinander (p.398).

Hacks is critical here of the implication that society and the individual are opposed. His own view is that love and the world are both important to the individual. Moreover, from a formal point-of-view, when a playwright is working on a love story with a philosophical substance, he finds that each theme has a dynamic of its own, but 'keine von beiden, finde ich, will gern voran ohne die andere' (p.400). It is not only permissible, but also quite human, if the two threads become entangled.

Rosie träumt is a free adaptation of several works by Hrosvith von Gandersheim, a tenth-century nun and reputedly the first German woman writer. In her plays and historical writings, Hacks discovered strict fathers of the conventional sort, and self-willed young daughters refusing to marry their pagan fiancés. The other Bridegroom, in Hrosvith's formula, was Jesus, who appears as a strong, handsome rival to claim Hrosvith's moral young heroines. In *Rosie träumt,* however, he makes no entrance, and therein lies the irony of Hacks's version. Rosie, a warm and vital girl, forever sucking sweets and casually working miracles in God's name, refuses to participate in the decline of the decadent Roman Empire and longs to be martyred, so that she can join Jesus in Heaven. She finally arrives there, along with her sceptical, earthly husband, Gallikan Caesar, only to be informed by the Virgin Mary that Jesus has been eaten by the bishops and that nobody is really sure whether God exists, since there are so many more heavens above.

Rosie's world is an unattractive one, wallowing in wars, executions and loveless prostitution. Her Christian faith, on the other hand, seems attractive, but it is no more than an illusion. Although Hacks remarks that the difference between history and modern socialism is that formerly 'der Unfug die Hauptseite war, und daß es heute der Fug ist' *(75)*, Rosie's unrealistic idealism does have a contemporary political significance. Whatever the faults of the actual world, total rejection of it is impractical and undesirable. That is the rationale behind Hacks's apology to Hrosvith:

> Ich habe ihren Standpunkt in Zweifel gezogen. Ich habe sie von dem göttlichen Platze des Autors auf den anfechtbaren eines Schäfchens zu seiner Ultralinken zurückversetzt (p.402).

Rosie herself is hard pressed to resist the temptations of this world. Like her female predecessors in Hacks's work, she loves flattery, and is delighted when Gallikan proposes to her:

> GALLIKAN: Sieh her, ich will dich heiraten, Rosvitha.
> ROSVITHA: O wunderhübsch.
> DIOKLETIAN: Du willigst ein?
> ROSVITHA: Ich darf nicht.
> GALLIKAN: Du sagtest: wunderhübsch.
> ROSVITHA: Ich mag Anträge.
> Ich hatte lange, fast sechs Wochen, keinen (p.70).

In spite of her commitment to Jesus, Rosie artlessly admits to God that the offer is alluring:

> *betet*
> O strenger Schöpfer, zitternd im Gebet
> Fleh ich den Mut von dir, die Neigung mich
> Zu widersetzen und der Pflicht zu folgen.
> Denn meine Lust, du kennst sie, ist sehr groß,
> Zu tun, was ich nicht sollte (p.71).

God luckily inspires Rosvitha with the idea that, by agreeing to go as Gallikan's slave, she will have the chance to save a pagan soul. Even so, she has recourse to a miracle or two in order to avoid being raped by her lustful owner, and she participates in the conversion of Thais, the notorious prostitute to whom Gallikan sends her for lessons. The exploitative sexual favours which Gallikan demands of her are certainly unpleasant, as is the general tenor of Rome, but when Rosie learns that she will never, after all, be embraced by Jesus, her virginity proves to have been a pointless achievement.

Rosie is determined to avoid earthly marriage, but she is by no means averse to the fripperies of material existence which conventionally absorb vain young ladies of leisure. As a result, just like a stereotyped woman, she is always late. She arrives in Heaven after Gallikan because she stopped to wash her dress, and she misses the chance to share her sisters' martyrdom for similar reasons:

ROSVITHA: Der Vater ruft?
DIOKLETIAN: Das Kind verweigert sich?
ROSVITHA: Nein, nein, was sprichst du da? Ich bin ja hier.
DIOKLETIAN: Doch später als die andern.
ROSVITHA: Ist es möglich?
Wie kann das sein? Ich höre den Befehl,
Lege das Kleid ab, richte mir die Haare,
Schlüpf in das gute Kleid, das will nicht sitzen,
Zieh in geschwinder Hast ein andres an
Und such zu dem die passenden Sandalen,
Und räum die Truhe auf, füttre die Spitzmaus
Und steck die Tute Bomboms ein und gehe.
Vater, ich ging im selben Augenblick,
Worin du riefst (p.69).

Rosie is a thoughtless creature. In her resolution to convince Gallikan that hers is the true God, she blithely calls for a miracle storm to strike thousands of warriors dead. She is obliviously sure of her own virtues, but she is so good-natured about her superiority, the basis for much of the play's humour, that she is extremely likeable. She may be foolish in comparison with her practical soldier husband, but she brings a note of cheerful humanity into his morbid, unfeeling world.

Nevertheless, in spite of the many comical idiosyncracies which make Rosie a more clearly delineated personality than Omphale or Eva, she is in many ways a stereotyped 'Schäfchen', as Hacks acknowledges. In drawing on biographical material for his play *Ein Gespräch im Hause Stein über den abwesenden Herrn von Goethe*, Hacks made a more complete break with the adoption of symbolical figures as abstractions of their sex and ontological status.

Hacks's interest in classical theories of art, and in the *Sturm und Drang* period in particular, brought him into repeated contact with eighteenth-century Weimar. This play is an exploration of the relationship between Goethe and Charlotte von Stein, a relationship which has given rise to speculation and many assumptions, but which have rarely been based on an interest in Charlotte herself. Biographers have seen her as a wronged mistress or as a demanding interference in the poet's life, according to their image of Goethe as a lady-killer or a sensitive genius. Hacks, freely interpreting letters and contemporary references, constructs a possible individuality for Charlotte, and portrays her love, not as a universal female sentiment, but as the unique experience of one woman. He is careful to stress this in countering a number of common misunderstandings of the play:

Insonders dies: das ist kein Stück über *die Frau*. Ich handle

> über eine einzige Frau: die Charlotte Stein, eine Frau also, die aus ihrer Angst ein Geschäft macht, so wie andere aus ihrer Schwerhörigkeit oder ihrer Dummheit Vorteil zu ziehen gelernt haben, und ich handle über eine einzige Weise zu lieben: die ihrige. Diese Liebe wird in gleichsam generalstabmäßigen Begriffen beschrieben. Ich weigere mich, eine solche Fühlart für ein unänderbares Ergebnis hormonellen Zwanges zu erachten. So wünschbar mir Spannungen zwischen den Geschlechtern erscheinen, für so überflüßig halte ich die dauernden Mordversuche zwischen ihnen. Ich bitte das weibliche Geschlecht, welches unfehlbar den Hang haben wird, sich in der Stein wiederzuerkennen, in dieser Sache ausnahmsweise eine prüfende Haltung einzunehmen. *(76)*

The specificity of the relationship between Charlotte and Goethe is essential. The form of the play itself underscores Charlotte's individuality. It is a monodrama. Only Charlotte appears on stage, reminiscing over her letters from Goethe. Herr von Stein is present throughout, with pipe and riding boots, in the form of a stuffed dummy. A distinct profile of Goethe is also constructed through Charlotte's musing. And yet, although Hacks dwells on the personal traits of these two characters, the fascination that their strange liaison had for him can be explained partly by the generalized view of love which Hacks expresses in his myths. Love, for him, is a contradiction, an impossible attempt by two individuals to lose their own identity in that of the beloved, to bridge an unbridgeable divide. What better material, then, than a relationship between two people whom literary history has pronounced incompatible? The feelings between Charlotte and Goethe bear the same extremes of attraction and repulsion as those between Omphale and Herakles. The difference lies in the complexities of the historical entities that were lacking in the lyrical symbols. The incompatibility does not stem from the exclusively loving nature of the woman confronted by the ceaseless social distractions of the man. Such abstractions could not account for all the ideological, temperamental and economic conflicts, set against the political background of the Weimar Court and the French Revolution:

> Wer an dem Bruch die Schuld trage? - Keiner; der Grund für das Scheitern der Liebe lag außerhalb ihrer eigenen Regel. Es ging nicht um Charlottes kalte oder Goethes überheizte Zimmer, es ging nicht um ihr Nichtempfangenwollen von geschlechtlicher Lust oder sein Nichtgebenkönnen; es ging nicht einmal um den Pudel: es ging um die Steuern für Kochberg (p.395).

What has happened with *Ein Gespräch im Hause Stein über den abwesenden Herrn von Goethe* is that, in developing a preoccupation unprecedented in East German drama with the unique facets of two historical individuals, without intending to illustrate the connexions between social structure and personality as general laws of dialectical materialism, Hacks has turned from the sphere of human abstraction and once more rooted his characters firmly within their own environment, this time without caricature. In truth, the quest for 'das pure Gattungswesen' in the world of myth had been riddled with all the contradictions of the cultures that had created and reinterpreted the myths. As structures, they offered powerful vehicles of expression for aspiration and endeavour, but individuality - and the love between individuals - had to be explored within its own historical context.

Chapter 10

HEINER MÜLLER: *DIE (UNBEWÄLTIGTE) DIALEKTIK VON OBJEKTIVER ENTEIGNUNG UND SUBJEKTIVER BEFREIUNG*

Although it is possible - whilst respecting the individuality of authors - to trace a shadowy pattern of evolution for East German drama, embracing shifts in purpose and method as a response to social and aesthetic developments, the work of Heiner Müller would defy incorporation into any such general scheme. In almost three decades of playwriting, covering the whole history of the GDR, he has remained outside the dominant modes of East German theatre, admitting to phases of keen interest in Western writers such as Samuel Beckett, Jean Genet and Edward Bond. Müller's career has embraced a wide variety of styles, from the didactic Brechtian *Lehrstück* to psychologically suggestive montage, from poetic myth to critical pantomime. His development has never been linear, and a chronological assessment of his work is almost impossible, since he has often reused old material in new plays, and a number of his plays consist of fragments pieced together from various periods. Furthermore, his works have not always been published or performed immediately after completion. *Die Umsiedlerin*, for example, which was performed briefly by the Leipzig student company in 1961 before being withdrawn, reappeared almost unchanged as *Die Bauern* in 1976 on the Berlin *Volksbühne*. *Der Bau*, a dramatized reinterpretation of Erik Neutsch's *Spur der Steine*, was first published in 1965 and never performed, but it was republished in 1975, and in March 1978 *Theater der Zeit* sought to revive interest in the play. *(??) Philoktet* (1958) was produced at the *Deutsches Theater* in 1978. Like several other plays, it had its première abroad, and it is in West Berlin that *Rotbuch Verlag* have been the most consistent publishers of Müller's writing.

In spite of the admonitions, and even censorship, that Müller's work has sometimes cost him, he has never been marginalized by the theatrical world. His dramatic talent and experimentation, his perceptive and provocative observations of socio-literary issues, and his knowledge and understanding of Brecht have won Müller a place at the centre of dramaturgic debates. Many of his plays, old and new, have been performed in the seventies, especially in Berlin, a city more receptive than most East German towns to innovation. The *Henschel* publishing house has now published most of his plays, with a volume of *Stücke* in 1975 and, in 1977, a smaller tome containing the more recent, montage works *Die Schlacht/Traktor* (1974) and *Leben Gundlings Friedrich von Preußen Lessings Schlaf Traum Schrei* (1977).

Müller is a close disciple of Brecht: not only Brecht the socialist classic, absorbed into school syllabuses as a committed Marxist and founder of socialist realism, but also Brecht the theatrical revolutionary, who aimed to transform the social relations of theatre, breaking down the barrier between stage and audience and making stern demands on the intellectual energy of his public. Müller, too, sees theatre as a process in which the members of the audience are co-producers of the drama, making their own judgements (especially in his early didactic plays) and associations (through his use of myth, fragments and montage). He has never wanted to obscure the medium through which he works by conforming to naturalist conventions, but has sought, rather, to involve the audience in the creative act. His characters rarely create the illusion of being real people who can set an example or induce a moral reaction. The theatre is always evident, in costume or make-up, stylized language, images of the absurd, or other alienating techniques. The figures are obviously tools in the structures of dramatic communication, incarnating attitudes in the didactic plays, moving between the worlds of history and myth in, for example, *Zement* (1973), or springboards for metaphor, resisting classical unity in an attempt to ignite the spectator's associative imagination in the more recent fragment montages.

If there is any major strand running through Müller's highly productive and diverse career, it is the belief that the socialist revolution outlined by Marx is far from complete, and that many contradictions still exist (in spite of the historic achievement of a socialized economy and a liberating political base), particularly in the psychological and anthropological spheres. Dramatic optimism must, therefore, mean more than formal happy endings or promising developments for characters in a play. In this respect, Müller takes Brecht's part in the debate with Friedrich Wolf about *Mutter Courage*. A recurring motif in Müller's work is the reminder that the human material of socialism is itself problematical. People are too complex to identify with a whole social system for conscious, moral reasons, and, in any case, socialism is not an abstract model, but an amorphous phenomenon in a state of flux, an erratic process of emancipation. There are still widespread attitudes of submission and authoritarianism, unconquered remnants of a psychology which complied with fascism, not only as a form of politics, but as a deeply engrained creed which permeated human relationships at work and in the family. At the same time, moralizing exponents of a socialist ethic have failed to acknowledge the force of sensuality, a vital drive which can be channelled in a positive and fulfilling manner when relationships cease to be exploitative. Müller's provocative drama assumes that there will be many people in his audience who are not ready to accept full and open responsibility for their life experience. In fact, he once characterized this transitional stage in the development towards socialism in terms of 'der (unbewältigten) Dialektik von objektiver Enteignung und subjektiver Befreiung'. *(78)*

How different is Müller's assessment of the epoch for which he is writing from that of Hacks, with his 'post-revolutionäre Dramaturgie'. Both have the professed intention of stimulating ideological and emotional creativity, but while Hacks yearns for harmony and laments the unattainability of the ideal, Müller is more concerned to unleash the subjective potential of socialism by breaking free from the psychological constraints of an historically authoritarian and submissive culture. To do this, one must recognize the more selfish forces within one's personality, and express social and emotional frustrations, however incoherent or unacceptable they may seem. The formal difference between the two authors is also considerable, although both are masters of language, form and theatrical business: Hacks seeks to inspire with his craftsmanship, whereas Müller prefers to expose the inadequacy of artistic expression, and to incite audience participation in the medium, even by resorting to techniques of revulsion. Müller is an entertainer who demands constant effort from his audience, assailing it with images and ideas that are a challenge to powers of identification and interpretation. His methods divide the public into enthusiastic supporters and sceptical, sometimes angry critics, and his houses are not so consistently full as those of his less exigent colleague.

The themes of Müller's plays are complex. His powerful and yet concise command of language enables him to incorporate a wealth of incisive observations, indicating connexions and contradictions for the spectator to explore. Together with his determination to enter uncharted waters and tap undeveloped sources of human psychology and sensuality, this makes Müller's dramatic output a forbidding object for detailed scrutiny in so short a space. Relationships between men and women, as a specific indication of social emancipation in general, are an essential part of almost all his plays. In fact, because of Müller's particular reliance on his characters to express contradictions in a verbal and physical form, they exist above all through their relationships to one another. Müller has shown a deeper insight and a broader understanding than any other East German playwright of the many ways in which oppressive attitudes towards women are integrated into restrictive social practices. His work has posed many unusual questions, not simply about the role of women in production and their growing self-confidence and social presence, but also about the validity and significance of patriarchal assumptions concerning female sexuality and male sexual aggression. Moreover, Müller does not find it necessary to devote a play specifically to the *Frauenfrage* in order to raise these issues. *Die Bauern*, for example, traces the effects of *Bodenreform* into three extremely intimate heterosexual relationships, linking economic developments to the rebellion of three women against particular forms of domestic and sexual oppression. In a play ostensibly 'about' peasants, Müller thus succeeds in observing patterns of patriarchal domination that have not been considered anywhere else in East German drama, from the underestimation of female labour in the reproductive sphere to the painful physical rejection suffered by both pregnant and ageing women. These experiences are not considered in isolation: they are manifestations of an exploitative society which must be eradicated at all levels of human interaction. Müller's female characters do not exercise a pedagogical function as such, but their demands on the revolution cover a broader range than do those of the men. They extend the horizons of socialist emancipation beyond male priorities, and as a result their revolutionary understanding tends to be more comprehensive.

In Müller's earliest plays, however, which are set at the point of production, women have subsidiary (but not insignificant) roles. This is a concession to the nature of the subject-matter. The industrial workers and functionaries in *Der Lohndrücker* (1956) and *Die Korrektur* (1958) reflect male predominance in these economic sectors. At the same time, the absence of female labour is itself a basis for Müller to explore the specific 'male' ethos of these industrial settings, and marks the beginning of his prolonged interest in sensuality in both its patriarchal and liberated manifestations.

These didactic plays drew attention to conflicts between new socialist tendencies and the legacy of reactionary attitudes which they encountered. In adopting Brecht's method from the *Lehrstücke*, and highlighting 'Haltungen' in various characters, Müller attracted criticism. He was defying the political and dramatic conventions of that time, which portrayed retrogressive ideals either as flaws in complex personalities which could be overcome, or else in the form of negative characters who would lose the historical battle in which they were engaged. Müller's approach demonstrated ways in which people sometimes brought their blinkered, selfish practices with them into the socialized economy, and ways in which progress could be generated by individuals with no conscious commitment to socialism.

In *Der Lohndrücker*, for example, the activist Balke is apolitical. The material is drawn from the same historical incident as Brecht's uncompleted *Büsching* (1953), in which the worker Hans Garbe mended a furnace while it was still hot to save production. Neither Müller's character nor Brecht's takes this risk as a political gesture, and yet the implications for the socialist economy are considerable. Balke is honoured by the party, but his workmates are hostile towards him because he has raised the norms and cut their private bonuses.

In the original version of this play, there are two women who reflect patterns of female labour, but it is not their function to encourage women to participate in industrial production, nor to prevail upon men to accept them there. One is the saleswoman in the canteen, an outsider and counter-figure to the troublemaking workers. The other, Fräulein Matz, is the director's secretary. Her only defence of her sisters' interests in the new state consists of complaints about the quality of lipstick, and whenever opportunity allows she dedicates herself to painting her lips. Unlike the similar figure of Miss Undertone in Vladimir Mayakovsky's *The Bathhouse* (1929), Fräulein Matz offers no suggestion of the pressures on women to use cosmetics, and the figure is conceived as an illustration that narrow self-interest determined many popular demands on the economy in those early years of *Aufbau*. (Cosmetics had, after all, been frowned upon by Hitler, and the DFD never chose to remind German women of Bebel's view that decorations of this nature were a remnant of female oppression.)

There is a further female character, a small, silent role used - like the incident with the canteen lady and the butter - to demonstrate the workers' selfish obsession with their own, unliberated interests. A girl stops on the evening street to observe a nude scrawled on the wall, only to be pursued, uninvited, by a man making allusions to her shape. This walk-on part makes the point that contemporary culture still channelled male sexuality in a manner which degraded women, and which was incompatible with the spirit of socialist equality and the collective ethic.

The revised editions of *Der Lohndrücker* are expanded by the addition of wives playing supportive (or noticeably unsupportive) roles in the activities of their husbands, who are involved in the central conflict. This aspect is absent from the 1975 *Henschel* edition, which dates from 1956, but appears in the *Hofmeister* edition of 1959, and in the *Reclam* collection *Der Weg zum Wir*, edited by W. Adling in the same year. There are two new scenes, one showing Balke's wife approving his decision to mend the furnace, and one showing Krüger's wife agreeing with their student son that Krüger is allowing himself to be exploited by the new state, just as he was by the old one, thus working counter to Krüger's dawning understanding of socialist economics. (This scene varies between the two 1959 editions.) The importance of wives for moral support is also discussed by party secretary Schorn and the Direktor. Schorn's wife committed suicide in the war when she believed he was to be executed due to Balke's denunciation. This element was introduced to sharpen the tension between the old Communist Schorn and his turncoat ally Balke. In talking to Schorn, the Direktor recognizes the value of a good woman to a man with a heavy burden of work and responsibility, and resolves to ask his own estranged wife to return to him. The introduction of these wives also had the effect of moderating the dispassionate, didactic mode of the play, thereby reinforcing the moral appeal of socialism and, presumably, appeasing those who had condemned it, ostensibly by accusing the author of dogmatic sectarianism.

The usefulness of a good wife is a theme reiterated briefly in *Die Korrektur* (p.58), but there are important new elements to the projection of women in this play, and it is tempting to attribute these, at least in part, to the collaboration of Inge Müller. Women appear as productive workers alongside men, although not in equal numbers. The representational function of the characters has been intensified, and there is one woman to embody the female workforce, just as there is one peasant, one young worker and one old worker, one Communist and one Nazi, one progressive and one conservative engineer. In the revised manuscript, these characters introduce themselves at the beginning, and the woman puts her historical claim:

> Die Frauen, die sich nicht gefallen lassen,
> mitbaun am eignen Haus, mitfahrn auf eignen Straßen (p.67).

She makes her appearance in a scene where various complaints are brought to illustrate how incentive bonuses can encourage workers to act dangerously or selfishly. This scene exposes aspects of unliberated thinking and selfish prejudice. The socialist perspective of the woman contrasts with the short-sighted attitudes of the Heiserer, a member of the works committee, towards his fellow humans. He betrays racialist sentiments when a complaint is lodged by a Sorb farmer, and then waves aside the woman's allegation that a driver on a productivity scheme caused an accident to the mother of four children:

> Wenn wir immer auf euch Weiber warten wollen, kommen wir nie zurecht (p.53).

This figure demonstrates that workers committed to the expropriation of capitalists and the socialization of the economy are not yet necessarily free from unjust and oppressive behaviour towards other groups. He is a precursor of the proletarian hero Gleb in *Zement*, of the militant Communist Flint in *Die Bauern* and of the caricatures of chauvinism in *Weiberkomödie* (1969).

Die Korrektur takes issue with a number of aspirations about women. Bremer's imagery in describing wartime Germany, for example, is a challenge to the view that the war was a strictly male affair. Class, not sex, was the determining factor. Bremer describes the petty-bourgeois women at home parading the booty of war, and the mothers who proudly sent their sons to the *Volkssturm*. He also objects to the bitterness of the young worker Heinz B., whose girlfriend sold herself in times of poverty, by drawing attention to the social context of prostitution. The woman was not responsible, although Bremer's terminology, typically for Müller, is terse and almost brutalizing:

> Wer hat sie zur Hure gemacht? (p.80)

The specific form of male consciousness reflected in the language of the old worker, Franz K., expresses an attitude already evident in *Der Lohndrükker* which was to recur in a number of Müller's plays. It relates to the 'male' comfort found in alcohol and womanizing:

> Wer nicht mit dem Schacht absoff, soff ab im Schnaps. Wen der Schnaps nicht fertigmachte, den brachten die Weiber auf den Hund. Es war schwer, sich heraushalten: aus den Schächten, aus den Weibern, aus dem Schnaps. - Jetzt hat sich das verbessert: Die Schächte sind gesichert, und die Weiber sind verheiratet (p.47).

The model of this mode of existence was to be Fondrak in *Die Bauern*, but such language is used in various kinds of play by Müller, corresponding as it does to his awareness that men have traditionally been the agents of history, and that women have been projected as the objects of male activity. The hedonistic devotion of his male characters to wine, women and song always implies some irony or exploitative sentiment, culminating in the disgust that the Hamletdarsteller feels in *Die Hamletmaschine* (1977) for his own oppressive sexuality, and for the unsavoury role of men in history as a whole.

The material that Müller chose for his earliest plays was fertile ground for this kind of male culture. The ethos of the shop floor emerges as one of untrammelled 'manliness'. Women have yet to forge a cultural image for themselves as 'Kumpel'. Müller traces the beginnings of this female intervention in *Der Bau*. There are two women in this play, set on a building site. Once more, one is the director's secretary, who conveys messages and exercises no influence. The other character, however, is the new young engineer, Schlee. The attitudes that she encounters among the workforce as a woman, and the way in which she counters prejudice with the argument of action, form a fundamental theme in the play.

Schlee's arrival on the building site is greeted by crude, mocking suggestions from the workers. Their insolent language is something that few writers have permitted themselves throughout the course of East German drama, but Müller is an enemy of palliative measures, and he believes that an underestimation of the legacy of oppressive values inherited by socialism is also an underestimation of the task of socialist forces and the contradictions within them. Schlee's function is to prove to these workers her value as a woman, as an engineer, and as a Communist, three identities which they view with deep suspicion. However, the lesson she teaches is not conveyed in straightforward political terms. The effect which Schlee has on the workers is a radical one which permeates their whole being, and Müller renders this by the striking change in their language from the first to the last scene. Initially, male sensuality is based on conquest and possession:

> SCHLEE: Ich bin als Ingenieur hier, die Frau ist Nebensache.
> GABLONZKI: Da kennen Sie uns schlecht.
> BARKA: Hände weg. Sie sind Ingenieur? Sie wollen hier arbeiten?
> Warum? Eins nach dem andern, erst der Einstand.
> *Er will sie küssen, und sie ohrfeigt ihn* (p.123).

By the final scene, when Barka and Bastian have learnt to respect Schlee, their poetic language is a contrasting expression of their new appreciation of women and of love. Sensuality becomes a positive force that can link individuals in an intimacy founded in mutual endeavour and fulfilment. The illegitimate child that Schlee is carrying, rejected by its father, party secretary Donat, becomes a symbol of unity and hope:

> BARKA: Du wärst mir leichter, wärst du schwer von mir.
> So lang der Weg reicht bist du meine Last.
> Hinterm Ural ist Nacht. Die Liebespaare
> Gehn in die Sträucher oder in die Betten
> In jeder Minute auf dem Flugstern hier
> Mit Baggern umgraben und mit Bomben
> Mit unserm Schweiß gewaschen und mit Blut
> Mit Kraut bewachsen und bebaut mit Steinen
> Über dem Lärm aus Stimmen und Papier
> Geht einem Mann in einer Frau die Welt auf. -
> Siehst du die Städte, die wir morgen baun? . . .
> Könnt ich die Zeit zurückdrehn auf den Punkt
> Knapp wie die Spanne zwischen Schnee und Wasser
> In dem er eins gewesen ist mit dir
> Gern laß ich mich in jeden andern sperrn
> Ob er der erste war oder der letzte
> Von dem dein Schoß blüht (pp.162-3).

Müller's acknowledgement of sensuality as a driving force in human nature is unconventional. On the rare occasions when physical desires are articulated in drama, they are usually represented as deriving from a primary bond of affection between two lovers, but not as a basic urge which exists in itself and seeks an outlet. The controversy and experimentation in matters of love that followed the Russian Revolution were never matched in the GDR, and the code of behaviour known as 'sozialistische Moral' has taken a reserved stance on the subject, tending to foster belief in the socialist family as the most prudent, natural and satisfactory outlet for sexuality. Latterly, sociologists and scientists such as Heinz Dannhauer have quietly undermined the psychological and biological validity of such sentiments *(79)*, but their findings have, as yet, had little public impact. Dominant morality continues to influence the production and reception of Müller's plays, and above all the image projected by women who express unconventional sensuality. In the *Volksbühne* production of *Die Bauern*, for example, there was unsympathetic, unambiguous treatment of the farm-hand Schmulka, who longs for the excitement of a physical liaison to relieve the monotony of her life. Müller portrays Schmulka's attempts to seduce the tractor drivers and the sober, puritanical FDJ activist Siegfried with humour, but the producer and actress found her sensuality funny in itself, turning her into a buxom pantomime wench. In an interview with tha author, Müller agreed that this interpretation did not do the character justice:

> Sie steht für alles, was man so unter Sinnlichkeit begreifen kann, und eigentlich das, was nur partiell realisiert wird in so einer Entwicklungsphase hier. Deswegen finde ich auch, daß sie ausschließlich karikiert wird. Da ist mir zuwenig die positive Seite, der positive Aspekt dieser Sinnlichkeit, in den engen Verhältnissen dieses Dorfs, die zu dem Zeitpunkt nicht ihre Bedürfnisse befriedigen kann. Das wäre eigentlich der Punkt, aber die Bedürfnisse werden zu sehr denunziert bei der Darstellung durch dieses negative Symbolisieren. *(80)*

In 1971 the same company, under the same producer Fritz Marquardt, had treated *Weiberkomödie* with similar suspicion. The plot of this lively, thought-provoking satire was taken from Inge Müller's radio play *Die Weiberbrigade* (1960), and concerns the assembly of a crane by a team of trained women mechanics in the face of male opposition.

The incident which is the cause of this momentous occasion is a nude bath taken by team-leader Jenny Nägle in a gravel pit on her building site. Several of her male colleagues are injured in the brawl which ensues, so that there are not enough men available to mend the crane of Nägle's boyfriend Häcksel. The women's brigade is happy to accept the party secretary's suggestion that they should assemble the crane, a job which they have never been allowed to do before, but some of the men see this either as an absurd impossibility, or else as a threat to their position. Finally, the men help the women to complete the job, for various motives, although they dress up in women's clothes to do so. Sectarianism is thus overcome, and there are opportunities for the actors to subvert gender roles by playing with properties and costumes.

The *Volksbühne* company was sceptical about the implications of this material. The notes to the rehearsal of 18 May 1971, which were published in *Sonntag*, labelled the central character, Jenny Nägle, as an extremist and an object of ridicule,

> die mit Bronchialgewalt ihren Emanzipationsanspruch durchsetzen will, deshalb zu törichten Übertreibungen neigt und ihr persönliches Glück sowie ihr Ansehen im Betrieb starrköpfig aufs Spiel setzt. Die unrealistisch gewählten Mittel erfüllen ihr Zweck nicht, utopische Verhaltensweisen werden preisgegeben. *(81)*

Apart from an incongruous desire to apply naturalist criteria to non-naturalist comedy, rooted in the company's lack of faith in Müller's comic method *(82)*, such criticisms betray a misunderstanding of the questions which Nägle's behaviour poses. From the notes we learn that Häcksel is funny, not because of the chauvinism which Müller ridicules, but because his courting methods are old-fashioned and fail as a strategy for winning his girl; and the personnel officer Zabel is funny, not because he cannot grasp the meaning of Bebel's teachings on the emancipation of women, but because he allows himself to be distracted from his work by Nägle's naked antics. The nude bathing itself also comes in for more criticism by members of the company than the social attitudes which greet it, although Müller appears to be attacking not Nägle's lack of conventional decorum, but the limitations of women's (and men's) emancipation in contemporary society. If Nägle is censured by her superiors, who talk of withdrawing her delegation to a conference, and if her male colleagues behave like jealous cock-birds fighting over a mate, then it is against these manifestations of prudish and patriarchal psychology that Müller directs the brunt of his humour. The irony that Nägle is blamed for the disruption, when it is the prejudice and chauvinism of the men's reactions which are at fault, is, in fact, one of Müller's complaints. Nägle, to be sure, is an exaggeration, a part of the comedy, but her self-defence raises neglected issues of female liberation. She quotes Bebel to remind Zabel that women in socialism shall have rights over their own bodies (p.75), and she draws his attention to the persistent evaluation of women in terms of physical beauty:

> Baden Sie mit, dann kann ich mir den Rest
> Von Ihrer Predigt unter Wasser anhörn.
> Da tuts uns beiden nicht so weh, wenn Sie
> Ihr Soll erfülln. Geniern Sie Sich? Ein Mann
> Ist keine Frau und muß nicht immer schön sein (p.86).

Some *Volksbühne* actors felt that the play was no longer relevant. It is ostensibly set in 1950, and by 1971 women had long enjoyed their right to work alongside men. (East German legislation, even so, unlike Soviet law up until 1 January 1981, prohibits women from carrying out a number of heavy jobs, a debate which Müller avoids, as the sexes finish the task together.) The crane, however, stands for an ideological construct which declares certain things to be the exclusive realm of men. Using anachronisms to place his challenge squarely in the present, Müller lampoons many aspects of gender stereotyping in his numerous sub-plots, and indicates his own view clearly in the 'Prolog' (absent from the *Henschel* edition):

> Wir sagen: wer A sagt, muß nicht nur B sagen, sondern auch,
> bitteschön, Z.
> Weil aber, wie der Marxismus lehrt
> Die herrschende Klasse der Macht nicht freiwillig den Rücken
> kehrt
> Setzen zu ihrem und unserm Glück
> An unsre Männer wir den Hebel der Kritik
> So lange bis der letzte Mann einsieht
> Daß zwischen Mann und Frau der Unterschied
> Nur dazu da ist und nur dafür gut
> Daß man für sein und ihr Vergnügen damit etwas tut (p.67).

The prejudice which comes under attack in the main plot is male deprecation of women's productive power. Not all the men, however, doubt the women's ability to assemble the crane. Amongst both doubters and non-doubters, there are those who welcome the women's attempt, and those who oppose it. The male characters express differentiated attitudes towards the opposite sex, which are linked into the main plot by the sub-plots in which each is involved.

Most of the workers gauge manliness in terms of beer consumption and conquests of women. The value of beer and women is interchangeable, as their bartering shows. Terminology such as 'Hahnenkampf' (p.69) and 'Hörner' (p.69, p.82) also illustrates their conventional pride in possessing women. Häcksel's workmates mock him when they learn that he was born under the sign 'Jungfrau', and Nägle under 'Stier', because this reverses their assumptions. But although Häcksel is part of this culture, issuing ultimatums to Nägle about what she may or may not do as 'his' woman, his reaction to a female team mending his precious crane is guided, above all, by his love of the machine. He has no objection in principle to women doing the job, but, because he is frightened that they might wreck the crane, he suggests that the men should dress up in women's clothes and help unnoticed.

Zabel, the personnel officer, is amazed at the proposal that the women might do this work, and his first reaction is to treat it as a joke. He has read Bebel, he boasts to Nägle, 'als du noch nicht/Gewußt hast, daß du eine Frau bist, Mädchen' (p.75), but in spite of this he has obviously not grasped the spirit of women's emancipation. He hypocritically tries to hide his interest in Nägle's bathing with moral lectures, and it is he who assumes that relationships between men and women can only be sexual, pretending to his wife on the telephone that Nägle, who is sewing on a button for him, is a man (p.77). Zabel has never learnt to do such things for himself, since he has firm views about the role of husbands and wives, and has prevented his own wife, Anna, from taking the job she would like, and for which she has trained. Zabel thinks that Nägle has forfeited the right to be a conference delegate, but he realizes that he must make a token gesture in support of *Frauenförderung*. He grumbles to the party secretary that it is hard to find women who will accept nomination, totally failing to understand their dilemma:

> Die eine kann oder sie will nicht reden
> Auf einer Konferenz. Aber nach Platz
> Im Kindergarten schrein, nach Waschanstalten
> Das können alle. Da ist keine schüchtern.
> Ich kann mich nicht zerreißen, Kaderleiter.
> Beruf und Haushalt und die Kinder und
> Mein Mann macht keinen Finger krumm zu Hause.
> Ja, wenn Sie meine Wäsche waschen und
> Bekochen meinen Mann, ich bin die erste (p.72).

He informs Nägle patronizingly, 'Wir haben Sie qualifiziert . . . von der Küchenhilfe zum Bauschlosser,' forcing her to retort, 'Was geraucht hat, war mein Schädel' (p.74). As a picture of a conservative, 'tokenist' bureaucrat, Zabel is unique in East German drama.

The Meister does not even pay lip service to the women's equality. He cannot argue rationally about his belief in the inferiority of women, and has recourse to innuendo (p.94). He has no faith in the ability of Nägle's team to assemble a crane. The Meister functions as an indication of the economic value of acknowledging female labour, even though he himself is so sceptical, because he is a pragmatist. His constant complaints relate to the labour shortage which prevents him from meeting plan requirements, but that is because he refuses to consider the women's potential.

The political value of setting a precedent of female achievement is emphasized by Prill, the 'Multifunktionär' (p.70). He is convinced that the women are capable of doing the job, and feels that the men should not participate, as this would ruin an historic occasion. Prill has his direct counterparts in the two injured workers, who are also certain that the women have the ability to assemble the crane, but are anxious to prevent them from doing so because the deed would mark a setback for male power. The Erster Blessierter warns the Zweiter Blessierter that women are becoming too rebellious:

Ich bin schon beinah über jede Mark froh
Die ich nicht hab. Ein Geld zu viel im Haus
Und meine Frau kauft eine Waschmaschine.
Staubsauger hat sie schon, Kühlschrank, was weiß ich.
Und mit jeder neuen Maschine reißt sie
Die Klappe drei Etagen weiter auf.
Die Technik macht die Weiber renitent (p.102).

The Erster Blessierter has read a book about a South Sea island where the familiar patriarchal roles are reversed. The comedy lies in the fact that the picture he paints, of one sex enjoying itself while it exploits the labour of the other, only horrifies the men because it is the women who have power. Like Wolf's Lehmkühl, these men envisage women's emancipation as a new kind of oppression. They have no intention of relinquishing their own position. However, the dramatist has his revenge on these two selfish and dishonest characters: until they are more reasonable, they are excluded from the joint repair work, and the stage manager removes the women's wigs that they called for in order to take part in the fun.

The other male to show his faith in the women's skills is the party secretary. This is a small role for, although the character has his own comic faults, his main purpose is to put the case for a non-sectarian resolution to the play, and to show that both political and economic aims will be furthered by an amicable acceptance of the women as qualified mechanics. He does this, not by moralizing, but in three brief and timely interventions: first, to make the suggestion that female labour should be used to solve the Meister's problem (p.73), secondly, to ask the women why they reject male assistance (p.95), and thirdly, when asked for his comment at the end, to paraphrase Lenin, 'Nichts gegen Träume. Wenn sie richtig sind' (p.115). This guiding function is necessary because such balanced observations lie outside the nature of the other characters.

The militancy of the women can only be appreciated in the light of the male attitudes outlined above. Nägle's provocations are primarily a challenge to Häcksel's possessive, dictatorial manner. By parading her own sexuality, or threatening to, she shocks Häcksel into realizing that the dual standards which he applies to male and female morality are based on false assumptions. While Häcksel swears he will bruise any other man who has anything to do with her, Nägle makes it clear to him that she is responsible for her own actions. The blank verse is a framework for rapid repartee, as Nägle plays havoc with Häcksel's traditional patterns of thought, and his only satisfaction lies in violence:

HÄCKSEL: Ich bin der Clown, wenn die Kollegen sich
Das Maul zerreißen über dich. Ich glaub
Kein Wort von allem, was sie dir nachreden
Aber ich hab ein Recht drauf, ich wills wissen.
Hast du mit ihnen oder hast du nicht.
NÄGLE: Und wenn.

HÄCKSEL: So ist das also.
NÄGLE: Das hast du
Gesagt.
HÄCKSEL: Das kann nicht wahr sein, Jenny. Du hast nicht -
NÄGLE: Das hab ich nicht gesagt.
HÄCKSEL: Ja oder Nein.
NÄGLE: Frag ich dich, wieviel Frauen du gehabt hast.
HÄCKSEL: Ein Mann ist keine Frau. Das ist was andres.
NÄGLE: Du mußt es wissen. Wenn du fertig bist
Mit unsern Möbeln, anderswo gibts mehr.
Ab. Häcksel fährt fort, das Möbel zu demolieren.
HÄCKSEL: Ich bring sie um. Ich bring sie alle um (pp.99-100).

When Häcksel proposes, Nägle questions why he wants to marry her, and suggests he would be better served by a dog (p.99). In the conciliatory atmosphere of a tea-break, when they have been working on the crane together, Nägle overturns the custom by proposing to Häcksel, instead. The 'Junge' that she has been visiting at weekends turns out, to Häcksel's joy, to be a four-year-old son.

Working as a mechanic is also the solution to Anna Zabel's estrangement from her husband. Anna rebels against Zabel's moratorium and leaves home to join the women's brigade. There is nothing for Müller to satirize in this character, although her retaliatory action is a little rash. Apart from illustrating the selfish narrowness of husbands preventing their wives from exercising their own rights, Anna challenges Zabel's double standards in love, which are similar to Häcksel's. Her argument with Zabel runs simultaneously with Nägle's verbal routing of Häcksel, so that they form a two-pronged attack, in scene 5, on male abuse of monogamy:

ANNA ZABEL: Wenn dir mal eine andre Frau gefällt
Ich bin nicht eifersüchtiger als andre
Und mir gefällt auch mal ein andrer Mann. -
HÄCKSEL: Ich hab dich was gefragt.
NÄGLE: Und ich dich, Häcksel.
ZABEL: Ein andrer Mann -
ANNA ZABEL: Ja, hast du was dagegen.
ZABEL: Ob ich . . . Natürlich hab ich was dagegen.
Wer -
ANNA ZABEL: Bist du eifersüchtig?
ZABEL: Nein.
ANNA ZABEL: Ich auch nicht.
ZABEL: Du auch nicht. So.
ANNA ZABEL: Störts dich?
ZABEL: Mich. Nein. Warum auch.
ANNA ZABEL: Dann ists ja gut. Und aus dem Märchenalter
Bin ich heraus. Die Ehe als Versteckspiel - (p.98).

Anna and Nägle are reunited with their men, once these are less domineering, but young Vera does not willingly renounce her own sectarian position. She is thus a more comic figure than the other two, indicating Müller's criticism, although her wagers with her boyfriend Karli are appealingly subversive. Karli is unwilling to accept Vera's skills as a mechanic. He bets that she cannot start the faulty motor bike. He loses, and his forfeit is that he must learn to knit. Karli is seen sporadically knitting throughout the next few scenes, to the ridicule of his workmates and to the delight of Vera, who hopes to have a properly tamed husband. The humour is ambiguous:

on the one hand, it is salutary to see a man learning domestic tasks, but on the other, Vera is too disrespectful towards Karli, just as she is the most opposed of all the women to men helping with the crane. When Karli doubts that the women can do this job, he foolishly promises to wear Vera's bridal gown if the crane stands. This provides one of many opportunities, at the end of the play, for pantomime which disrupts expectations concerning male and female appearance.

If Vera hopes to maintain her power over Karli by training him to do the housework, the older woman, Kaschiebe, represents a more traditional form of female government in the home. Kaschiebe bears many stereotyped characteristics of the elderly, more conventional housewife. She is superstitious, likes to gossip, and her corpulent figure is the butt of jokes about her sex appeal. Kaschiebe's size is also an expression of female physical strength, but, while she is eager for her brigade to prove women's worth in the productive sphere, she has an absurdly false idea of emancipation in relationships. She advises the other women that the only way to keep men in their place is to *prevent* them from learning how to look after themselves. She demonstrates how to use this bargaining power when her husband refuses to lend her his bicycle:

KASCHIEBE: Ich zähl bis drei, dann bricht die Revolution aus.
Dann kannst du deine Socken selber stopfen.
MANN: Hier ist der Schlüssel.
KASCHIEBE: Da bricht ihm der Schweiß aus.
So muß man mit den Männern umgehn, Mädchen (p.101).

The other woman in the cast is not a member of the brigade, but the chairwoman of the *Frauenausschuß*. Hilde Prill is the token woman who usually goes to conferences and who is called in to find nursery places and solve arguments between canteen staff and men who flirt with them. This work she refers to as the 'Kampf der Geschlechter' (p.83), but she is marginalized from the real battles: the issue of women assembling the crane, and challenges that individual women make to their menfolk in personal matters. Hilde's relationship with her husband Prill is almost non-existent, as both are too busy with their political functions to leave much time for married life. Prill is teased by the men for this, because he does not keep his wife in her place. Nevertheless, although the Prills are an object of mirth throughout the play because of their political rhetoric and their apparent lack of human interests, they plead at the end of the play for more sympathy:

PRILL: Kollegen, wenn wir schon beim Ändern sind
Was mich angeht und meine Frau, ich find
Wir stimmen mit dem Leben sozusagen
Nicht überein. Das muß man doch mal sagen
Ich meine, will man uns karikieren.
ZABEL: Das mußt du mit dem Autor diskutieren (p.114).

At this stage in the play, Müller can afford himself the luxury of such disclaimers. The stage business is becoming increasingly 'out-of-hand'. Once the relatively serious matter of repairing the crane has been settled to the satisfaction of everybody, Müller begins to play havoc with the gender of his characters. Many of the men have dressed in women's clothing to help on the crane, and when a long-haired person arrives looking for Häcksel, there are disputes about the sex of the newcomer. Since the person is called Häcksel, some characters assume that Häcksel is secretly already married, particularly as the stranger adopts a falsetto voice. However, the person turns out to be Häcksel's long-haired, good-for-nothing brother, Franz. When Franz tries to flirt with Nägle, Häcksel is angry and takes 'control' of the play:

> Das Ganze hält. Das Stück geht so nicht weiter.
> Zur Liebe brauch ich keine Mitarbeiter.
> Ich bin kein Witz für die Theaterkasse.
> In meiner Eigenschaft als Arbeiterklasse
> Greif ich jetzt ein in die Dramaturgie
> Und übernehme selber die Regie.
> Kollegen, zu eurer Information:
> Ich bin der Held. Ich mach euch nicht den Clown.
> Drum hab ich jetzt beschlossen, daß ihrs wißt
> Daß dieser Bruder meine Schwester ist (p.113).

To complete the confusion, the woman who now appears removes her long wig to reveal a page-boy hairstyle. With Karli wearing Vera's bridal gown because he has lost his bet, the stageful of wigs and costumes illustrates the inadequacy of artificial distinctions between men and women, and reinforces the appeal in Kaschiebe's closing speech for mutual understanding between the sexes.

Müller 'grants' Häcksel his intervention to remind the audience of the play's historical context. He was aware of the limitations of his penetrating satirical attack on patriarchal images of women. The ridicule he was seeking to arouse against attitudes which inhibited both women's liberation and general social advance was effective as a criticism, but his caricature of the male workers and functionaries obscured the dynamics of historical change. Müller acknowledged this in a supplementary note to the text:

> Den Schwank unterscheidet von der Komödie, daß er das kleinbürgerliche Moment mehr zum Gegenstand des Amüsements als der Kritik macht. Daß die ökonomischen Grenzen der Emanzipation in WEIBERKOMÖDIE nur Theater (als Requisiten eingesetzt) und nicht, in ihrer dialektischen Einheit mit ihrer Geburtshelferrolle, reflektiert sind, hält den Text auf dem Niveau einer Art (sozialistischer) Bierzeitung. Er sollte nicht als mehr gelesen werden. Solange Arbeit mehr Notwendigkeit als Bedürfnis, braucht das Theater, wenn es den Hintern zeigt, keinen Ausweis (p.116).

Zement (1972) raises similar issues from a totally different formal perspective. The play stresses the liberating potential of the socialist revolution, and the characters incarnate not just attitudes, but internal conflict. They thus carry within them the seeds of change. However, there are no lighthearted resolutions to the historic incursions on traditional emotions which threaten to tear them apart. Müller delves into the painful psychology of upheaval, as the characters glimpse new dimensions to human relationships, and wince at the challenge of breaking out from oppressive patterns of security.

Based on the novel by Fyodor Gladkov about Russia in the early twenties, *Zement* is a play of merciless dialectics. It shows the revolutionary process as a Hydra: whenever Hercules/mankind succeeds in cutting off one of its heads, another grows in its place. The dramatic contradictions are therefore rife and violent. A continuous plot can be identified, but it is of comparatively little significance, since Müller deliberately uses a fragmentary scene sequence as a means of involving the audience in many unresolved questions. The basic development is positive: the mechanic Gleb Tschumalow returns home from the war a hero to find that the cement factory, the hub of productive activity in the village of Novorossisk (a microcosm of New Russia), has ceased to function and is overrun by goats. Gleb gathers the forces of socialism, secures the aid of the bourgeois engineer, Kleist, and sets the factory into operation again. Gleb is a working-class hero, but his treatment of his wife, Dascha, is steeped in the oppressive traditions of feudal, patriarchal Russia. Dascha's transformation from a housewife into a revolutionary overturns every aspect of her relationship with Gleb: their emotional, intellectual and physical behaviour, and also the spheres of their economic, social and domestic responsibilities. Müller highlights the psychological torment inside Dascha, and the confusion into which she throws Gleb, when she questions the whole basis of monogamy. Her doubts remain unanswered. There is no solution to them in the play, and the challenge to family morality was curtailed in Soviet society in subsequent years. Badjin's claim that 'die Familie ist ein Relikt und wird die Revolution nicht überleben' (p.347) has not yet been realized. Müller's play raises the issue again, and his setting is both specific and general:

> Das Stück handelt nicht von Milieu, sondern von Revolution, es geht nicht auf Ethnologie, sondern auf (sozialistische) Integration aus, die Russische Revolution hat nicht nur Novorossisk, sondern die Welt verändert, Dekor und Kostüm sollten nicht Milieu zeigen, sondern den Entwurf der Welt, in der wir leben (p.389).

Although Dascha's questions are given contemporary relevance, Müller's characters do not represent right and wrong. They embody historical conflicts, existing within contradictory and overlapping discourses, through their counterposition to other characters. Nevertheless, Müller clearly feels some sympathy for the issues which Dascha raises. But the reception which Dascha was given by audiences at the *Berliner Ensemble* in 1973 was often unfavourable. The same suspicion of female sensuality which greeted Nägle, and later Schmulka, was reinforced by what Walter Benjamin called the 'Sphinxgesicht', the shocking sight of the woman with political power. *(83)* The actress Christine Gloger's ability to project Dascha's contradictions with sympathy was further prejudiced by the techniques of the company, which, since Brecht's death, has tended to emphasize 'Haltungen' at the expense of emotional conviction. The critic Irene Böhme judged Gloger's interpretation to coincide emphatically with Gladkov's subsequent recantation and his condemnation of Dascha as a warning to women *(84)*, but the *Dramaturg* Hans-Jochen Irmer denied that this was the intention:

> Der Meinung, Dascha Tschumalowa werde mit beinahe unmenschlicher Härte gegen ihr Kind und ihren Mann dargestellt, konnten wir nicht zustimmen. Es geht hier um den ersten und den letzten Klassengegensatz, und der Ausbruch aus der Haussklaverei ist in der Tat ein Gewaltakt, insbesondere unter den Voraussetzungen des kleinbürgerlich-patriarchalischen Kapitalismus . . . Es entstehen Fronten, und die Beurteilungen dieser Dascha hängen sehr von den sozialen, politischen, individuellen Dispositionen der Beurteilenden ab. *(85)*

Müller's adaptation of Gladkov's novel is certainly provocative. To sharpen the dramatic form and underline his own insistence on the intense struggle of contradictions, he has stressed the conflicts in the novel with his violent metaphors and a decentralization of Gleb's role. The latter is achieved by heightening Gleb's internal conflict, and by separating the mythical symbolism of the revolutionary gains from the figure of the working-class hero and transferring it to the intermezzos. The implications for the character Dascha are that her own contradictions become more acute and her torments harsher. In the novel, Gladkov goes to great lengths to illustrate Dascha's love for her little daughter Njurka, so that when the child dies of starvation in the children's home, the reader shows more understanding for Dascha's dilemma, torn between the care of her child and the demands of the Revolution. In the play, Dascha's determination to pursue her independent political tasks is thus more pronounced, and Gleb's fury is reinforced, although at the same time Müller suggests that Gleb is equally responsible for Njurka, and that he cannot apply one code to himself and another to his wife. Dascha is also more pressurized in the play to confront Gleb with her metamorphosis, without the time allowed the novel character to prepare him for the shock. Their conflict is, therefore, all the more embittered, intransigent, and even violent, and this violence in turn emphasizes the world-historical significance of the tumultuous events informing their new relationship. The aggression of the play as a whole is designed to provoke, and also to make the spectator aware of the Revolution's impact, not only on the means of production, but also on personal relationships.

That the action in Novorossisk heralds a new epoch is further accentuated by Müller's use of myth. Like Peter Hacks, he turned to the Greeks for material, but his interpretation is rather different. Whereas Hacks considers that, in a classless society, the humanist aspirations of these myths can be rehabilitated, Müller uses them as a forceful expression of mankind's struggle to control the environment. As a result, where Hacks establishes a rigid antithesis between reality and ideal, Müller shows the harrowing process of contradiction and qualitative transformation. Where Hacks has recourse to harmonious classical forms, Müller defies the dramatic traditions of unity, presenting his myths in disjointed form, alternating with and commenting upon the historical action. Hacks turns to myths for simplified concepts: Müller uses them to diversify the level of action and to promote the associative complexities of language and symbol. Hacks identifies the poetry of post-revolutionary society with that of primitive classless society, sometimes tampering a little with the versions handed down by intermediary, authoritarian and patriarchal cultures: Müller, on the other hand, underlines the difference between the old and the new by subverting the relationships in the myths altogether. This occurs many times in *Zement:* five of the fourteen scene titles refer to Greek myths, and another to Christ. The purpose is twofold: to demonstrate that the significance of the action extends far beyond Novorossisk in 1920-21, and to question the basis of the original myths.

The scene 'Heimkehr des Odysseus' shows that Dascha bears no resemblance to the patient, loyal Penelope, sitting at home and carrying out her women's duties until her husband returns from the war. The apolitical Motja reveals this to Gleb on his return:

> Lang hast du sie allein gelassen, Krieger.
> Dascha-wo-ist-sie-wartet-sie-auf-mich.
> Wo soll sie sein. Bei ihren Freiern ist sie.
> Frag die Partei nach deiner roten Witwe (p.328).

Dascha's emancipation from Penelope's role, introduced in this hostile (and distorted) manner, is not something which the audience is permitted to condone without question. Motja, herself a contradictory figure, who believes that the role of women should be domestic and maternal and yet comes to blows with her patriarchal husband, describes Dascha in a negative light, alluding to her liaisons with Red Army soldiers and condemning her for leaving the child to grow thin. Nevertheless, Motja's own children have all died in the famine, so that her criticisms are alienated by the knowledge that Njurka is probably no worse off in the children's home than with her mother. Gladkov, in his novel, shows the children's home to be a comfortable, happy and loving place. Müller, whose concern is not to argue the virtues of Soviet welfare policy but to observe a psychological revolution, does not emphasize this point. He does not give Dascha easy excuses.

Dascha's ensuing entrance, in the company of other Communist women, makes a more favourable impression, since she is clearly offering a valuable contribution of her own to the Revolution. Gleb's refusal to be called 'Genosse' by his wife is seen as an undesirable prejudice. At the same time, however, Dascha's companions are disconcerting in their defiance of conventional feminine images: Polja has a romantic view of military struggle, and the features of the Bärtige Frau add to the unprepossessing appearance of these political women.

Further discriminatory practices and jokes on the part of the Communist men at the works committee are illustrated in the next scene, and this is followed by 'Das Bett'. The name symbolizes the battle between Gleb and Dascha for control over Dascha's sexuality, and the only property on an otherwise bare stage is the bed. The previous scene, by exposing the backwardness of the men in their regard for women, provides a favourable context for Dascha to justify her emancipation, but here, too, her language is harsh and alienating. She rejects the illusion of comfortable domesticity, and refuses to console her war-torn husband. Müller thus projects Dascha as a victim and an agent of the gruelling conditions in which the protagonists are struggling to defeat famine and counter-revolution.

Gleb tries a number of arguments to preserve his pre-war position, but each time Dascha parries with clearer logic, demonstrating that Gleb is still trapped in authoritarian ideology in certain respects. Gleb begins by evoking a religious order:

TSCHUMALOW: Bist du noch ein Weib.
Soll ich dir zeigen, wozu dich Gott gemacht hat.
DASCHA: Langsam, Genosse. Die Sowjetmacht hat ihn
Liquidiert, deinen Gott (p.334).

He then resorts to his rights of possession:

TSCHUMALOW: Wer fragt den Gaul, wann er geritten sein wird . . .
DASCHA: Kühl dich ab, Besitzer.
Aus welcher Fibel hast du dein ABC
Gelernt als Kommunist (p.335).

Gleb now turns to emotional pressure, accusing Dascha of losing her loving nature. Dascha recounts a little of her political involvement, which has taught her sacrifice and achievement, and reminds him of the acute social deprivation. She has changed, and Gleb cannot appreciate her individuality:

Soll ich begraben im Familienbett
Ersticken unter dir auf einem Laken
Was mir so teuer ist, weil es so viel
Gekostet hat, Tränen Schweiß Blut: meine Freiheit
(pp.335-6).

When Gleb plays on Dascha's maternal guilt, she turns the argument against him:

> Gut, Gleb. Wenn du sie füttern willst. Bleib du
> Zu Hause. Spiel die Mutter für dein Kind. Ich
> Hab keine Zeit (p.336).

Because he cannot begin to comprehend Dascha at this point, Gleb assumes that her political work must be quite unimportant, and that her much-prized liberty is the result of lasciviousness. The idea of female sexuality revolts and excites him. He later defends the soldier Makar, condemned to death for rape, by arguing that women incite men to seduce them, but his standards are inconsistent, and he does not accept that Dascha was just as entitled as he was to sleep with strangers during the war. His anger and contempt are expressed in metaphors of disgust, which deny Dascha's humanity, while, in an act of supreme irony, he starts to rape her:

> Und so. Und so. Hast du noch eine Brust.
> Sie regt sich. Unter wieviel Händen schon.
> Die Schenkel. Heiß. Der Gaul braucht Auslauf, wie.
> Die Frucht ist noch nicht taub, der Acker will
> Gepflügt sein (p.337).

After Dascha defends herself with a rifle, Gleb weeps for his confused presumption:

> Schieß, mach ein Ende, wenn du willst. Alles
> Hab ich gegeben für die Revolution.
> Ich kann nicht mehr. Verflucht die Bourgeoisie
> Die Seele hat sie uns vergiftet. Dascha
> Sag, können wir uns nicht verstehen (p.338).

Now that Gleb has arrived at this state of accessibility, Dascha is able to articulate her own feelings and doubts. The new times have brought an end to possessive relationships, but the form that love between men and women will take in their place is still unclear. Gleb must allow time for adjustment:

> Was auch geschehen ist, Gleb, ich liebe dich
> Und nur auf dich hab ich gewartet. Ich
> Weiß nicht was werden wird. Alles ist anders
> Laß mir Zeit, Gleb. Auf die alte Art wirst du
> Deine Frau nicht mehr finden. Etwas hat aufgehört
> Was anfängt ist noch blind. Wenn es dir schwer wird
> Ich bin nicht eifersüchtig. Manche Frau
> Ist ohne Mann geblieben. Das ist mein Ernst, Gleb (p.339).

Dascha's questions were not unusual at the time. They were expressed in the essays and stories of Alexandra Kollontai. But debates about love and morality waned as the twenties drew on, partly due to the political situation and partly to widespread concern that young people in particular were being hurt as a result of emotional insecurity and exploitation of a freer sexual morality by an unscrupulous minority. (In the novel, Badjin is an example.) As the climate changed, Gladkov made continual changes to his novel, so that later editions were less tolerant of Dascha.

In scene 7, 'Die Frau am Baum', which is highly charged with the sexual and violent terminology of psychoanalysis, Dascha faces death at the hands of rebel Cossacks. She rejects the proposition of the Cossack officer that she can save her life by sleeping with him. His insinuations are an insult to her, and she is not prepared to co-operate with an enemy of her party.

The Cossack officer is historically moribund, and to her he represents death:

Ich bin kein Wurm, der sich von Aas ernährt
Wie kann ein Toter mir das Leben schenken (p.354).

For the Cossack, Dascha's proud stance deserves the ultimate accolade:

Du hast dich gut behalten. Wie ein Mann (p.355).

His normal expectation of women is that they are inevitably 'whores'. The Communist women, with their cropped hair and brave demeanour, are a mystery to him. He has always believed that the predicate of womanhood is that it is weak, and that it desires flesh and offers itself to men. As a result, although it is he who wishes to exploit Dascha, and not the other way about, he expresses himself as though he would be performing her a service. In deceptively more chivalrous tones than Gleb, he, too, compares women to horses:

Du wirst mit mir zufrieden sein
Ich kenn mich aus mit Pferden und mit Weibern.
Und deine Brüste schrein nach einem Mann.
Die Schenkel haben Lenin nicht gelesen (p.354).

Dascha hates the man who seeks to humiliate her by threatening either to rape her himself, or else to hand her over to his men (who, he implies, are inferior). Therefore, in spite of the Cossack's decision to reward her courage with freedom, when Badjin returns with soldiers to wipe out the enemy, Dascha riddles the officer's corpse with bullets. Dascha has not wanted to sleep with Badjin before, but now she needs release from her traumatic experience. In contrast to the officer, Badjin stands for life and hope. The close encounter with death has galvanized Dascha into a fresh desire for life, and she informs Badjin that she wishes to sleep with him.

The intermezzo 'Herakles 2 oder die Hydra', recited by any of the actors (at the *Berliner Ensemble* it was done by a woman), recounts a male myth. Müller's Herakles is in some ways similar to and in others very different from the Herakles in *Omphale*, which was in the *Ensemble* repertoire at the same time as *Zement*. Hacks's Herakles is intended to represent virility. Heroic action is, for the purpose of the encounter with Omphale, intransigently male. In Gladkov's novel, too, the Herculean metaphor is integrated with the portrayal of Gleb, the revolutionary worker who heaves the productive forces of socialism into motion. Müller separates this symbolism from the figure of Gleb, introducing the metaphor as a comment on the struggle of all the revolutionaries. If we look back to Müller's earlier play, *Herakles 5* (1964/66), we find a Herakles who is distinctly male in so far as he is tempted by Zeus to clean the Augean stables with the reward of a naked Hebe, who floats past on a cloud to inspire the hero. But Herakles is not male in so far as he performs his deed in the name of humanity as a whole, rebelling against the patronizing taunts of the deity. By forcing the river to wash out the stables for him, Herakles demonstrates humanity's control of nature and, by implication, the development of the means of production in the interests of the people. The imagery echoes the words of Heinz B. in the revised version of *Die Korrektur*, spoken on behalf of all the progressive groups in the play, including the women:

FLUSS, STEH STILL! DEIN LAUF WIRD KORRIGIERT
PLATZ DA, ERDE! WAS DU HAST, GIB HER! (p.80).

This metaphor was adopted by Müller in other works. The river becomes a symbol for the forces of history. The waters in which Ophelia drowned in Shakespeare's *Hamlet* represent the subjugation of women to these historical forces. In *Die Hamletmaschine*, Ophelia refuses to be drowned and grasps for emancipation, shaking off her time-honoured role with rancour, and giving vent to the indignities that women have suffered at the hands of men who, as statesmen, have killed them (most of the references are to images from Müller's own plays and recall specific historical situations) and, as seducers, have humiliated them. Scene 2 suggests this rebellion:

DAS EUROPA DER FRAU
Enormous room. Ophelia. Ihr Herz ist eine Uhr.
OPHELIA (CHOR/HAMLET)
Ich bin Ophelia. Die der Fluß nicht behalten hat. Die Frau am Strick Die Frau mit den aufgeschnittenen Pulsadern Die Frau mit der Überdosis AUF DEN LIPPEN SCHNEE Die Frau mit dem Kopf im Gasherd. Gestern habe ich aufgehört mich zu töten. Ich bin allein mit meinen Brüsten meinen Schenkeln meinem Schoß. Ich zertrümmre die Werkzeuge meiner Gefangenschaft den Stuhl den Tisch das Bett. Ich zerstöre das Schlachtfeld das mein Heim war. Ich reiß die Türen auf, damit der Wind herein kann und der Schrei der Welt. Ich zerschlage das Fenster. Mit meinen blutenden Händen zerreiße ich die Fotografien der Männer die ich geliebt habe und die mich gebraucht haben auf dem Bett auf dem Tisch auf dem Boden. Ich lege Feuer an mein Gefängnis. Ich werfe meine Kleider in das Feuer. Ich grabe die Uhr aus meiner Brust die mein Herz war. Ich gehe auf die Straße, gekleidet in mein Blut (pp.91-2).

The image of the woman drowning in the river also appears in the montage *Germania Tod in Berlin* (1956/71), another nightmarish sequence that indicts slaughter and oppression, and fascism in particular. In the early part of the play, women are present only as street prostitutes, degraded by their patriarchal society, and in the symbolic role of Hitler's commander, Germania. At the end, however, a hopeful era dawns, and a girl comes to join the Communists. Hilse identifies her in his fantasy as 'die rote Rosa', who drowned herself in the Spree when pregnant. Now she is red, not with blood, but with her convictions:

HILSE: Das Wasser hat dich nicht behalten, Rosa (p.78).

When women seize emancipation, they haul themselves out of the water that has swept them helpless down the centuries, and reach for the right to be mistresses of history, subjects, in the Marxist sense, alongside men. Herakles thus becomes the representative of all humanity. The metaphor of the intermezzo in *Zement* is generalized. There is nothing in the language that confines it to manhood.

The complement to Herakles, the legend of action, is Prometheus, the legend of human intellect, another familiar figure in Müller's work. The Revolution frees intellect to develop in the interests of humanity. This is shown in the early scene 'Die Befreiung des Prometheus', which falls into two halves. The first portrays an historical struggle between Gleb and the petty-bourgeois engineer Kleist. Gleb wins Kleist's intellectual power for the workers. The act is performed by men, given its specific context, but it is of symbolic value for all the revolutionaries. The recitation of the reworked Prometheus legend in the second half again expresses the general significance of the alliance.

The Herakles intermezzo is the sign for an interval in the play, and the second part begins with a long and demanding scene, involving considerable psychological confession, first between Gleb and Dascha, and later with the addition of Polja and Iwagin. The scene is 'Medea-Kommentar', a mythical reference which lends tragic significance to the news of Njurka's death. At the same time, there are challenges to simple comparisons. Medea, jealously in love with Jason, kills the children of her womb to reconquer their father's faithless attention. The social context of Njurka's death undermines the abstractions of the myth. The emancipated Dascha has as much right as Gleb to pursue her political commitment; or else Gleb has as little right as Dascha to neglect the child. To complicate the dilemma, it was famine that caused Njurka's death, and her parents were absorbed by fighting the famine and building an economy to end poverty. Müller's play is more severe than Baierl's *Frau Flinz* in placing the myth of Motherhood in an historical perspective.

Müller maintains this historical approach to maternity throughout his work. In exploitative societies, where violence and subjugation are inherent in the system, motherhood, as a life-giving principle, is a mockery of itself. The crippled Ophelia in *Die Hamletmaschine*, assuming the role of Elektra, rejects this role:

> Ich stoße alle Samen aus, den ich empfangen habe. Ich verwandle die Milch meiner Brüste in tödliches Gift. Ich nehme die Welt zurück, die ich geboren habe, zwischen meinen Schenkeln. Ich begrabe sie in meiner Scham. Nieder mit dem Glück der Unterwerfung. Es lebe der Haß, die Verachtung, der Aufstand, der Tod (p.97).

In socialist societies, pregnancy retains its connotations of hope and optimism. The girl who drowned herself in *Germania Tod in Berlin* was the victim of poverty and strife, but Schlee's pregnancy in *Der Bau* betokens an inspiring future, and for the quiet, submissive Niet in *Die Bauern* it is a motive for breaking with the lazy Fondrak. Encouraged by Flinte 1, the 'Umsiedlerin' Niet accepts a piece of land under the *Bodenreform*, a brave act for a single woman. This unobtrusive character, the only 'Identifikationsfigur' in a sharply critical comedy, thereby draws attention to the new horizons opened up for unsupported mothers by the socio-economic transformation of agriculture. Niet survives without having to resort to the stratagems of a Mutter Courage or a Shen Te in fending for her child, and has the real choice of rejecting her honest suitor Mütze, because she is wary of attaching herself to another man.

In 'Medea-Kommentar', where the battle for socialism is still raging and the contradictions are fierce, pregnancy, in spite of all the turmoil, is again an expression of hope. The juxtaposition of Dascha's sorrow and Motja's joy is poignant:

> MOTJA: Was sagst du, Nachbarin, zu meinem Bauch.
> Mir ist als ob ich neu geboren wär.
> Fühl wie es sich bewegt. - Dascha, verzeih mir.
> Vergessen hab ich, nur an mich gedacht.
> Ach was bin ich für eine Bestie. Njurka
> Tot und begraben. Und ich spiel mich auf
> Mit meinem Bauch vor dir. - Es hat schon Füße.
> Verzeih mir, Dascha, daß ich glücklich bin.
> DASCHA: Warum sollst du nicht glücklich sein (p.361).

As in the other plays, the relationship between motherhood and its social context works in both directions: general morality and practice define motherhood, while mother characters become symbolic indices of the historical system.

The tragedy which draws Dascha and Gleb together and drives them apart is a catalyst for Dascha to explain her evolution to Gleb. Contrary to the Medea legend, it is the woman who has torn away from the marriage, and the man who wants to win her back. Dascha feels a need to account for herself. She tries to convey to Gleb the process of her involvement in the party, starting with her desire to help her husband's cause in his absence, the tortures inflicted on her by the enemy, including rape by their officers, her increasing contacts with the Red Army and her inability to refuse sexual consolation to its soldiers, identifying them at first with Gleb, and then swimming in the anonymity of their numbers. Dascha talks freely of her new awareness of her own sexuality. Her night with Badjin was an unforgettable experience, but based entirely on carnal passion. He is an animal, and she has no love for him. She loves Gleb, but she will not let him touch her because she does not know what this love means. She is afraid of the possessiveness that goes with love:

> Was ist das für eine Liebe, die am Besitz klebt.
> Warum schlagen wir nicht die Zähne du
> In mein Fleisch und in dein Fleisch ich und beißen
> Uns einer aus dem andern unsern Anteil.
> Wenn mich die Weißen totgeschlagen hätten
> Du hättest einen ruhigeren Schlaf jetzt (pp.366-7).

Gleb, however, now more receptive to Dascha's conflicts, cannot accept these views. The image of Dascha with other men torments him. He acknowledges that Dascha was right to remind him of their equality, and that he has acted unjustly towards her, but he cannot understand why she is cold towards him, and not other men. Dascha likens him to a bourgeois in love: incurably possessive. She packs her belongings to leave.

The arrival of Polja and Iwagin brings a new dimension to the debate. Iwagin, an intellectual and son of a rich house, rejects the family as a concept, and yet he wants Polja to live with him. He talks of the strife within his own family, deducing from this that families should be abolished. Iwagin later shoots his brother in a battle with the White Army. He has renounced his bourgeois mother in disgust and ridicule but, illogically, shows a great respect for the tragedy of Medea, whose torment was to murder the children she had born. In a certain respect, Iwagin is more like Medea than Dascha could be: he openly rejects his parents in front of his comrades in an (unsuccessful) attempt to win their political approval. Meanwhile, Dascha invites Polja to take care of Gleb, but Gleb wants only Dascha, and in threatening to draw nearer to Polja he is making an appeal to his wife. The scene ends with a tableau that clearly illustrates the confusion that the Revolution has sown in relationships between men and women:

> *Tschumalow geht auf Polja zu, die weicht aus, zu Iwagin, der ihr ausweicht. Sie geht zurück, Tschumalow geht auf seine Frau zu, die bleibt stehn, er geht zurück, stellt sich mit dem Gesicht zur Wand* (p.373).

The story between Dascha and Gleb has no resolution in the play. Their last encounter is brief and open-ended. After the workers have beaten off the White Army attack on the factory, in the congratulatory exchanges which follow, Dascha cannot commit herself to Gleb, but she does express her pride in him:

TSCHUMALOW: Wie lebst du, Dascha. Wann kommst du zurück.
DASCHA: Gleb. Ich bin froh, daß du es bist, kein andrer
Den unsre Arbeiter auf Händen tragen (p.380).

Helen Fehervary suspects that the reason for Dascha's eclipse from the latter stages of the play is Müller's own inability to resolve her crisis:

> The author simply could not continue to 'write' her. He himself was at a loss and did not go on. This is where he was most honest, most 'progressive' - if we still want to employ that term. *(86)*

Her suspicion is reasonable, but there is surely some truth, too, in her initial reaction to Dascha's disappearance, that she has had no room in history itself to come to terms with her self-discovery.

It is not Heiner Müller's practice to preach any morality to his audience, nor to weigh heavily in the direction of a particular creed. He is more concerned with human potential, and the way in which it fights to express itself in new ways. Dascha and Gleb represent two sides to a conflict, and they also embrace internal contradictions, and it is out of oppositions such as this that change is generated. Dascha's experiments with free love are an honest outlet for her sexuality in a turbulent age, but at the same time they cause pain, not only to her husband, but also to herself, because both of them have been moulded to fit a possessive structure of emotional security. Dascha does not have the answers to her questions. She cannot yet grasp the potential connexions between desire and love and comradeship. She defends her new self-awareness, but her attitude is still ambivalent:

Vielleicht muß ich die Liebe
Oder was man so nennt, mir auch ausreißen
Und meine Lust, die manchmal mit ihr eins war
Und manchmal nicht, wie einen Nagel, der
Ins Fleisch gewachsen ist, daß endlich aufhört
Der Walzer aus Gewalt und Unterwerfung
Der uns zurückschraubt in die Bourgeoisie
Solang es auf der Welt Besitzer gibt (p.364).

Dascha's significance, in the context of East German drama, is that she probes areas of sexual psychology that have otherwise remained unexplored. The idea that desire and affection (Kollontai's 'winged Eros') may not always correspond is discussed at most by sexual psychologists as a form of delinquency requiring treatment and as a problem of broken marriages and sexual crime. But Dascha is a mouthpiece for Müller in one fundamental plea not to repress feelings traditionally evaluated as improper:

Sind wir Kommunisten oder nicht.
Können wir leben mit der Wahrheit. Oder
Baun wir die Welt neu mit verbundnen Augen (p.366).

For Müller, sensual experiences require liberation in the same way as labour. He does not advocate free love in particular. Dascha is not his ideal but an expression of conflicting emotional needs and ideological rationalizations. The tenderest relationships in Müller's works are based on respect and desire entwined. Barka's encouragement to Schlee, and Mütze's courtship of Niet are examples. The power of the montage plays, however, operates in a quite different way. *Die Schlacht, Leben Gundlings Friedrich von Preußen*

Lessings Schlaf Traum Schrei and *Die Hamletmaschine* provoke associations drawn from subliminal realms of audience experience, demanding their acknowledgement and ventilation. The historical connexion between violence and sexuality, made in *Zement* through simile and the recurrent theme of rape, is even more striking in these later plays. Exploitative societies - bourgeois Denmark, autocratic Prussia, fascist Germany - generate exploitative and repressive psychologies. Coercion and humiliation determine relations between men and women, just as they determine the nature of motherhood. These plays contain images representing the female body as a consumer object. Hamlet, like the young Friedrich, treats women as prostitutes, and this also colours his Oedipus complex and his disgust with his own birth. Love between husbands and wives, where it exists, is distorted by the politics of death and violence. The nightmare of the butcher's wife in *Die Schlacht* reflects her anguish at encouraging her husband, for social protection, to join the fascists. She wishes him dead.

These images are designed to repel and to anger because of the human indignity they represent. There are no solutions within the repressive societies they describe. The Hamletdarsteller can only seek escape from his male role as an oppressive agent of history by identifying instead with the oppressed. He laments, 'Ich will eine Frau sein' (p.92), but there is nothing glamorous about being a victim, and his transformation by Ophelia into a masked whore is equally grotesque. As in 'Die Frau am Baum', lust and death are linked, here in the imagery of the coffin. The words that emerge from it, 'Was du getötet hast sollst du auch lieben' (p.92), have no single, obvious meaning. The symbols and images in the scene suggest both male abuse of women as objects for their own selfish sexuality, and the catastrophic course of history in general over which Hamlet/men have presided. Audience response is allowed free rein.

The metaphors of oppressed womanhood in *Die Hamletmaschine* incite reactions to the specific relationship between men and women in patriarchal society, but the fundamental mood of the play is a more general rejection of all forms of psychological subjugation, to which the Hamletdarsteller himself is prey. Out of the welter of allusions and images describing women as the victims of history comes a reversal, whereby poisoned motherhood and prostitution symbolize the human condition wherever there is psychological coercion and emotional inhibition. The revolutionary ethos is evoked to counter stagnation, not only in the broad social sense, but in individual terms. The spectator is provoked into anger about himself or herself.

Of these montages, only *Die Schlacht*, which has more direct points of historical reference, has been performed to date in the GDR. But even this production, at the *Berliner Volksbühne*, was met with widespread incomprehension of the part of the public. Müller's refusal to formulate his material discursively demands a new epistemology from the theatre-goer, and a new interest in the complex mechanics of revolutionary anthropology. If the plays which Müller wrote in the late seventies are to be produced in the GDR, the suspicion which they must overcome is not simply political, or even technical. Joachim Fiebach, whose vast knowledge of Western and Third World theatre qualifies him to surmount the barriers of naturalist illusion, is one of a small number of people in the drama profession who have attempted to alleviate the bewilderment of readers and audiences. In his 'Nachwort' to the *Dialog* edition, he explains that Müller's defiance of conventional 'Zuschaukunst' is deliberate:

> Das Darbieten von punktuellen Vorgängen, Ereignissen, Entwicklungsansätzen, das sich dem Modellieren zu einem

glatten, abgerundeten Ganzen sperrt, zwingt den Betrachter zu verfeinerter Sensibilität, zwingt zu Wachheit der Sinne und der Vorstellungskraft, setzt Fantasie voraus und zugleich in Bewegung, stärkt Vorstellungsvermögen. Man muß Dinge, die voneinander geschieden sind, zusammensehen, versuchen, sie zusammenzudenken . . . Genuß ist nicht ohne geistige Arbeit und Anstrengung der Wahrnehmung, Übung der Sinne möglich. Die Collage gibt als solche, als Produkt aus Bruchstücken, die Mühe des Künstlers mit den Dingen, seine Arbeit, Welt in Kunst zu bewältigen, unmittelbar durch Form wieder . . . Oberflächlichem Aufnehmen und Verarbeiten der widerspruchlich-schwierigen künstlerischen Ebene und der durch sie bedeuteten Realität wird vorgebaut. Daher vielleicht auch mancher Unwille, manches Unverständnis und Distanz gegenüber solcher Kunst, wie sie in der Inszenierung der Berliner Volksbühne dokumentiert sind (pp.114-5).

Chapter 11

VOLKER BRAUN:
DIE SCHAUBÜHNE NICHT ALS EINE MORALISCHE ANSTALT BETRACHTET

Like Peter Hacks and Heiner Müller, Volker Braun does not believe that the advent of classless society heralds the demise of dramatic antithesis. In the naturalist mode of drama, antagonistic contradiction ended with the historical defeat of the class enemy, incarnated on stage as the 'Gegenspieler'. The contradictions which Braun feels are underestimated by most of his contemporaries are not antagonistic in the sense that they do not derive from the existence of classes with irreconcilable interests. Nevertheless, the clashes of will and opinion which characterize the more conversational stream of East German drama, he contends, are merely superficial manifestations of the contradictions within socialism, whose resolution ultimately determines the evolution of communist society. Without contradiction and resolution, there can be no change:

> Bisher hat sich unsere Literatur oft damit begnügt, *Symptome* für die treibenden und hemmenden Vorgänge unserer Revolution zu zeigen, aber sie hat kaum diese Vorgänge selbst gezeigt, geschweige denn ihre Wechselwirkung, ihre Notwendigkeit erklärt. Die Symptome erscheinen da in einem nationalen oder gar geschichtslosen Raum. Sie erlauben selten Schlußfolgerungen, sie wirken da in ihrer geschichtlichen Abstraktheit (Zufälligkeit) eher lähmend als beflügelnd. Die Theorie, die das trägt, ist blaß; die Praxis, wo sie ihr folgt, ist pragmatisch. Die Literatur operiert da innerhalb der Grenzen dieser Revolution, statt *mit ihr* die Grenzen aufzuspringen. *(87)*

For a dramatic plot to aspire to poetic significance, the author must identify the general, historical pattern which underlies the anecdote, and ensure that its significance emerges clearly. For Braun, the challenge of forging history is a natural inspiration for poetry. It was the fundamental theme of his lyrical work before the potential which the stage offered for showing several individuals interacting to make history drew him into the theatre. His drama thus became a 'vieldimensionale' extension of his lyrical writing. *(88)* Like Hacks and Müller, Braun uses verse and heightened prose in his plays to emphasize the grandeur of human endeavour and to enable the characters to articulate meanings beyond the confines of naturalist conversation.

As a former student of philosophy, Braun shows a committed familiarity with the Marxist concept of subjectivity. The appropriation by socialist citizens of their environment, and the transforming effect of this on their psychology, are a constant theme. In relation to this celebration of human subjectivity, Braun steers a course somewhere between the 'post-revolutionäre Dramaturgie' of Hacks and the 'unbewältigte Dialektik' of Müller. Unlike Hacks, he does not consider his own time to be post-revolutionary. For him, the revolution is still in progress. Therefore, while the drama of Hacks and Braun shares formal reliance on the tension between the real and the ideal, Braun's characters do not lament the unattainability of Utopias. Their world is not 'die beste aller wirklichen Welten' *(89)*, but a world to be bettered. They do not experience the blissful agony of striving unsuccessfully for their absolutist objectives, but express the satisfactions and frustrations of mastering one challenge only to be confronted by a new one. In this, they resemble certain characters in Müller's works, although they have advanced further along the path of history: Braun's characters strain towards the future, whilst Müller's are disentangling themselves from the past. Volker Braun is, after all, Müller's junior by ten years, and more properly a child of the German Democratic Republic. In spite of his father's death at the front and the bombing of his home, Dresden, when he was a small boy, the war and the eradication of fascism were not major formative influences on his work, and his earliest poetry reflects rather the youthful optimism of constructing a new society.

Braun has attempted to avoid the pitfalls, as he understands them, of the approaches adopted by Müller and Hacks. The latter, by projecting his aspirations into some intangible future, enables the establishment to feel complacent about present reality; the former, on the other hand, prises a grey poetry for today out of the awful reality of yesterday, but the establishment is too ignorant to appreciate it. *(90)* Braun, like Hacks and Müller, and like the authors of moral *Konversationsstücke*, seeks to provoke his audience to accept the challenge offered by socialist society for the development of individual integrity and humane relationships. His particular method is to impress upon them the enormity of this challenge, and to excite them, as individuals, to share in the poetry by grasping their opportunity to mould their own environment and, in the process, themselves. His plays take tragic turns. Characters are killed to underline in parable form the existential urgency of self-assertion through honesty, solidarity, love and unalienated labour. But the mood of the plays is optimistic, because the aspirations of the author emerge through his characters, even when they fail, as a result of selfishness or individualistic actions, to meet their challenge. The audience, in so far as they can refrain from indignation about the political immaturity of spontaneous responses by the characters, should feel inspired:

> Die Bühne hat nicht mehr Urteile zu sprechen sondern Veränderungen vorzubereiten. Sie hat nicht mehr Moral abzuliefern sondern Moralisierung auszutreiben. Sie hat nicht mehr Ergriffenheit zu lehren sondern Ergreifen der Möglichkeiten. *(91)*

Any attempts to interpret Braun's work by treating his protagonists as exemplary figures are misguided. These figures may be sympathetic, like Goethe's Faust, by dint of their absolute commitment to the pursuit of an attractive goal, but, like Faust, they have their own myopic flaws. They are not heroes. Furthermore, they do not stand alone against their enemies, nor do they lead one camp against another. Their vision may be the impetus for other characters who outpace them where they have failed. Their own function may oscillate so that they are positive forces at one point and negative at another, but all the time they are part of the confrontations which generate social progress:

> Diese menschliche Befreiung ist ein langer Prozeß, und die jeweiligen Widersprüche, die ihn machen, müssen wir stückweise, in Stücken, sich äußern lassen; es ist müßig, aus den abzusehnden Zielen der gesellschaftlichen Entwicklung eine Dramaturgie aus der Zukunft auf heutige Stoffe zu pressen.
> Der aufwühlendste Widerspruch zwischen den Leuten, die in die sozialistische Revolution verwickelt sind, ist der neuartige zwischen den politisch *Führenden* (die bewußt die Umgestaltung der Gesellschaft organisieren oder bewußt oder unbewußt hemmen) und den *Geführten* (die bewußt oder unbewußt die Pläne realisieren oder kritisieren). Auf beiden Seiten Aktivität und Trägheit,

> Hoffnung und Resignation. Auf beiden Seiten Entbehrung und Wohlleben, Anerkennung und Verlust. Es unterscheidet sie nicht der Charakter, kaum der Besitz, aber sehr die Mittel ihrer Macht. Dabei sind die Leute nicht in Klassen auf eine Seite genagelt, sie werfen sich selber hin und her. *(92)*

It is a daunting task to distill all this social movement into a play, and the Faustian analogy is not incidental. Braun's third play is a modern reference to Goethe's classical work. It was originally to be called *Faust, 3*, was first performed in Weimar in 1968 with the title *Hans Faust*, and was reworked to emerge in Karl-Marx-Stadt in 1973 as *Hinze und Kunze*. Although tempted by the early bourgeois specimen of an individual striving to become the complete master of his environment and to stretch human powers beyond their familiar limits, Braun realized whilst he was working with this material that a writer cannot tamper with the drama of an outmoded society to produce a play of contemporary relevance. Dramatic structures derive from social structures. Eighteenth-century plots and characters are unsuitable vehicles for twentieth-century, socialist questions. In the final version, therefore, *Faust* is present 'als Zitat, als heitere Erinnerung' *(93)*, but the functions and personalities of Hinze (Faust), Kunze (Mephistopheles) and Marlies (Gretchen) are original products, not new pegs fitting into old holes.

The plot has its own dynamic, although there are occasional parallels to Goethe's play. The scene 'Straße', for example, recalls 'Trüber Tag. Feld' in so far as it represents a lament about the terrible predicament into which Marlies has fallen as a result of Hinze's departure. But it is Kunze who laments, because he is not 'der Geist, der stets verneint', but a socialist citizen whose similarity to Mephistopheles lies in the powerful position that enables him to propel his partner forward. The cause of Kunze's sorrow is not Marlies's pregnancy, but her abortion, and his comment, 'Sie ist ganz frei, und befreite sich vom Schönsten' (p.134), is an ironic twist to Faust's protest:

> Erbärmlich auf der Erde lange verirrt und nun gefangen! Als Missetäterin im Kerker zu entsetzlichen Qualen eingesperrt, das holde unselige Geschöpf! *(94)*

Other verbal echoes, such as Hinze's monologue:

> Ich kann schachten, mauern, zimmern -
> Und stehe im Dreck und klopf
> Ziegel und kratz im Sand. Für ein Fressen
> Und ein halbes Bett schlag ich mir zwei
> Arme wund und renne mir
> Die Füße ab, damit was klappt
> Was? was ohnehin klappen müßte.
> Und klappts am Ende, kann ich mich dann freun? (p.77),

are parodies which provide both humour, and also an historical dimension which works in two ways: the Faustian references reflect upon *Hinze und Kunze* so that its subject-matter is associated with some of the grandeur still attributed by modern audiences to *Faust;* and the differences between Goethe's society and Braun's are drawn into the foreground.

These differences are exemplified in the story of Marlies as a literary granddaughter of Gretchen. When Hinze is first called upon by Kunze to renounce domestic comforts and dedicate himself, allegorically, to building socialism, he describes his relationship with his wife Marlies as one of protector and dependant:

Sie hängt an mir
Wie eine Klette oder wie Honig
Am Brot, so süß. Ich kann nicht von ihr los (p.91).

Like Faust, he is lured by greater things, but unlike his predecessor he advises Marlies not to mope at home in his absence:

Wenn du einen Tip willst: lern einen Beruf, du wirst ihn
brauchen (p.92).

Marlies is downcast because Hinze does not confide in her or ask her opinion about his task. He does not see her as a partner. Marlies is eclipsed at this point by the male team, Hinze the worker and Kunze the politician. She remains in the background while Hinze rises to the challenge of *Aufbau*, setting a record by breaking productivity norms, mastering knowledge at university, and returning to the building site to replace his mentor, Kunze, as director. Hinze does not meet Marlies again until scene 10, when she reappears as the laboratory technician on his site. He is staggered by her indifferent reception. She relates to him as her director, not as her lover. It is Kunze who reveals the significance of Marlies's transformation to the audience:

Ja, sie ist ihr eigner Mann, das hat er
Auch erreicht. Und frei wie Arbeit Menschen macht
Also ist sie ein Mensch und macht Arbeit
Das sind zwei Dinge, über die man sich
Nähertreten kann, wenn Zeit ist -
Erst Öl für alle, dann auf deine Lampe (p.105).

The hardest, earliest years of *Aufbau* militated against the enjoyment of marital and romantic relationships, but now fruitful partnership is not only a possibility, but a necessity if greater aims are to be achieved. Kunze now wants Hinze and Marlies to be reconciled, because Hinze needs Marlies to carry out his historic task.

When Hinze comes to her in her laboratory, Marlies talks to him as a scientific worker, in a language Gretchen would never have learnt:

Ja, die Destillationskolonnen, schönes
Glas, die Kühler, an den Wänden die
Glassäulen, da wird Öl gaschromatografisch
Getrennt, das willst du sehn. Gefällt es dir? (p.107).

Marlies is inspired by her own work. Her existence is not defined by her love for a man. Hinze has to court her afresh. His attempts to remind her of their past are unsuccessful. He revitalizes this relationship only when he explains that the laboratory is crucial to the concept of a new and better objective for the site:

Ich kanns nicht ohne dich, allein. Wir könnens nur zusammen (p.108).

This social partnership is a wonder for Marlies, and she begins to experience a new passion for Hinze, which she expresses verbally and physically in scene 12. For Marlies, this love springs from their shared social commitment and, in turn, the social objective symbolizes their love. This is a female emotion which differentiates her from Hinze. His passion is just as great, but he sees it nonetheless as a distraction from his responsibilities. It falls to Marlies, as it fell to Anna, Barbara, Ev, Dascha and countless other female figures, to make the links between social and domestic commitment. Hinze may need Marlies to carry out his plan for society, but he considers it, even so, to be *his* mission. In a similar way, he disregards the feelings of his workers, restricting the development of their subjectivity by not consulting them or adopting their innovatory suggestions. He does not have Marlies's sense of collective achievement, and believes that benevolence is sufficient to replace democracy:

HINZE: Bin ich nicht da und sorg für meine Leute?
MARLIES: Du sorgst für sie - wie schön.
Brauchst du sie wirklich, Hans - in deiner Arbeit?
HINZE: Die Gretchenfrage. - Ja, ich brauche sie.
Aber ich fang bei *mir* an, das muß jeder.
Ein 'Kollektiv' warn wir schon immer:
Eins von Nichtsen (p.115).

Hinze is still too reminiscent of Faust, revelling in his individualistic desire for the existential satisfaction of never being satisfied, and he has yet to make the democratic transition 'vom Ich zum Wir'. In spite of this, Marlies, whose privileged status as a scientific worker entitles her to cooperate in Hinze's scheme, decides to celebrate their partnership by conceiving a child. It is an act of love, but it is also a revolutionary act in terms of female history, because it results from her conscious choice, which surprises Hinze by being unilateral.

Hinze is now ripe to learn the lessons of democratic participation. After the frustration of an unexplained change to his plan by superior powers, he is then called upon to face rebelling workers in a representation of the strike of 17 June 1953. Hinze's reaction is to escape in despair to a forest. Marlies is obliged to choose between Hinze's wild dreams of asserting his personal right to carry out his own plan, and Kunze's pragmatic insistence that the current plan cannot be abandoned in mid-course, whatever its faults. Marlies knows that both attitudes are valid. To complicate the contradiction, she is aware that she has contributed to Hinze's disillusionment by sowing the seeds of democratic collectivity, although his reaction was not in keeping with her constructive intentions. The conflicting moments of historical progress are expressed in a tug-of-war in which Marlies is caught, with Hinze and Kunze urging her 'Komm mit!/Bleib hier!', 'Komm, Marlies!/ Bleib, Marlies!', 'Komm/Bleib!' (pp.123-4). Neither the dreamer nor the pragmatist is capable of accomplishing anything alone. Gretchen's granddaughter therefore finds herself invested by Kunze with a new historical role: she must combine these functions and complete the work that the Promethean partnership began. While Hinze and Kunze reel under the shock of their broken contract, Marlies becomes the pivot of dramatic action, the generator of progress. The experiments are successful, and after six months of stress Marlies perfects the technology planned by Hinze.

However, even though Marlies has proved herself capable of the ultimate in professional skill and dedication, she retains her female attribute of surprise at her own powers. Kunze, who is still the political visionary directing his new executive, Marlies, tells her that only she can now involve all the workers in her innovatory scheme by persuading them to return to their schoolbooks. Marlies does not have the faith in her new self that Kunze has. For her, it is another 'Wunder' (p.131). Kunze shows her how to talk with the workers so that they can identify their interests with the project, but it must be Marlies, not Kunze, who carries out the task.

The duality of the Kunze/Hinze and Kunze/Marlies partnerships, inherited from the diabolic pact between Mephistopheles and Faust, created one problem from which Braun could not extricate himself, despite textual revision. Although the powers which Hinze and Marlies develop at Kunze's instigation have nothing magical about them, they are nonetheless dependent on another character, Kunze, for their initiation. Kunze emancipates Hinze, and Kunze emancipates Marlies. Unlike Hauser in *Am Ende der Nacht*, Braun is not suggesting that Kunze represents the Soviet mentor and benefactor guiding Germans out of the fascist night. Braun's characters are not naturalistic, not even naturalist representatives of a social force. They are poetic expressions of different aspects of socialist subjectivity: the aspiration and the agency, political power and spontaneous response. Sometimes they are in conflict, and sometimes in harmony. These are the major contradictions in socialism which Braun is attempting to make visible through the medium of theatre. Kunze *is* the political power and vision of Marlies.

By convincing the workers of the value of her project, Marlies completes her transformation from a self-effacing, dependent wife into a woman who leaves her impression on the lives of others. Kunze pays homage:

> Jetzt redest du mit allen, Große.
> Bist du vervielfacht? alle hören dich! (pp.133-4).

Marlies's words echo through the workforce as each labourer argues his case with the next using the ideas which she has implanted. But Marlies, although socially and financially independent of Hinze, is by no means emotionally estranged from him. Her love has grown as it has shaken off its passivity and deference. At the moment of her triumph, therefore, Marlies is still vulnerable. When Kunze mentions her absent husband, Marlies pales and collapses. Kunze realizes that her dedication to the project has cost her the other symbol of her self-fulfilment: she has aborted the child.

Abortion was finally legalized in 1972. This was the year in which Braun was reworking the play which became *Hinze und Kunze*, and it absorbs much of the debate that surrounded this measure. The controversy was not, in the main, articulated in discussions concerning the right of women to control their fertility and the definition of human life, as in Britain. The social problems of childrearing were also quite different, with a climate generally favourable to children, both economically and culturally, and financial and practical aid to compensate for some of the burdens of parenthood. Women, moreover, expected and had access to employment. However, at the same time, the main responsibility for children was still attached to women. Debates therefore emphasized the conflict between a woman's wish to follow a career and her desire to raise a family, and there was demographic, as well as religious, opposition to the proposed legislation.

The dramatic conflict in which Marlies is placed reflects this dilemma. In scene 20, she succumbs to the rival pressures on her energy and her emotions. The project is her social commitment, stimulating her creativity and responsibility in the productive sphere:

> Jetzt hab ich eine Möglichkeit
> *Mich* zu beweisen, wie vielleicht nie mehr! (p.128).

Motherhood is another manifestation of her personality, a commitment in the reproductive sphere and also an act of giving, not to the collective, but to a loved individual:

> Ich will für es *dasein!*
> Das ist doch nicht nur, daß ich es zur Welt bring!
> Ich will Mutter sein, wenn ichs sein kann (p.128).

Because it is the historical contradiction of female aspirations which Volker Braun wishes to highlight, and not the social possibilities for reconciling conflicting roles (such as are presented in *Regina B. - Ein Tag in ihrem Leben*), Marlies's crisis is extreme. Both commitments require total involvement. They cannot be reconciled. Hanna, the room-mate who functions solely in this scene as a counterpoint to Marlies, a woman, and so a potential childbearer, who sees motherhood as a joy, first advises her to give up work; but when she remembers how crucial Marlies is to the project, and realizing that Marlies plans an abortion, she quickly tries to convince her that a baby is not so very demanding:

Das bißchen Windelwaschen, Breikochen
Trockenlegen! Dann, wir helfen dir
Oder ich, irgendwie - (pp.127-8).

Her reaction is one of shock and horror, not, as a Christian might think, because of any offence against the sanctity of life, but because children represent happiness, and she knows that Marlies will regret her loss. Marlies knows this herself, but she sees that her dilemma cannot be resolved. She does not want the help of the collective, or of a friend, because she wants to devote herself to motherhood with the same exclusive zeal as she has dedicated to the project. At this point in time, the project is urgent: a child can wait until a more appropriate period in her life. She will not summon Hinze, and is bewildered by her own independence. Her final line of the scene

Kann ich doch machen was ich will -! (p.129),

while it is an emancipated echo of the traditional song,

Laß sie reden, sei fein still!
Kann ja lieben, wen ich will,

is nonetheless fraught with despair.

Hanna's reaction is articulated by Kunze, who carefully distances himself from the moral outrage which may be felt by sections of the audience. His monologue in scene 23 summarizes the topical questions for female self-expression:

Sie ist ganz frei, und befreite sich vom Schönsten. Wollte ihr Kind nicht! und es hilft ihr nichts, daß sie jetzt traurig ist über sich selbst. Und ich versteh sie; o ihr habt gut reden, in euern sichern Betten, ihr Großväter und Jungfern, euch macht kein Regen naß im Herbarium eures Lebens, das ihr schaustellt und nicht genießt, und reißt das Maul auf über die lebende Natur! Ihr redet! - Wilde Zeit, da die Frau wählen kann, ob ihr was blüht im Schoß oder im Betrieb! Sie hat alle Rechte und kann alle Arbeit tun oder lassen - aber nicht wie es ihr paßt und wie sie lustig ist! Ihr redet und redet! - Sie wollte nicht das Opfer sein und kein Objekt der Pläne, sondern ihr Leben packen und selbst entscheiden, und sei es falsch! (pp.134-5).

In Kunze's view, Marlies made the worst possible decision. The gravity of Marlies's decision is certainly intensified by the personal symbolism of her pregnancy. The child was to be the fruit of her social partnership with Hinze and of their love. The news of the pregnancy and abortion shatters Hinze in his forest retreat. He believes that Marlies could not have loved him, and that his love oppressed her:

Was mich aufhob wie im Flug - wie ein Stein lags auf ihr! Wie

> ein Fels, von dem ich die Aussicht genoß, und ihr lastete er auf den Gedanken, daß sich aller Sinn verkehrte! . . . Sie hat mich nicht geliebt (p.135).

The play ends in disarray at the point where Hinze is totally demoralized and must start afresh in partnership with Kunze. But the wheel has not turned in a circle, but a spiral, although Hinze is too shattered to realize this. History has been changed, and so have Kunze, Hinze and Marlies. The play proceeds, like history in Braun's dialectical materialist view, as a series of stages, contradictions resolving themselves in advances or setbacks and making way for new contradictions. The dynamic shifts over to Marlies when Hinze loses his motivation, and this is only possible because the arena of human subjectivity has widened to take in more agents, so that autocracy yields a little to collective responsibility - a process which Marlies continues when she encourages the workers to qualify under her scheme. Even here, Marlies is still the indispensable pivot, and she is crushed by her ambition to live a more challenging life than Hinze, as the prologue predicts:

> Weil sie nicht weniger will als er:
> Leben, und zwar menschlicher (p.76).

Marlies disappears from the closing stages of the play, defeated by the very aspirations which make her a more progressive figure than Hinze, and throws herself bitterly into a new task. In the female tradition, she combines political and personal commitment. It is she who introduces an awareness of love and shared involvement into Hinze's single-minded consciousness, teaching him solidarity and democratic principles. Her pregnancy is an expression of this intense emotional, intellectual and physical love. Yet, because her desire for self-assertion is absolute in everything she undertakes, she is torn apart.

In this respect, Marlies is a forerunner of Tinka in the play of the same name (1974). This subsequent work corresponds to a later stage in the history of the Republic. The protagonist does not have to struggle, as a woman, for a social identity, but is presented from the first as a qualified engineer conscious of her own skills and political commitment. Tinka is a character who has attracted the attention of New Left and feminist writers in the United States, where her role in combining political and personal principles has been investigated by, among others, Christine Cosentino. *(95)* Tinka is destroyed because she loves a colleague who betrays her democratic ideals, although she herself fails to make her fears comprehensible to those around her. The men in the factory, whose consciousness of female equality has not developed apace with social changes in women's status, dismiss Tinka's disruptive behaviour in the belief that marriage will cure her: she will find her true identity and satisfaction in being the wife of a man she despises politically. Tinka, showing greater moral consistency, demands that her lover should change. Her insistence oversteps the bounds of tolerance, and her lover inadvertently strikes her dead.

However, because *Tinka* reflects a more advanced stage of social development than *Hinze und Kunze*, rooted in more securely established collectivity, history does not stand or fall by the fate of this individual. The subsidiary roles in *Tinka* are less subsidiary, and the protagonist, while herself too absolute and self-orientated to succeed, influences other characters positively, including the (male) party secretary, Ludwig. The childbearing function is ascribed here to Tinka's colleague Helga, who learns from Tinka to question the nature of her own love and to assure herself that her lover believes in certain social and personal values, before she acknowledges him gladly as the father of her child. Helga undermines Meister Kessel's faith in marriage as an automatic solution to women's problems, including pregnancy. Helga insists that marriage must be a free choice. She is more consistent that Tinka in making her decision.

Throughout Volker Braun's dramatic work, women assume the unusual function of articulating the physical joys of love. This is an area where feminine modesty has traditionally demanded reserve, and in Braun's poem 'Liebessonett' it is the poet's mistress who shies away from physical passion outside of marriage. When Goethe was revising the *Urfaust*, he was at pains to modify Gretchen's erotic desires, replacing the explicit 'Schoß' with the more prudent 'Busen' in her song at the spinning wheel. It would be illuminating to learn whether propriety or his own concept of female sexuality guided him in this. In any event, as Peter Heller has pointed out, Gretchen is still not 'das reine deutsche Mädel' that subsequent reception has puritanically made her out to be. Gretchen desires Faust, just as Lessing still permitted his heroines to desire their seducers, but in the nineteenth century such feelings were shocking in female characters. *(96)* Braun's heroines, though, are moral. Whilst the attitude of his male characters towards women is reductive, from *Die Kipper* (1965) until *Tinka*, and lacking in the social and private ideals expressed by Marlies, Tinka and Helga, the passions of these women are intensified by the aspirations which make them take their historical fate into their own hands. Their eroticism is social. Moreover, they need no longer fear the biological consequences.

In *Die Kipper*, pregnancy is clearly an index of female erotic pleasure. Even amongst the sand tippers in this early setting, there is female labour, represented by Marinka, for whom physical love is communion with nature. The organic relationship between mankind and nature is a major theme of Braun's lyrical work, including his drama, as a context for human domination of the environment in socialism. Thus the act of love between Marinka and Bauch sixty metres up amongst the concrete and machinery of their work is a sensuous experience. Twice, once in the past and once in the play, Marinka makes love with three men, and finds herself pregnant. The relationships are not necessarily gratifying: some of the men help her to sense her identity by making her feel beautiful, whilst others use her. Bauch, the dubious hero of the play, is one of those who exploit her for selfish pleasure. Marinka, however, is attracted to him because he does not want to possess her emotionally. Her fear of permanent bonds in love is parallel to Bauch's fear of settling to one job, an inability to accept the challenge of real commitment deriving from the alienating nature of unskilled labour, in Bauch's case, and of unstimulating relationships with men in Marinka's. Their attitudes are symptomatic of the underdeveloped stage of socialism in the 'Gründerjahre'. Both begin to learn to apply themselves constructively as they and socialist society progress together. Marinka's second pregnancy does not leave her ostracized.

Marinka's free love is appealing for its self-assertion, but not for its abdication of commitment. Helga's determination to be sure of her love rather than enter a conventional marriage also evokes sympathy. Marriage is no longer the automatic destiny of Braun's women - in spite of the state generosity cited in *Tinka* by Kessel:

> Er erpreßt die Leute schon dazu: mit Wohnung, Steuergruppe, Kindergeld und Kredit. Das Vergnügen wird honoriert statt daß es kostet (p.180).

Marinka, Marlies, Tinka and Helga all refuse to depend on a man simply because he has made love to them or fathered their child. These women go further than asserting their right and ability to work: they also want to determine their own sexuality, demonstrated explicitly by the characters in both language and bodily action in a manner not customary on the East German stage. Tinka's reunion with Brenner in scene 2, and Marlies's declaration of love to Hinze in scene 12, are examples. This sexuality reflects their political desire to 'master' their own lives and to grasp what they want without institutional coercion.

The transformation of female self-awareness has not permeated the consciousness of all the male characters. There is a tendency, in all three plays, for working men to see their womenfolk as domestic havens of leisure who will brighten their husbands' and lovers' lives after tedious labour. In reaction against Tinka, Brenner seeks out a wife who will make no demands on his moral integrity, enabling him to carry on dividing his life into two watertight compartments: work and marriage (in that order). Karin is a sexual instrument for him. Most of the men in *Die Kipper* look for self-gratification in women, and, as in *Tinka,* women are expected to yearn for a domestic role above all else: party secretary Reppin is advised to overcome her professional zeal by settling down to marriage. In *Hinze und Kunze,* men are still the predominant suppliers of labour, and especially of hard, manual work. (Marlies, after all, is a scientific worker.) Women signify respite, the non-working, cosy world of home against which men measure their sacrifices:

> ERSTER ARBEITER: Wir arbeiten, und sie schrauben den Plan hoch. Wir kommen hierher in die Taiga, und sie schrauben den Plan hoch. Wir arbeiten in Frost und Winter und von Frau und Kind weg, und sie schrauben den Plan hoch (p.118).

A wife is not somebody who is consulted about political and economic matters. Hinze does not discuss his decision with Marlies when he first leaves her. He calls her 'Schatz', 'Maus' and 'Lieschen', all terms which betray his paternalism. Brenner believes that he can satisfy Tinka's curiosity about the plan by telling her he loves her. But from *Die Kipper* onwards, the women challenge these assumptions, demanding first a part in their husbands' lives and then, increasingly, setting their own standards, making their own interventions in history. When they function as independent subjects, in social partnership with men, they offer a new definition of harmonious love, as Marlies observes when she is reunited with Hinze:

> Was ich jetzt tu für ihn - ich will es selbst.
> Geh zu ihm hin, und gehör doch mir.
> Nach meinem Sinn geht nun meinen Tag (p.111).

Chapter 12

STEFAN SCHÜTZ: *EIN NEUER GIERIGER GRIFF NACH DEM LEBENDIGEN THEATER*

From the mid-sixties and into the seventies, literature was concerned less and less with stating the case for socialism as a finite political and economic structure, distinct from its imperialist counterpart. Increasingly, socialism was treated as an accepted foundation, and it was the moral, political and intellectual choices facing the individual which now dominated cultural discussion. Attention was drawn, not only in literature, but also in political and economic debate, to the internal dynamic of socialism itself, and to the alternatives posed by its evolution. The concept of 'der entwickelte Sozialismus', widely used as a definition of contemporary society in the seventies, was a concession to growing consciousness that progress itself was relative. Volker Braun's Tinka, playing upon the opportunism of Kahlfeld and Windelmann, her modern Rosencrantz and Guildenstern, hammers home the significance of this shift in political theory. Either socialism was simply a model which the citizen could only support or reject, in which case 'der Kommunismus ist eine ganz andre Zeit und hat nichts damit zu tun' (p.157), or else, logically, socialism was a transitional phase and 'keine selbständige geschloßne Gesellschaftsformation, was ein nutzloser Begriff ist' (p.158).

Against this background, the role of the committed writer underwent a considerable transformation, from argumentation in favour of a basic way of life, to observation of weaknesses and criticism of undesirable practices. The extent to which an author overstepped prevailing parameters of debate, and the form in which he or she did so, varied considerably, but there was, nonetheless, a mood which united the majority: an intolerance of complacency and acquiescence, of individual and social stagnation.

Stefan Schütz is an author with a preference for historical motifs whose work is, nevertheless, a clear appeal to his own society. Although his plays are set firmly in the past, so that the characters operate within the structures of their own culture and age, there are points of modern reference, and abstractions can be made. Schütz makes a plea throughout his work for individual courage and adherence to principle, and for the emancipation of human energy from stultifying social pressures. Like Müller, he is grimly opposed to any manifestation of psychological coercion. His drama, a difficult combination for the stage of legend, fantasy, documentation and poetry, is a spirited and evocative part of the general onslaught on historical passivity.

Material culled from history has a number of advantages for the playwright. On the one hand, a play set in a bygone age carries intrinsic value as an exposition of a different society, and offers areas of comparison by which modern times may be measured and evaluated. On the other, material drawn from distant myths and turbulent eras can establish a more powerful dramatic basis for a conceptualized conflict of contemporary relevance, since the playwright can make use of heightened antithesis and the emotional effects of war and death. Mythical tales in particular lend themselves to symbolic abstraction and allow the writer greater interpretative licence. Schütz has experimented with various combinations of documentation and imagination in his plays. *Odysseus' Heimkehr* (1972) and *Die Amazonen* (1974) suggest whimsically what might have happened to Odysseus when he arrived home at the court of Penelope, and to Theseus when he returned to Athens with his Amazon bride. *Heloisa und Abaelard* (1975) and *Kohlhaas* (1976, after Kleist) are more strictly historical, drawing on documented sources, with surreal additions. *Majakowski* (1971) and *Fabrik im Walde* (1973, after Karavayeva) take their framework from the more recent, uncompleted past of the Russian Revolution. The former borrows its nightmares and visions from the work of the poet himself, and in the latter the presence of the saw mill is personified by Schütz as a ghost haunting party secretary Ognjew. In all of these plays, human productivity, whether it be primarily economic *(Odysseus' Heimkehr, Fabrik im Walde, Kohlhaas)*, artistic *(Majakowski)*, intellectual *(Heloisa und Abaelard, Kohlhaas)* or loving *(Heloisa und Abaelard, Die Amazonen)*, is extolled by the author and, with the ambiguous exception of *Fabrik im Walde,* falls prey to inhibiting social forces.

Schütz's early play *Odysseus' Heimkehr* bears a marked affinity to the work of Heiner Müller, to whom it is, in fact, dedicated. By this time Müller had frequent recourse to Greek mythology, which he interpreted freely, for plots to serve as vehicles for his projections of mankind forging history. Schütz took the legend of Odysseus, who returns to the green and prosperous shores of Ithaca after heroic battles and dismisses the rival suitors living like parasitical leeches at the court of his faithful and sorrowing wife, Penelope. Schütz's version is a grotesque distortion. Odysseus returns to an Ithaca prematurely aged and exhausted by a plague of scabs, which are painstakingly measured and cultivated by his bureaucratic son, Telemachos. Penelope, herself a parasite, takes her suitors to her bed in turn, hoping to find a virile force that will satisfy her withering body, but all these men are hopelessly debilitated by inactivity and uselessness. Some of the mood, the anger that the playwright aims to provoke with this morbid inhumanity, could have been created by Müller. Certainly, the metaphors which Schütz generously wields - bestial, anal, cannibalistic, lustful - are directed against the same tabus and exploitative psychologies that Müller has often challenged. Relations between the sexes are founded here on alienated desires for satisfaction, where there is no love, and men are the labouring parties. The swineherd Kryton's metaphor recalls Gleb:

> Nur die Herrin hat ihren Garten gehegt und wartet auf deinen Pflug (p.16).

Penelope's role in the play reflects her passive sexual behaviour. She awaits Odysseus's return, not out of fidelity or virtue, but because, after exhaustive experimentation, she has discovered that no other man can satisfy her. In a country where time plays no part except to testify to senile decay, where productive activity is discouraged by the parasite class, and where the creativity of the people has been repressed so that they, too, are an unattractive mob, Penelope is more of an inhibiting than a dynamic factor. Her function is to delay and prolong. The eagerly awaited decision concerning her remarriage has an unwelcome twist to it: it threatens to demand some initiative on the part of the suitors. Change will mean having to make adjustments to ensure that their useless life remains unchallenged by a sudden outburst of productivity by the people. The suitors therefore conspire to maintain the *status quo*. Telemachos, meanwhile, resolves to establish his position permanently by bedding his own mother. Penelope's objections are shortlived and unconvincing. Although the disguised beggar Odysseus succeeds in quenching her carnal thirst, he exasperates her superiority when he claims to be her husband, and she rejects him, yielding to her son. The web of corruption, perversity and incestuous stagnation is now complete, and Odysseus, who grows during the play from an intolerable braggard into the only life-force on Ithaca, is destroyed, in an act of cowardly treachery instigated by his own family.

This symbolic Penelope has little in common with the female characters in Schütz's later plays. The unsympathetic male image of woman as Eve the Seductress, prostituting herself to satisfy her own selfish lust, is evoked in the language of Herakles and the Eupatriden *(Die Amazonen)*, Abaelard and the Betrunkener *(Heloisa und Abaelard)* and Sachar *(Fabrik im Walde)*, but in each case their condemnation of female sexuality is a thin veil across their own exploitation of the female body. The image is overturned by the sincere and humane experience of love proclaimed by the Amazon queen Antiope, the communist Elena Pechtina, and, most decisively, by Heloisa, who develops Abaelard's hypocritical glorification of Eve into a philosophy of erotic vitality. Penelope, however, is not so much a woman as a fantastic representation of decadent power, seeking private gratification at the expense of the people and even of its own executives, and returning nothing to society to enable the growth of social wealth and prosperity. In the context of antiquity, new social relations encouraging cosmopolitan trade would eventually replace the system of booty and tribute which restricted economic progress. A peasant uprising to save Odysseus would have been anachronistic in this historical context, and so the common people rebuff his incitement to fight off their disease. Even so, Telemachos, measuring his scabs and opposing all manifestations of initiative amongst his peasants, is a satirical figure used by Schütz as an indictment of unimaginative bureaucracy wherever it hinders productive energy. The play launches a universal attack on sluggish acquiescence amongst the gullible masses and on restrictive systems of power and wealth which thwart individual and social potential.

The outstanding female roles subsequently created by Schütz are quite the opposite of this grotesque Penelope symbol. Antiope, Elena Pechtina and Heloisa all experience a breakthrough in consciousness in their relationships with their lovers, from which each emerges with the superior social understanding and vision. Antiope, queen of the Amazons, learns through Theseus to love men, only to be cast aside by him for diplomatic reasons. When Ognjew is excluded from the Bolshevik party for his tempestuous personality, at the end of the play, his mistress Elena is admitted in order to continue the struggle with her greater insight into the feelings of the peasants. Heloisa, initiated into the ways of the secular world by her teacher Abaelard, rejects suffocating religious dogmas while he recants, and accepts responsibility for her liberating immersion in love.

There is a familiar pattern to this fusion of female romantic and visionary/pedagogic functions, and once more the identification of these women with loving ideals does not leave them confined by their amorous roles. Love enables them to find new strength and direction and hence leads to advanced political awareness. Antiope denounces the militarist economy of Athens and its mercenary senate. Heloisa spurns the intellectual and emotional straitjacket of the Holy Roman Empire. Both are destroyed by the inauspicious forces of their age. It is Elena Pechtina, although her part is smaller and less central, who has the historical opportunity to place her energy at the disposal of progress, against the rigorous and uncertain backcloth of the Russian Revolution, hunger, disease, and counter-revolutionary sabotage.

At least until the changes in social relations which permit Elena Pechtina to intervene in the political and economic process as a working woman, history has trapped the female sex in a corner. Patriarchal society did not allow women to nurture their intellectual and emotional potential because it excluded them from productive activity in the realms of economic, political and ideological influence. Women therefore constantly appear in Schütz's plays who are naively religious, since they are isolated from practical experience of worldly ways by which to measure their views. Sinowjeka, in *Fabrik im Walde*, and Lisbeth Kohlhaas pay the price for their trust in human goodness with their lives. Heloisa learns through her relationship with Abaelard that Biblical exegesis is not an accurate means to knowing the world, but the Church is not interested in her views, only in Abaelard's. He is the man, and so the active factor in its ideological hegemony. Heloisa flourishes in love and proves herself Abaelard's intellectual superior, unshackled by the professional expediencies which hold him back. But Heloisa has no outlet for her understanding. In history, she entered a cloister: Schütz takes poetic licence to have her strangled by Abaelard in a nightmarish landscape after their child is born dead. The historical structures which inhibit female development are always sufficiently in evidence to discredit any reduction of Schütz's characters to 'natural' gender roles. The specific oppression of women's creativity over the centuries makes them especially suitable to demonstrate the tragedy of human potential crippled by social systems with no respect for life.

Schütz maintained his historical perspective even when he returned to Greek mythology in search of material to express the ugly effects of greedy power on human relationships. In *Die Amazonen*, the struggle between matriarchy and patriarchy is the context for an exploration of love and oppression between men and women. The myth might easily lend itself to polarization of the sexes, each representing a set of values. Peter Hacks had taken advantage of the opposition between the original matriarchal legend of Omphale and the patriarchal deification of Hercules to suggest a male and female essence which could not fuse. Rudi Strahl, in *Wie die ersten Menschen*, and Joachim Knauth, in *Die Weibervolksversammlung* (1965), his adaptation of Aristophanes's *Ecclesiasuzae*, and also in his unfinished interpretation of the *Lysistrata*, had made comical use of a battle between the sexes to criticize the political priorities of (male) class history, identifying women with peace, equality and non-exploitative love. These values were again associated with women in a short story by Karl-Heinz Jakobs, whose *Quedlinburg* is a travesty of matriarchy, in which the women seem to hold power but, in fact, are abused by lazy and loveless men.

Schütz avoids setting up an antithesis between the sexes. Although there is a quantity of passionate generalized defamation of each sex by the other, the trajectories of the protagonists, Theseus and Antiope, are deliberately defined by their social situations. There is, moreover, clear differentiation between the men and between the women in the degree to which each character is prey to unloving and exploitative sentiments. The production in Basle in 1977 accentuated this with its careful use of masks. Representing insincerity, they could be full facial masks or else half-masks. They were worn by the women in Athens who adapted to the male system by becoming prostitutes; and they could be discarded, so that Theseus wore his mask at the beginning and end of the play, but not while his love for Antiope allowed his nobler characteristics to prevail. Of course, even this symbolism incurred the danger of simplifying Schütz's subtle differentiations and his historical perspective, as Hans-Rainer John observes in his review for *Theater der Zeit*. *(97)*

The two opening scenes of *Die Amazonen* establish the opposition between the warring camps. At the same time, however, they reveal varying attitudes to war itself, thus modifying the appearance of absolute sexist hostility. The first scene presents the encampment of the male alliance, Herakles and

Theseus. Their respective patriarchal intentions are distinguished. Herakles, an unattractive bully aspiring to deity, has to capture the girdle of the Amazon queen as one of his twelve labours. He is convinced of the loathesome worthlessness of the female sex. Theseus, by contrast, sees women as a source of pleasure, for which he has developed a connoisseur's appreciation. He is a strategist and diplomat, rather than a thug, and has been driven to war by his expansionist burghers. (His alliance with the legendary Hercules was an Attic addition to the myth of the Twelve Labours.) Herakles, then, represents the anti-feminist principle of Greek thought, while Theseus is the unenthusiastic agent of political and economic forces. Herakles's language is coarse and brutal: Theseus speaks with calculation and, when referring to women, a hedonistic, aesthetic sense of life which distances him from the destructive urge of his cousin. Herakles is the ugly reflection of the heroic achiever in *Omphale*. Believing that 'gemacht ist der Mann für die Tat, und siegreich, liegt er für immer auf den Zungen der Geschichte' (p.64), he is prepared to eliminate anything that stands between himself and immortality. His belligerence is currently aimed at the Amazons, for whom he uses animal images: 'Hündin', 'Schildkröte' and, by extension for Theseus, 'Hurenbock' (p.64). He also subscribes to the view that the Amazons (from *a-mazos*) cut off their right breasts, reputedly to make holding a bow more comfortable, and this enables him to include them alongside other monsters he has fought.

Theseus, who prefers to compare women with 'Krüge voll Wein' (p.64), is more cautious, and the arrival of a two-breasted Amazon prisoner elicits his wise response:

> Bei den Göttern, eine Zeitungslüge (p.65).

This anachronism recalls the technique used by cruder forms of modern propaganda to dehumanize advocates of alien ideas. Theseus proves by his scepticism in this matter that he is not so easily stirred into irrational hatred as the warmonger Herakles.

The entrance of a captive, Iope, supplies a comical challenge to the self-assured Herakles. Not only is he taken aback by her normal appearance, he also finds himself floored by a judo throw. Iope's pride and refusal to betray information, illustrating the strength and proud solidarity of the women, so anger the boastful hero that he stabs her, although the other men have to hold her for him.

The second scene, in Antiope's palace, reveals that the Amazons are in a defensive position. Antiope's instruction of her sister Oreithyia in the character of men is bitter and generalized, expressed in metaphors as hostile as those of Herakles, but Antiope's theory is based on experience of male power and greed, and for this reason she describes men, like Heloisa, as wolfish predators. Historically, the fall of matriarchy is attributed by Marxist anthropologists to the replacement of primitive communal structures by privatized property in the hands of men. Antiope's hatred of male society is therefore rooted in a moral evaluation of this development which the audience is tempted to accept. It is in order to be able to continue living their own way of life against the mercenary currents of historical change, and in order to avoid confrontation and bloodshed, that the Amazons, steely warriors as they are, have retreated to Themiskyra, protected by impenetrable defences. Moreover, while the alliance between Theseus and Herakles is uneasy, based on personal interest, amongst the Amazons there reigns an attractive sense of sisterly affection, and Arka's report of Iope's capture conveys real grief. Compared with the plundering greed and dishonourable cunning of male society, the Amazons' alternative lifestyle is idyllic. The one element which it lacks is the experience of love between the sexes, and the price that the Amazons pay to maintain their freedom and independence is forbidding: for the purposes of procreation, weaker men, 'jämmerliches Fleisch' (p.65), are imported into Themiskyra, and no lasting relationships are permitted.

In contrast to Heinrich von Kleist, in his wild and desperate tragedy *Penthesilea*, Schütz emphasizes the Amazons' desire for peace. Although they are evidently capable of matching the fighting skills of the men, they shun combat, and the task of the men is to lure them out of their fortress to force a battle. For similar reasons, Schütz's Amazons do not share the custom of Kleist's women according to which they are obliged to conquer their mates. The Amazons of Themiskyra take a pragmatical view of reproduction. They need the biological services of men, but they cannot allow themselves the dangerous luxury of passion. They recognize the oppressive consequences of male lust, and create an ideology which preserves their solitude. Antiope is unremitting in her condemnation of men, whom she identifies with death and barrenness:

> Oh ich will mit Haß verzehrn diese Männerseuche, und aufspießen ihre Unfruchtbarkeit . . . Wagt den Schrei nach Herrschaft, und ist doch nur ein Samengeber, lustloser Wind, der eitel und faul aus dem Maule riecht. Euer Frauenglück ist ihr Leichnam, den ihr nach eurem Geschmack euch legt, und der verwittert dann und ausgekaut auf dem Misthaufen vergeht. Ihr Geier sucht nur Leichfrauen (p.65),

> Herakles ist ein Mann, auch die Götter sinds, und männliche Macht tötet Weiber aus Prinzip (p.65).

She sees no value in sexual relations, which are simply an expression of male exploitation:

> Ihre Züge sind Grimassen, kocht das Blut ihnen im Unterleib. Der Trieb ist tierisch. Hüte dich davor! (p.65),

> Diese Penisbrut, Muskeln nur und After, und der Kopf ist eine Kläranlage (p.65).

The vivid disgust with which Antiope views patriarchal society implies that there must be an alternative. The repulsion which she expresses begs for something better. For Antiope and her Amazons, loving partnership with men is an historical impossibility, for patriarchy is consolidating its influence. The dramatist, however, is addressing his plea to men and women who have the choice of eradicating the morbid values which first crushed the matriarchal order, without resorting to new forms of sexual conflict.

The inevitable defeat of the Amazons is precipitated by the characteristic cunning with which Theseus lures them from their city. (Strategists such as Theseus, in pursuit of power, are insincere individuals.) However, although history decrees that the Amazons must surrender, signifying the collapse of matriarchy, Schütz makes the battle a close one and depicts the courage and martial dexterity of the women, as well as the surprised indignation of the men, who betray a modern underestimation of female abilities. The skirmish is represented in the third scene by two duels. In the first, both the man and the woman are killed, the man first. They are followed on a parallel by Herakles and Antiope, and the previous confrontation seems to have been incorporated partly in deference to Kleist's example, for it provides an opportunity for a woman to prove her superiority in swordplay, as Penthesilea did in her first combat with Achill. The struggle between Herakles and Antiope is long and equal. Herakles eventually prevails, but he does not kill Antiope. He considers it more fitting that she should be punished for her impudence in raising arms against men by being raped by his army. The man who berates women as 'Huren' thus exposes himself as the real agent of female sexual humiliation.

In the fourth scene, then, Antiope experiences the indignity of being owned and bartered for by men. Penthesilea's great tragedy is thus reversed, f whereas Kleist's character suffers from her failure to subjugate Achill, Schütz's heroine is insulted by a callous desire to own and exploit her which is alien to Amazon civilization. Schütz suggests that it is symptomatic of the inhuman morality pertaining in patriarchal society for relationships to be determined in this manner by possession and power. Theseus saves Antiope from the sentence passed by Herakles when he exchanges her for all his booty, which the soldiers divide amongst themselves (thus sowing the seeds for Theseus's political crisis in Athens). Antiope's new situation is further confused by another new experience: Theseus claims to love her. He therefore offers her freedom. Antiope is now caught up in two dilemmas. First, she cannot accept liberty from a man who has power over her, because this will bind her to him in debt. Secondly, Theseus's protestation of love raises doubts in her mind. She is unable to dismiss him completely as a false flatterer, and her desire to die subsides - indicating an unfamiliar emotional involvement with her enemy which bewilders and distresses her. The audience, from what they have seen of Theseus, are no better placed than Antiope to judge his sincerity.

The fifth scene, an interlude in Athens, shows two consequences of the fourth. Set outside a brothel, it examines the logical extension of the mercenary relationship between the sexes which Antiope is beginning to discover. There is no more erotic love in Athens than there is in Themiskyra. Some Athenian women adapt to their new environment by selling themselves to men. The Kupplerin is sycophantic towards her respectable bourgeois customers, but secretly curses and despises them. To this extent, she shows a humorous vitality. She is pleased that her girls are enjoying the more virile and lucrative attentions of the booty-ridden soldiers, and, with a twinkle of irony, suggests to her dislodged middle-class regulars that they should make love to their wives for once, for which she sells them a potion:

> salbt sie kräftig, in solcher Not verdoppeln sich Empfindung
> und Geschlecht, ihr werdets überstehen (p.67).

It is quite in keeping with the money-grabbing lovelessness of the Athenian economy that the burghers should choose this forum to voice their discontent towards Theseus. Their king has failed to represent the interests for which they equipped him in the war against the Amazons. He has exchanged his booty for, of all horrors, a woman, and so paid them nothing for their investment. At the same time, the soldiers have returned with their pockets full and displaced the burghers from their brothels and, presumably, from other markets. It is this monetary crisis that will prompt the senate, on behalf of the burghers, to propose that Theseus should marry the Cretan princess Phaidra. In the meantime, the burghers vent their anger and contempt on the woman and enemy, Antiope:

> Sie maßt sich Rechte an, die nie eine Frau besitzen kann. Uns
> regiert ne Amazone; Athen, dein Blut ist weibisch (p.67).

(The word 'weibisch' has become implicitly pejorative.)

In this hostile environment, Antiope is feeling the full force of her new love for Theseus. Her monologue in scene 6 betrays the crisis incipient in scene 4:

> Verrat schreit mein Volk, Hure flustert Athen. Eingeschlossen
> in Dolchmauern aus Verachtung, quält mich unsagbar das Lichtloch
> der Freiheit. Gefesselt und doch nicht in Fesseln, erfüllt der
> Mann mir alle Liebe, oh ich Zerrissene (p.67).

In scene 2, Antiope showed that she had all the attributes of an attractive, positive personality, except that she did not know intimate love for a man. Now that she has experienced this, and has been inspired by a passion which melts her hatred, she finds herself in a society where everything conspires to prevent the expression of her love, which itself becomes a prison. Throughout Schütz's work, love is the great emancipatory force of mankind, freeing self-knowledge and individual vitality, and encouraging compassion and the rejection of useless moral strictures. Antiope's very being, however, opposes the foundations of Athenian society, 'eine Männerstadt, Roheit des Marktes und Gewalt von Geld' (p.67). The social reflection of her love would be a world of peace, but Athens thrives on the profits of war.

When Theseus arrives, the couple embrace and declare their great passion, but with a difference. Antiope cannot forget her country and her convictions: Theseus, in the masculine tradition, sees his romance as an escape from the political intrigues he despises. Furthermore, in despising the expediency which governs his life, he ignores the threat sensed by Antiope, which then materializes in the deputation of Eupatriden.

The senate's proposal for a marriage with Phaidra is based on state pressures. The measure would secure a rich dowry to boost the economy, and a powerful naval ally for future wars. Theseus, impetuous and unstatesmanlike in the heat of love, offends the senators. As the net closes over Antiope, the interval delays a rapid build-up of machinations.

Oreithyia, inspired by what her sister has taught her about the evils of men, has brought an army to Athens to free Antiope, forging an alliance with the Scythian Androkus. But all men *(andros)* are untrustworthy in their lust for power, and Androkus plots against Oreithyia. In the city, the Eupatriden, furious that Theseus should be so committed to Antiope, are also conspiring to ensnare their king. They have called Deukalion of Crete to their aid, and Theseus will be obliged to wed Phaidra out of gratitude. Theseus, moreover, seems to be sensing the forces which are gathering against him, as he advisedly rejects Antiope's suggestion that they should marry. He manages to make her feel guilty and faithless for asking, making protestations of his undying love. Again, it is impossible to judge his sincerity.

Cunning, as Antiope warned in scene 2, is a male trait. In contrast to all the political intrigue, which casts respect for love and life to the winds, the reunion of Antiope and her sister is honest and moving. While Oreithyia pledges the determination of the Amazons to overcome hardship and death to save their queen, Antiope has the painful task of revoking her own teachings and explaining to Oreithyia that she is a willing slave to her lover. Both women are trapped in a fatal contradiction. Antiope, although she has found love, paints a forlorn backcloth to her choice. The age of humanity is over, she says, and she has chosen a heavenly love in a desert. Hers is the creed of a dying morality, expressed with tragic poetry. Oreithyia rages in disbelief. She is caught up in the 'Ideologie der Rache' (p.69) with which she has spurred her army on. The sisters can still embrace, and arrange together to avoid war, but they have been divided by Antiope's love for a man. Theseus, in the background, makes unworthy interventions which reveal that he has no sympathy with Amazon independence and pacifism:

> Streicht diese Schlacht aus eurem Kalender. Ruft zur Ordnung euer Heer und schlachtet anderswo. Wir wollen keinen Krieg aus Eifersucht. Seid endlich ein Weib und begreift, daß die Schwester geliebt wird am anderen Ufer (p.69).

Once more, the Amazons' desire for peace is to be thwarted. Athens wants war, Deukalion wants war, Androkus wants war, and in any case we know that Oreithyia is going to a treacherous death. In fact, as the Hirte recounts in scene 9, a summary which provides further historical commentary on the inevitable fall of matriarchal principles, she is stabbed from in front and from behind as she leaves the city. Androkus and the senators are united in their hatred of the Amazons. There is no room in the age for peace, love and solidarity, characteristics which enable individuals to grow. Both Antiope and, to a limited extent, Theseus have been transformed by their love, for all its limitations, but it cannot survive, and the final scene marks its grotesque termination.

The palace of Theseus is preparing for the marriage of the king to Phaidra of Crete. The Eupatriden celebrate their victory and alliance, distorting the truth with their patriarchal perspective. Athens 'ist zum Mann geworden. Dem Herakles gleich' (p.70). Deukalion is their saviour, and Antiope is the culprit of all their woes. Three prostitutes are sent for to dance a ritual symbolization of the love between the bride and groom. The irony scarcely disguises a further symbolism: these women have been paid to excite the male guests with their bodies, thereby exemplifying sexual relations in Attica. Deukalion makes the monstruous and demagogic claim that he has brought love among mankind, just as Prometheus - whom he condemns as a troublemaker - once brought fire. In his drunken stupour, he demands, 'Schafft ran Frauen und Narren, ich möchte meinen Geist mästen' (p.71). Theseus, still in love with Antiope, acquiesces to the political necessity of this marriage, certain that she will understand.

In the midst of this nightmare, cast aside as a meaningless shadow, Antiope laments her tragedy and summons her former strength and resolution, determined, in a fit of madness which parodies *Penthesilea*, to make her impression on this obscene festival:

> *Erhebt sich.* Ich muß sehen, wo ich bin? Die Wände tanzen. Aus dem Holz springen Töne. Licht und Stein mischen sich. Dies ist nicht Themiskyra. Athens Mauern begrüßen mich. Bin ich zu spät! Man erwartet die Braut, und ich in solchem Kleide. Ich muß eilen, mein Hochzeitsgewand mir umzulegen (p.71).

Antiope returns armed with a sword, and the finale is her duel with Theseus. In Schütz's version, this last confrontation does not shame the Amazon queen: it is she who initiates it as a gesture of uncorrupted pride. Still fired by the self-assertion of her people, she will fight for her lover or die in the process. Antiope sways between jealous love and deadly enmity. As a wronged mistress, she demands to know why Theseus has deserted her, pleading 'erlagst du der Staatsräson, oder dem Blick der Königstochter?' (p.71). Rejected, she is still a warrior:

> Die Spitze meines Schwertes ist auf deinen Leib gerichtet! (p.71),
>
> Tränen sind kraftlos, wie soll ich weinen (p.71).

Antiope is not consumed, like Penthesilea, by animal-like hatred. When she wounds Theseus, she tears her own clothes to make a bandage, admitting:

Sein Blut ist mir zu teuer! (p.72).

The lethal battle is simultaneously erotic:

THESEUS: Die Mulde deiner Wut ist schön wie das erstarrte
Wasser in der Schlucht. Eisrosen! Mach es weich!
Ich will die Schmelze sehen!
ANTIOPE: So ists gut, mein Körper bebt.
THESEUS: Um dich zu trinken kämpf ich.
ANTIOPE: Dir nicht zu widerstehen bin ich hier (p.72).

When Antiope is wounded, she and Theseus almost embrace, but the encounter is treacherous, and she runs onto Theseus's sword. The ambivalence of their relationship is conveyed in the last tableau, where Antiope dies in the arms of her murderous lover. Theseus is at first disbelieving, then he lies with her corpse and recalls their passion, but soon, ultimately the politician, he returns to his wedding table and calls for music.

Formally at least, Schütz draws extensively on Kleist, and the provocative wildness of his predecessor seems to have appealed to him. However, as with the adaptation of *Michael Kohlhaas*, the events in *Penthesilea* have been reshuffled, reversed and reinterpreted to meet a new purpose. Antiope is queen of a life-giving society which can only protect its values by repressing erotic love. Antiope's own emotional productivity is liberated by her feelings for Theseus, but the dishonest, destructive principle of expansionist patriarchy prevails over this individual outburst of authenticity. The festival in the final scene is the perverse celebration of a marriage of convenience: the roses of love are icy cold.

In all his plays, Schütz shows how human energy has been prevented from expressing itself creatively by coercive codes and compromising institutions. Women are closely identified with the life-force, as a result of their biological and social functions, hence their allegorical value. The basis of matriarchal Themiskyra was the production and protection of human life, and in later ages women's role as life-givers is reflected in the pregnancies of Heloisa, Sinowjeka and Elena Pechtina. Sinowjeka and her child are murdered by her seducer, the counter-revolutionary Sachar in *Fabrik im Walde*. Heloisa, too, comes to a grotesque end when, nursing her stillborn baby on an ashen heath, she encounters Abaelard and her father, symbolically crippled and blinded. The exceptions to this female function are the mythical travesty of Penelope, and the witches in *Kohlhaas*, ugly distortions of womankind who accept the destructive aims of their Lord, Satan.

Nevertheless, there is hope for the male race and for communion between the sexes - and, by extension, for the communist future of humanity. In the new historical conditions of *Fabrik im Walde*, the Bolshevik Ognjew learns to accept his fatherhood, coming to his child when it is sick and, eventually, conquering the gulf between political and domestic responsibility which traditionally divides male and female experience. The process which integrates Ognjew into family life, giving him the insight into personal feelings which was previously lacking in his political judgement, is the same process which enables Elena Pechtina to apply her womanly compassion productively in the world of politics. In 1917, Schütz is claiming, foundations were laid for overcoming the dichotomy which set matriarchy and patriarchy at war in antiquity. These foundations put an end to the rule of property over human relations, and gave women the same rights to social expression as men.

This is the political assumption underlying much of the *Frauenliteratur* which has been developing in the GDR since the late sixties. Novelists and short-story writers in particular have explored the emotional psychology of masculinity and femininity to discover the deeply entrenched barriers which must be surmounted if humanity as a whole is to break free from the fetters which still inhibit personal relationships. There has been a tendency to look for refreshing values in the female sex. Writers such as Christa Wolf, Günter de Bruyn, Irmtraud Morgner, Brigitte Reimann and Gerti Tetzner have illustrated some of the ways in which men have been emotionally atrophied by their narrow involvement in a professional ethic, losing touch with spontaneity and compassion. The inspiration for this interest was the humanism expressed in Marx's early works, notably the *Ökonomisch-philosophische Manuskripte*. Annemarie Auer, in the concluding remarks of her essay for the anthology *Blitz aus heiterm Himmel*, containing seven short stories which made a major contribution to this theme, explains the contemporary relevance of Marx's argument:

> Die revolutionäre Aufhebung der gesellschaftlichen Arbeitsteilung der Geschlechter verspricht, zum erstenmal in aller Geschichte, auch in der Liebe einen Abbau der Entfremdungen: den uneingeschränkten Austausch menschlicher Wesenskräfte und Kreativität. Eine Demokratisierung der Liebe bahnt sich an, deren bezaubernde Perspektiven noch niemand absehen kann. Da treten die Träume in ihr Recht. *(98)*

Schütz, whilst he similarly understands socialism to be the basis for this emancipation, is adamant that the process is far from complete. Were it not, there would be no need for theatre to inspire audiences with a desire to eradicate the ugliness of stifled human creativity. Schütz uses patriarchal distortion of heterosexual love as a parable for socio-political suffocation of human aspirations in any form, although this does not mean that he glosses over the issues raised by the allegory itself. His plays expose specific manifestations of sexist ideology and its language with unusual perception and forceful conviction. *(99)* By berating restrictive structures on both the particular and the general level, his work implicitly demands their transformation, as Elli Jäger acknowledges in her assessment of the author:

> Die Schönheit der Fabel und ihre gestische Qualität eröffnet überraschend neue Aspekte der Dialektik von Sein und Werden, von Zustandsschilderung und Veränderung . . . Schütz stellt an den Leser und Zuschauer hohe Anforderungen des Mitdenkens, Forderungen, die sowohl auf Zustimmung als auch auf Widerspruch aus sind. Möglichkeiten - und Grenzen - des Subjekts unter objektiv-geschichtlichen Bedingungen werden vorgeführt. Schütz wählt Stoffe aus der Geschichte, doch zielt er mit seinen Stücken immer auf das Hier und Heute. *(100)*

And yet, in spite of the praise with which a number of professionals and academics in the GDR have greeted his work, there is still a body of criticism that is unable to accept drama which relies on antipathy rather than empathy to achieved the desired state of social stimulation. Ernst Schumacher, for example, reacted in horror against an observation by Schütz in *Theater heute* that 'ein Stück, nur aus einem Schrei gebaut, das wäre ehrlich'. *(101)* Schumacher accuses Schütz of projecting a 'schwarzes Welt- und Menschenbild', and he associates this with what he calls the existentialist nausea promoted by Heiner Müller in *Die Hamletmaschine*. *(102)*

Müller's own reaction to Schütz, not surprisingly, has been favourable. He recognizes in his younger colleague not only the effective understanding of theatre which Schütz culled from his acting days, but also a kindred spirit, a revolutionary of the theatre who has no patience with drama that argues politely for moral reform, and who turns the full force of his vivid imagery against stagnation and stultification wherever they appear. Schütz, like Müller, is less interested in illustrating what has been achieved than in revealing what must still be done:

> Jedes neue Stück ist ein neuer gieriger Griff nach dem lebendigen Theater. Die Qualität der manchmal betäubend schönen Sprache liegt darin, daß er nicht geprägte Bilder ausmalt, sondern Bewegungskurven zeichnet, die der Wirklichkeit seiner Figuren und Vorgänge neue Aspekte aufzwingen. Die Grundform der Bewegung ist die Spirale, nicht der Kreis. Das hat mit Geschichte zu tun, mit einer kreativen Haltung zu Geschichte. Wenn er aneckt, liegt es daran, daß er hoch hinaus will . . . Hans Henny Jahnn hat einem seiner späten Stücke den Satz vorangestellt ALLMÄHLICH IST DIE LIEBE UNSER EIGENTUM GEWORDEN. Der Akzent liegt, hier und heute, auf allmählich, nicht auf Eigentum. *(103)*

SUMMARY

The female characters which we have observed are not conceived as theoretical models of womankind, nor as projections of how womankind might aspire to be. They are constructed from all manner of authorial considerations, formal and ideological, as part of a network of social commentary. They demonstrate elements of the contemporary female condition as the author perceives it, and to a greater or lesser extent they may incorporate some of his hopes for the female sex, if not humanity in general. At the same time, they are linked into a dramatic framework where they function as political teachers or pupils, social victims or rebels, jokers, messengers, motors of romantic tension, or pillars of antithesis. Their purposes, usually multiple, are defined by more than abstract postulations: they must correspond to the demands of the play. There is thus an interaction between, on the one hand, ideas which an author wishes to communicate to his audience about the character and position of his female figures and, on the other, the formal structure of his drama, which is itself determined by both stylistic preference and agitational intentions. This interaction affects the impression which a female character makes on an audience: she may be the confident incarnation of good sense, a probing adolescent maturing with her choices, the oblivious butt of satire, or a lyrical inspiration for psychological liberation.

The brevity of conclusions is insidious. It exaggerates unity where there is diversity and, in the interests of manageability, glosses over the fragmentary and even contradictory aspects of the subject-matter. However, having admitted the perils of ignoring the swirls and meanders of style, characterization and political priority which distinguish one writer from another and one play from the next, let us consider the currents which mark the flow.

In the early years, writers such as Wolf, Strittmatter and Sakowski appealed for commitment to the new, socialist order as a humanitarian alternative to feudal and capitalist exploitation and, ultimately, war. Their drama was formed out of a clear polarity between the attractive forces of socialism and the selfish, cunning supporters of counter-revolution. (This alternative was less sinister by the time of Sakowski's writing.) All these authors, like the young Baierl in his more didactic vein, created outstanding female protagonists, not only because they wished to argue for the basic right of women to use and develop political and productive talents, but also because the very strangeness of allocating women to such roles emphasized the startling newness of socialist society. Women, and especially country women, were, by nature of their double oppression under capitalism, particularly suitable as exponents of liberation from social structures which impeded personal development. Moreover, the symbolism of the caring society, providing for all its citizens, was conveyed in almost all these plays by the female function of child welfare: Anna's project was a school, while Hanna, Murawski, Lene, Lisa and Frau Flinz were mothers. Baierl's formal approach to this theme was different from that of his contemporaries, but in using comedy and alienation to subvert the intentions of his post-Brechtian mother-figure, his ideological analogy was the same.

Throughout the sixties, as class struggle waned and interest in the socialist personality grew, a new, less confrontational mode of drama evolved. After a dearth of female roles in plays set in industry and in the realms of international political intrigue, the established expectation that women could and would work was reflected in an increasingly equitable distribution of dramatic functions between the sexes, but the gender-orientation of career patterns was evident. After Hauser's first Barbara, the exemplary female protagonist became obsolete as the moral choices posed by drama became less antithetical. Women expressed their views and decisions with greater fluency than previously, although usually with a more gentle regard for others than was shown by men. The broader spheres of female responsibility, which transcended the barrier between domestic and public life, making women more concerned for relationships between people, continued to suggest women as a formal mouthpiece for humanitarian, progressive ideas. In this last detail, Claus Hammel was a notable exception: his male party activists were a sober influence on his more whimsical heroines, and in any case the symbolic function of his characters was submerged by their idiosyncracies to a considerable extent. The domestic settings which proliferate in the *Konversationsstück* were not intended as an escape from productive life, but as a more intimate mirror of social morality. At the same time, they provided an opportunity for some discussion of the frustrations felt by women confined to, or burdened with, the role of housewife by husbands still unaware of their own patriarchal faults. It was against such relatively minor pitfalls of moral laxity and political complacency that writers such as Hammel, Hauser, Kerndl and Strahl expressed their disquiet. Strahl's popular use of caricature, farce and romantic matchmaking was a lively alternative to the polemics of conversational drama, but it relied heavily on conservative stereotyping, albeit with updated social content.

The plays of Pfaff and Gozell dealing with problems of implementing *Frauenförderung* were more illustrative of the ideological and economic contradictions hampering women's emancipation. Pfaff's play was the most practical, if limited, display of motherhood in the naturalist repertoire. Pfaff set a new trend by breaking with the assumption that a single mother would automatically be happier with a husband, suggesting that community support was a solution to the additional burdens of parenthood. Gozell went further in undermining the confidence of his audience in the benevolence of average citizens. He also questioned prevailing evaluations of housework as nothing but stultifying drudgery. In spite of his obvious wit, Gozell did not establish himself as a dramatist, and his failure can be ascribed in part to his contravention of accepted codes.

From the late sixties and throughout the seventies, writers such as Müller, Braun, Schütz and, in certain respects, Hacks, sought to revitalize the challenge of theatre and to generate fresh energy for the revolution in human relationships. Female characters were still closely defined by partnerships in love, and their exigent personal commitments continued to make them attractive protagonists of advance. However, whereas romantic involvement was formerly a useful but modest vehicle for the conversion of retrograde males, the tabus which traditionally inhibited dramatic expression of sexuality, and above all female sexuality, were cast aside, and the self-assertive desires of Dascha and Nägle, Marlies and Tinka, Heloisa and Antiope were in themselves a stimulation for the eradication of oppressive psychology in personal and political life. Women's fertility was still a frequent symbol of a vital, loving nature. As a result, *Hinze und Kunze,* the first play to deal with abortion after its legalization relieved authors of the embarrassment of silence and diversion, takes a supportive but wistful view of female choice. These authors were impatient with drama that obscured the contradictions still inherent in contemporary socialism, but the conflicts which inspired their plays did not derive so directly from economic systems as from human relationships. Myth, history, and allegory were used to inject dramatic power into themes which topical naturalistic settings seemed too lame to convey.

The only play in East German drama to attempt a programmatic discussion of the unsolved issues of women's liberation in its own day, the satire *Weiberkomödie*, provoked controversy and a notable degree of incomprehension with its attacks on persistent forms of patriarchal and puritanical attitudes. The mixed reception which has greeted many plays written in the seventies, and especially those of Heiner Müller, can be attributed to both their violation of aesthetic conventions and their contentious refusal to be complacent about the achievements of modern socialism. Women's right to work, independence and legal equality had been established and widely realized, but there was a swelling current in drama, in literature of all genres, and in society at large, which sought to widen the aspirations of both women and men, and to explore the more intimate foundations of human relationships. The more psychological and sexual aspects which can be detected in Bürgermeister Anna's challenge to patriarchy, once lost to economistic interpretations, began to find new exponents.

As a genre, drama continued to attract an overwhelming majority of male authors, even though many women started to publish prose in the seventies. Although dramatists have provided many insights into patriarchal discrimination against women, female experience has tended to be used for its allegorical function, and this has weighed in favour of a rather more abstract projection of women's lives in drama than in prose. For this reason, although motherhood is a recurring theme, there is little evidence of mothering itself, whilst the symbolism of heterosexual love, which depends on powerful passions rather than long-term co-existence, has avoided the final tabu - lesbianism - which has been a major issue for Western feminism. Nevertheless, male dramatists have often drawn attention to sexist practices which have not been explored in public debate, practices which they, as men, will have confronted in their own experience, including the devaluation of women as objects of male desire and, most strikingly in the works of Müller and Schütz, the patriarchal assumptions of language.

FOOTNOTES

1 In the Bibliography, I have listed useful books by Mary Allen, Jenni Calder, Anthony Cockshut, Lloyd Fernando and Elizabeth Hardwick, but there is a growing body of research too broad for inclusion here. In the field of German, two initiatives taken in the United States have proved valuable. The first was the publication in 1977 of the proceedings of the second symposium of the *Women in German* collective, which included papers on the economic, political and, especially, literary history of women in modern Germany. The second was the 10th Amherst *Kolloquium* in the same year, which was devoted to the theme of 'Die Frau als Heldin und Autorin'. The proceedings were published in 1979 and they provide several detailed investigations into female authors, characters and readership from the Middle Ages to the present day.

2 See Renny Harrigan, 'The Stereotype of the Emancipated Woman in the Weimar Republic', *Women in German*, pp.47-79, and Wolfgang Emmerich, 'Identität und Geschlechtertausch', p.131.

3 'Notate des Zwiespalts und Allegorien der Vollendung', p.48.

4 For discussion of the disenfranchisement of women from the eighteenth century onwards, see Ann Oakley, *Housewife*, and, with specific reference to Germany, Wulf Köpke, 'Die emanzipierte Frau in der Goethezeit und ihre Darstellung in der Literatur', *Zehntes Amherster Kolloquium*, pp.96-110 (p.97).

5 'Innovation and Convention: Women in the GDR'.

6 See Emmerich, *op.cit.*, (p.154).

7 *Marx Engels Werke*, Ergänzungsband I, pp.465-588 (p.535). For discussion of this process see Damm and Engler, *op.cit.*; Eva and Hans Kaufmann, *Erwartung und Angebot*, especially pp.135-215; Alexander Stephan, 'The Emancipation of Man. Christa Wolf as a Woman Writer'; and Patricia Herminghouse, 'Die Frau und das Phantastische in der neueren DDR-Literatur: Der Fall Irmtraud Morgner', *Zehntes Amherster Kolloquium*, pp.248-66, and her essay in *Literatur und Literaturtheorie in der DDR*.

8 'Ein Brief', *Theater der Zeit*, August 1975, pp.58-9 (p.59).

9 This contention was the subject of a discussion paper which I gave at the conference 'The GDR under Honecker: 1971-81', Dundee, Scotland, 11-13 September 1981, reprinted in the conference proceedings under the title 'Women as Social Visionaries in the Prose and Drama of the GDR'.

10 'Die Funktion der Frau in den Komödien der DDR', p.189.

11 'Women and the Aesthetic of the Positive Hero in the GDR', *Women in German*, pp.121-132 (p.129).

12 'The Structural Development of the Novel in the GDR: 1949-69', p.13

13 Since completing this dissertation, I have had access to two doctoral theses submitted in the United States which are the result of parallel research and which throw useful light on complementary areas: Gerhild Stiewe, 'Die Rolle der Frau in der DDR-Literatur', Minnesota, 1979, is a thematic examination of women's roles in the works of several authors, both male and female, primarily of prose; Jochen Hoffmann, 'Das Bild der Frau im Drama der DDR: 1949-71', Massachussetts, 1980,

has devoted more attention than I to the history of cultural policy as an influence on the evolution of drama.

14 'Verfremdung', from 'Aus den "Katzgraben"-Notaten', *Schriften. Über Theater*, pp.521-44 (p.529).

15 *On the Emancipation of Women*, p.114.

16 For a detailed account of Kollontai's life and works, see the biography by Cathy Porter.

17 A useful study of this period is Jill Stephenson's *Women in Nazi Society*.

18 *Also sprach Zarathustra*, p.307.

19 Friedrich Wolf, 'Theater des Übergangs', *Aufsätze 1945-1953*, pp.57-64 (pp.58-9).

20 'Zur Frage der Kritik', *Berliner Zeitung*, 17 August 1945, quoted in *Theaterkritiken*, p.17.

21 *Die erste Stunde. Porträts*, edited by Fritz Selbmann, p.14.

22 Friedrich Wolf, in an untitled article from *Theater der Zeit*, January 1946, quoted from *Aufsätze 1945-1953*, p.50.

23 *Theater der produktiven Widersprüche*, p.306.

24 *Vom Geist und Ungeist der Zeit*, pp.100-101.

25 *Theater der produktiven Widersprüche*, pp.46-7.

26 February 1949, p.1.

27 'Kampfgenosse Volksbühne', *Aufsätze 1945-1953*, pp.383-5 (p.384).

28 'Formprobleme des Theaters aus neuem Inhalt', *Aufsätze 1945-1953*, pp.221-5.

29 '"Schwarzweißmalerei" im Drama', *Aufsätze 1945-1953*, pp.230-5 (p.233).

30 See, for example, the summaries in *Schauspielführer II/2*, pp.415-6, and *Geschichte der Literatur der DDR*, pp.161-3.

31 'Women and the Aesthetic of the Positive Hero in the GDR', pp.124-5.

32 See three articles in *Aufsätze 1945-1953:* 'Griffelarbeiten von Alice Lex-Nerlinger', pp.282-4, and 'Lilo Herrmann', pp.40-3 and 284-9.

33 'Die Waffe der Satire', *Aufsätze 1945-1953*, pp.493-7.

34 'Weshalb schrieb ich "Bürgermeister Anna"?', *Aufsätze 1945-1953*, pp.334-5 (p.334).

35 A study undertaken by UNESCO in Hoyerswerda in 1970 observed an average of 47.6 hours a week per household, of which 78 per cent was contributed by women. The GDR thus compared favourably with Western households in the division of labour, but fared worse than all other Eastern European countries, in spite of the wider acquisition of electrical aids. The situation has certainly improved since then, but the significance of housework has always been greater than its presence as a literary theme suggests. These findings are quoted in: Evelyn Leopold and Jutta Menschik, *Gretchens rote Schwestern*, p.146.

36 This was the title of a pamphlet issued by the *Frauenabteilung* of the

SED Central Committee as part of its agitational work amongst women working in agriculture during the fifties.

37 'Erwin Strittmatters "Katzgraben"', *Schriften. Über Theater*, pp.396-400.

38 'Aus den "Katzgraben"-Notaten', *Schriften. Über Theater*, pp.521-44.

39 *Also sprach Zarathustra*, p.96.

40 'Preface', *On the Emancipation of Women*, pp.7-14 (p.14).

41 H. Baierl, *Die Köpfe oder Das noch kleinere Organon*, p.13.

42 Werner Hecht, 'Die Kennerin der Wirklichkeit Helene Weigel', *Brecht: vielseitige Betrachtungen*, pp.225-34 (pp.226-7).

43 D. Schlenstedt, 'Ankunft und Anspruch - Zum neueren Roman in der DDR', and E. Röhner, *Abschied, Ankunft und Bewährung: Entwicklungsprobleme unserer sozialistischen Literatur*.

44 *Gegenwart auf der Bühne*, p.102.

45 'Untersuchungen zum kulturellen Aspekt der weiblichen Gleichberechtigung', p.94. This is not to say that there has been no discussion of the subject at all. (See page 75.)

46 *Brecht 73 - Dokumentation zur Brecht-Woche*, pp.200-1.

47 *Brecht 73*, p.217.

48 A principle of personality development listed by the *Philosphisches Wörterbuch* of 1965, p.416.

49 *Philosophisches Wörterbuch*, p.416.

50 *Philosophisches Wörterbuch*, p.416.

51 Peter Hutchinson has provided a detailed analysis of this interest as a central theme of East German fiction in his book *Literary Presentations of Divided Germany*. His observations about the conventions of the Traveller and the Representative place characters such as Barbara and Moritz, Sabine and Alfred in a literary context. My aim in this chapter is to relate these functions to their gender.

52 *Die Geschichte der Literatur der DDR*, p.639.

53 'Interview mit Claus Hammel', *Weimarer Beiträge*, 17 (1969), pp.325-36 (p.333).

54 Quoted by Bernhardt in his article '. . . auf dem Weg zu diesem Stück', in *Erworbene Tradition*, edited by G. Hartung, pp.226-55 (p.232).

55 I. Böhme, 'Interview mit Claus Hammel', p.332.

56 I. Böhme, 'Interview mit Claus Hammel', p.328.

57 Institut für Gesellschaftswissenschaften beim Zentralkomitee der SED (writers' collective), *Erkundung der Gegenwart*, p.156.

58 *Brecht 73*, p.208.

59 'Konflikte genießen?', *Theater der Zeit*, February 1974, p.4.

60 *Unsere Literaturgesellschaft*, p.49.

61 'Unser Werkstattgespräch mit Rainer Kerndl', *Theater der Zeit*, May 1965, p.7.

62 Quoted by Erika Stephan in her review of the Magdeburg première in *Sonntag,* 7 October 1977, p.4.

63 1981 brought the publication of a book, *Die berufstätige Mutter,* by Heinz Schmidt, which is a response to public debate about the double burden of working mothers and also to interest in some of the ideas of Western feminism. Schmidt reiterates the Marxist premise that culture is a changeable human artefact, and argues that the child*bearing* and early nurturing role of women, which is biologically fixed, does *not* imply that women are the sole natural rearers of children.

64 'Rebellierende Schatten', *Theater der Zeit,* March 1974, pp.8-9 (p.8).

65 'Die Funktion der Frau in den Komödien der DDR', p.197.

66 'Theater als Prozeß', *Theater der Zeit,* October 1972, p.9.

67 Kurt Richard Bach, *Geschlechtserziehung in der sozialistischen Oberschule,* p.13.

68 'Versuch über das Libretto', *Oper,* p.229.

69 *Erwartung und Angebot,* pp.185-6.

70 'Über "Adam und Eva"', *Die Maßgaben der Kunst,* pp.382-8 (pp.387-8).

71 'Über "Adam und Eva"', p.387.

72 'Interview', *Die Maßgaben der Kunst,* pp.106-12, p.106.

73 'Zu einigen Aspekten des Verhältnisses von Individuum und Gesellschaft in der sozialistischen Gegenwartsliteratur der sechziger und siebziger Jahre', in *Literatur und Geschichtsbewußtsein,* edited by Manfred Diersch and Walfried Hartinger, pp.87-126 (pp.98-9).

74 'Zehn Zeilen über "Rosie träumt"', *Die Maßgaben der Kunst,* pp.397-402 (p.397).

75 'Vorwort', from 'Das Poetische', *Die Maßgaben der Kunst,* pp.41-4 (p.44).

76 'Es ließe sich fragen . . . : Zu "Ein Gespräch im Hause Stein über den abwesenden Herrn von Goethe"', *Die Maßgaben der Kunst,* pp.391-6 (p.392).

77 It was subsequently produced at the *Berliner Volksbühne* in 1980.

78 'Ein Brief', *Theater der Zeit,* August 1975, pp.58-9 (p.59).

79 Dannhauer's *Geschlecht und Persönlichkeit* contains a Marxist reappraisal of the social and biological factors influencing sexuality.

80 From the typewritten transcipt of an interview given by Heiner Müller to the author on 11 October 1977, p.1.

81 'Wer lacht über wen?', 1 August 1971, p.5.

82 This lack of confidence was also noticed by Rainer Kerndl in his review for *Neues Deutschland,* 9 July 1971, p.4.

83 'Zement', *Die literarische Welt,* 3 (1927), no.23, pp.5-6.

84 'Ein Stück über Revolution', *Theater der Zeit,* December 1973, pp.3-5 (p.4).

85 'Die Aufführung am Berliner Ensemble', *Zement,* pp.507-13 (p.511).

86 'Women and the Aesthetic of the Positive Hero in the GDR', p.130.

87 'Geschichtsloser Raum', *Es genügt nicht die einfache Wahrheit*, p.37.

88 'Über die Bauweise neuer Stücke', *Es genügt nicht die einfache Wahrheit*, pp.139-46 (p.144).

89 P. Hacks, 'Vorwort' to 'Das Poetische', *Die Maßgaben der Kunst*, p.44.

90 'Provokateure oder: die Schwäche meiner Arbeit', *Es genügt nicht die einfache Wahrheit*, pp.40-41 (pp.40-41).

91 'Die Schaubühne nicht als eine moralische Anstalt betrachtet', *Es genügt nicht die einfache Wahrheit*, pp.45-7 (p.45).

92 'Es genügt nicht die einfache Wahrheit', *Es genügt nicht die einfache Wahrheit*, pp.17-8 (p.18).

93 'Interview', *Es genügt nicht die einfache Wahrheit*, pp.121-36 (p.132).

94 *Faust*, edited by Erich Trunz, p.137.

95 'Frau und Staatsbürger in Volker Brauns Schauspiel "Tinka"', *Women in German*, pp.114-20.

96 'Gretchen: Figur, Klischee, Symbol', *Zehntes Amherster Kolloquium*, pp.175-189.

97 'Die Liebe zwischen Theseus und Antiope', February 1978, pp.61-3 (p.63).

98 'Mythen und Möglichkeiten', *Blitz aus heiterm Himmel*, edited by Edith Anderson, pp.237-84 (p.284).

99 For discussion of the allegorical nature of female characters in the drama of the GDR, see 'Women as Social Visionaries in the Prose and Drama of the GDR'.

100 'Nachwort', in Stefan Schütz, *Stücke*, pp.236-44 (pp.236-7).

101 'Die Schlachtung der Wörter', *Theater heute*, 1978, no.1, p.11.

102 'Brecht und der sozialistische Realismus heute', in *Brecht 78: Brecht-Dialog Kunst und Politik 10.-15. Februar 1978*, edited by Werner Hecht, Karl-Claus Hahn and Elifius Paffrath, pp.87-103 (p.98).

103 'Über den Dramatiker Stefan Schütz', *Theater-Arbeit*, pp.123-4 (pp.123-4)

BIBLIOGRAPHY

The Bibliography is divided into three parts. The first lists major texts referred to in the course of the dissertation. It is not intended to be exhaustive, since there are very few East German plays in which there are no female roles and which therefore fail to lend themselves to some degree of observation. The second part contains a selection of *Frauenliteratur*, and exemplifies some of the preoccupations of that broad phenomenon that are mentioned in brief in the dissertation. The third and longest section gives details of secondary material which has been of some value. It includes literary theory and criticism, political and historical works of relevance, and fiction which does not belong in either of the first two sections.

Owing to difficulties in locating first editions, I have considered it more appropriate to quote from collected editions or from other editions which are widely available.

Unless otherwise stated, references to Berlin are to the capital of the GDR.

I - MAJOR TEXTS

Helmut Baierl — *Die Feststellung, Stücke*, Berlin, 1969, pp.5-38
Frau Flinz, Stücke, pp.39-120
Johanna von Döbeln, Stücke, pp.161-234

Volker Braun — *Die Kipper, Drei Stücke*, Berlin, 1975, pp.5-72
Hinze und Kunze, Drei Stücke, pp.73-136
Tinka, Drei Stücke, pp.137-98

Roland Ender — *Frauen sind Männersache*, (1977), typed copies available through *Henschelverlag Abteilung Bühnenvertrieb*

Rolf Gozell — *Der Aufstieg der Edith Eiserbeck*, (1970), typed copies available through *Henschelverlag Abteilung Bühnenvertrieb* (82 pages)

Peter Hacks — *Die Sorgen und die Macht, Ausgewählte Dramen 2*, Berlin, 1976, pp.85-184
Moritz Tassow, Ausgewählte Dramen 1, Berlin, 1971, pp.153-276
Amphitryon, Ausgewählte Dramen 1, pp.277-360
Omphale, Ausgewählte Dramen 1, pp.361-412 (operatic adaptation: *Oper*, Berlin, 1976, pp.109-54)
Adam und Eva, (1972), typed copies available through *Henschelverlag Abteilung Bühnenvertrieb* (98 pages)
Rosie träumt, Das Jahrmarktfest zu Plundersweilen und Rosie träumt, Berlin, 1976, pp.63-121
Ein Gespräch im Hause Stein über den abwesenden Herrn von Goethe, Ausgewählte Dramen 2, pp.389-454

Claus Hammel — *Frau Jenny Treibel oder Wo sich Herz zu Herzen find't, Komödien*, Berlin, 1969, pp.5-88
Um neun an der Achterbahn, Komödien, pp.89-186
Morgen kommt der Schornsteinfeger, Komödien, pp.283-375
Le Faiseur oder Warten auf Godeau, Berlin, 1972
Rom oder Die zweite Erschaffung der Welt, Berlin, 1976

Harald Hauser — *Am Ende der Nacht*, Autoren der DDR, *Sozialistische Dramatik*, Berlin, 1968, pp.37-104

	Barbara, (1963) and *Barbara: Drei Biographien in Zwei Akten*, (1968), typed copies available through *Henschelverlag Abteilung Bühnenvertrieb* (86 pages and 54 pages respectively). *Barbara* is also published in *Neue Deutsche Literatur*, 12 (1964), no.2, pp.57-114
Rainer Kerndl	*Schatten eines Mädchens, Stücke*, Berlin, 1972, pp.5-58 *Seine Kinder, Stücke*, pp.59-122 *Plädoyer für die Suchenden, Stücke*, pp.123-72 *Die seltsame Reise des Alois Fingerlein, Stücke*, pp.173-248 *Ich bin einem Mädchen begegnet, Stücke*, pp.249-90 *Wann kommt Ehrlicher?, Stücke*, pp.291-350 *Nacht mit Kompromissen, Neue Deutsche Literatur*, 24 (1976), no.9, pp.11-67 *Der vierzehnte Sommer, Theater der Zeit*, May 1977, p.56-9
Joachim Knauth	*Die Weibervolksversammlung, Stücke*, Berlin, 1973, pp.63ff
Alfred Matusche	*Die Dorfstraße, Dramen*, Berlin, 1971, pp.5-44
Heiner and Inge Müller	*Der Lohndrücker*, Heiner Müller, *Stücke*, Berlin, 1975, pp.5-32 (other editions referred to: Heiner and Inge Müller, *Der Lohndrücker*, Leipzig, 1959, and W. Adling, *Der Weg zum Wir*, Leipzig, 1959) *Die Korrektur*, Heiner Müller, *Geschichten aus der Produktion 1*, West Berlin, 1974. First version pp.47-59, Second version pp.67-80 *Klettwitzer Bericht, Junge Kunst*, August 1958
Heiner Müller	*Der Bau, Stücke*, Berlin, 1975, pp.115-65 *Die Bauern, Stücke*, pp.33-114 *Herakles 5, Stücke*, pp.167-78 *Prometheus, Geschichten aus der Produktion 2*, West Berlin, 1974, pp.27-55 *Weiberkomödie, Theaterarbeit*, West Berlin, 1975, pp.67-116 (see also *Stücke*, pp.221-72) *Germania Tod in Berlin*, West Berlin, 1977, pp.35-78 *Zement, Stücke*, pp.323-89 *Die Schlacht/Traktor* and *Leben Gundlings Friedrich von Preußen Lessings Schlaf Traum Schrei*, Berlin, 1977 *Die Hamletmaschine, Mauser*, West Berlin, 1978, pp.89-97
Siegfried Pfaff	*Regina B. - Ein Tag in ihrem Leben*, Berlin, 1970
Helmut Sakowski	*Die Entscheidung der Lene Mattke*, Berlin, 1961 *Steine im Weg*, Autoren der DDR, *Sozialistische Dramatik*, Berlin, 1968, pp.239-300 *Weiberzwist und Liebeslist*, typed copies available through *Henschelverlag Abteilung Bühnenvertrieb*
Rolf Schneider	*Der Mann aus England, Stücke*, Berlin, 1970, pp.5-46
Stefan Schütz	*Odysseus'Heimkehr, Stücke*, Berlin, 1977, pp.5-62 *Fabrik im Walde, Stücke*, pp.63-132 *Kohlhaas, Stücke*, pp.133-88 *Heloisa und Abaelard, Stücke*, pp.189-235 *Die Amazonen, Theater der Zeit*, February 1978, pp.64-72

	Majakowski, Stasch, West Berlin, 1978, pp.7-51
Armin Stolper	*Amphitryon, Stücke,* Berlin, 1974, pp.5-66
Rudi Strahl	*In Sachen Adam und Eva, Stücke,* Berlin, 1976, pp.5-52 *Wie die ersten Menschen, Stücke,* pp.53-112 *Keine Leute, keine Leute, Stücke,* pp.113-72 *Der Todestag, Stücke,* pp.173-88 *Ein irrer Duft von frischem Heu, Stücke,* pp.189-251
Erwin Strittmatter	*Die Holländerbraut,* Autoren der DDR, *Sozialistische Dramatik,* Berlin, 1968, pp.105-72 *Katzgraben,* Berlin, 1953
Berta Waterstradt	*Ehesache Lorenz,* typed copies available through *Henschelverlag Abteilung Bühnenvertrieb*
Friedrich Wolf	*Cyankali, Gesammelte Werke,* 16 vols, Berlin, 1960-68, II (1960), pp.81-345 *Tai Yang erwacht, Gesammelte Werke,* III (1960), pp.95-195 *Was der Mensch säet, Gesammelte Werke,* V (1960), pp.327-415 *Die letzte Probe, Gesammelte Werke,* VI (1960), pp.5-106 *Wie Tiere des Waldes, Gesammelte Werke,* VI (1960), pp.107-94 *Bürgermeister Anna, Gesammelte Werke,* VI (1960), pp.195-281

II - SELECTED *FRAUENLITERATUR*

Anderson, Edith, ed., *Blitz aus heiterm Himmel,* Rostock, 1975: anthology containing an essay by Annemarie Auer, 'Mythen und Möglichkeiten', and the following short stories -

Edith Anderson	*Dein für immer oder nie*
Günter de Bruyn	*Geschlechtertausch*
Gotthold Gloger	*Das Rübenfest*
Karl-Heinz Jakobs	*Quedlinburg*
Sarah Kirsch	*Blitz aus heiterm Himmel*
Rolf Schneider	*Meditation*
Christa Wolf	*Selbstversuch - Traktat zu einem Protokoll*

Brüning, Elfriede, *Partnerinnen,* Berlin, 1978

Bruyn, Günter de, *Buridans Esel,* Halle, 1968

Jendryschik, Manfred, *Ein Sommer mit Wanda,* Halle, 1976
- *Anna, eine Chronik, Neue Deutsche Literatur,* 25 (1977), no.4, pp.111-29

Kirsch, Sarah, *Die Pantherfrau: Fünf unfrisierte Erzählungen aus dem Kassetten-Recorder,* Berlin, 1973

Morgner, Irmtraud, *Leben und Abenteuer der Trobadora Beatriz nach Zeugnissen ihrer Spielfrau Laura,* Berlin, 1974

Panitz, Eberhard, *Absage an Viktoria,* Halle, 1975

Reimann, Brigitte, *Franziska Linkerhand,* Berlin, 1974. (A stage adaptation by Bärbel Jaksch and Heiner Maaß is published in *Theater der Zeit,* June 1978, pp.62-71.)

Schütz, Helga, *Lauter Leben,* Berlin, 1975

Smolka, Sigrid, ed., *Die Frau neben uns - Probleme und Perspektiven*, Leipzig, 1969

Tetzner, Gerti, *Karen W.*, Halle, 1976

Wander, Maxie, *Guten Morgen, du Schöne: Protokolle nach Tonband*, Berlin, 1977

Wolf, Christa, *Nachdenken über Christa T.*, Halle, 1968

Wolter, Christine, *Wie ich meine Unschuld verlor*, Berlin, 1977

III - SECONDARY MATERIAL

Abusch, Alexander, *Humanismus und Realismus in der Literatur*, Leipzig, 1966

Akademie der Wissenschaften der DDR, *DDR - Werden und Wachsen*, Berlin, 1975

Allen, Mary, *The Necessary Blankness: Women in Major American Fiction of the Sixties*, Illinois, 1976

Allendorf, Marlis, *Die Frau im Sozialismus*, Leipzig, 1975

Artery, ed., 'Stefan Heym: An exclusive interview', August 1975, pp.14-17

Bach, Kurt Richard, *Geschlechtserziehung in der sozialistischen Oberschule*, Berlin, 1974

Baierl, Helmut, *Die Köpfe oder Das noch kleinere Organon*, Berlin, 1974
- 'Interview', *Neues Deutschland*, 10 October, 1976, p.4

Barck, Karlheinz, and Brigitte Burmeister, *Ideologie - Literatur - Kritik: Französische Beiträge zur marxistischen Literaturtheorie*, Berlin, 1977

Bathrick, David, 'The Dialectics of Legitimation: Brecht in the GDR', *New German Critique*, 2 (Spring 1974), pp.90-103

Baumbach, Gerda, 'Theatralische Qualität poetischer Texte: "Der Bau" von Heiner Müller', *Theater der Zeit*, March 1978, pp.50-3

Bebel, August, *Die Frau und der Sozialismus*, reprint of 50th revised edition of 1909, Berlin, 1946

Becher, Johannes R., *Über Literatur und Kunst*, Berlin, 1962

Benjamin, Walter, 'Zement: Zum Roman von Fjodor Gladkow', *Die literarische Welt*, 3 (1927), no.23, pp.5-6

Birnbaum, Uta, 'Masken für die Amazonen', *Theater der Zeit*, February 1978, pp.62-3

Böhme, Irene, 'Interview mit Claus Hammel', *Weimarer Beiträge*, 17 (1969), no.2, pp.325-36
- 'Ein Stück über Revolution', *Theater der Zeit*, December 1973, pp.3-5
- 'Rebellierende Schatten', *Theater der Zeit*, March 1974, pp.8-9

Böttcher, Kurt, and Ludwig Hoffman, *Schauspielführer II/2*, Berlin, 1975

Böttger, Fritz, ed., *Frauen im Aufbruch*, Berlin, 1977

Bräulich, Heinrich, *Die Volksbühne*, Berlin, 1976

Braun, Volker, *Gedichte*, Leipzig, 1972
- *Es genügt nicht die einfache Wahrheit*, Leipzig, 1975
- *Unvollendete Geschichte*, *Sinn und Form*, 27 (1975), pp.941-79

Brecht, Bertolt, *Die heilige Johanna der Schlachthöfe, Gesammelte Werke*, 8 vols, Frankfurt am Main, 1967, I, pp.665-786

- *Die Mutter, Gesammelte Werke*, I, pp.823-95
- *Die Gewehre der Frau Carrar, Gesammelte Werke*, II, pp.1195-228
- *Mutter Courage und ihre Kinder, Gesammelte Werke*, II, pp.1347-444
- *Der gute Mensch von Sezuan, Gesammelte Werke*, II, pp.1487-608
- *Der kaukasische Kreidekreis, Gesammelte Werke*, II, pp.1999-2105
- *Büsching*, unpublished fragments, *Berliner-Brecht-Archiv* Catalogue nos.4470-4480
- *Schriften. Über Theater*, edited by Werner Hecht, Berlin, 1977
- *Arbeitsjournal 1938-1955*, edited by Werner Hecht, Berlin, 1977

Brecht-Dialog 68, Berlin, 1968

Brecht 73 - Dokumentation zur Brecht-Woche, Berlin, 1973

Brecht 78 - Brecht-Dialog, Kunst und Politik, Berlin, 1978

Brettschneider, Werner, *Zwischen literarischer Autonomie und Staatsdienst. Die Literatur der DDR*, West Berlin, 1972

Bütow, Wilfried, ed., *Zur schöpferischen Arbeit im Literaturunterricht*, Berlin, 1975

Buhr, Manfred, and Georg Klaus, ed., *Philosophisches Wörterbuch*, Leipzig, 1965

Calder, Jenni, *Women and Marriage in Victorian Fiction*, London, 1976

Cockshut, Anthony, *Man and Woman: a study of love and the novel*, London, 1977

Damm, Sigrid, and Jürgen Engler, 'Notate des Zwiespalts und Allegorien der Vollendung', *Weimarer Beiträge*, 21 (1975), no.7, pp.37-69

Dannhauer, Heinz, *Geschlecht und Persönlichkeit. Eine Untersuchung zur psychischen Geschlechtsdifferenzierung in der Ontogenese*, Berlin, 1973

Diersch, Manfred, and Walfried Hartinger, *Literatur und Geschichtsbewußtsein: Entwicklungstendenzen der DDR-Literatur in den sechziger und siebziger Jahren*, Berlin, 1976

Drenkow, Renate, and H. Konrad Hoerning, *Handbuch für Laientheater*, Berlin, 1968

Düwel, Gudrun, *Friedrich Wolf und Wsewolod Wischnewski*, Berlin, 1975

Eichhorn, Wolfgang, ed., *Dialektik im Sozialismus*, Berlin, 1976

Eichler, Rolf-Dieter, '"Weiberkomödie" von Heiner Müller', *Nationalzeitung*, 7 August 1971, p.7

Einhorn, Barbara, 'The Structural Development of the Novel in the GDR: 1949-1969', *GDR Monitor*, no.1 (Summer 1979), pp.13-28

Emmerich, Wolfgang, 'Identität und Geschlechtertausch: Notizen zur Selbstdarstellung der Frau in der neueren DDR-Literatur', *Basis 8*, edited by R. Grimm and J. Hermand, Frankfurt am Main, 1978, pp.127-54

Engels, Friedrich, *Die Lage der Arbeitenden Klasse in England. Nach eigner Anschauung und authentischen Quellen, Marx Engels Werke*, 39 vols, Berlin, 1960-65, II (1960), pp.225-506

- *Der Ursprung der Familie, des Privateigentums und des Staats, Marx Engels Werke*, XXI (1962), pp.25-173

Erpenbeck, Fritz, *Lebendiges Theater*, Berlin, 1949

Fernando, Lloyd, *'New Women' in the Late Victorian Novel*, Pennsylvania, 1978

Fiebach, Joachim, *Von Craig bis Brecht: Studien zu Künstlertheorien in der ersten Hälfte des zwanzigsten Jahrhunderts*, Berlin, 1977
- 'Nachwort', Heiner Müller, *Die Schlacht/Traktor, Leben Gundlings Friedrich von Preußen Lessings Schlaf Traum Schrei*, Berlin, 1977, pp.112-38

Fischborn, Gottfried, 'Helmut Sakowski', Hans Jürgen Geerdts, *Literatur der Deutschen Demokratischen Republik: Einzeldarstellungen*, Berlin, 1974, pp.387-402
- 'Künstlerische Subjektivität und Wirklichkeitsaneignung: Zum Schaffen der Dramatiker Hacks, H. Müller und Stolper', *Theater der Zeit*, January 1978, pp.52-5

Fischer, E., and W. Ruppert, *Kostümplastiken für das Theater*, Berlin, 1975

Fix, Peter, 'Nachwort', Peter Hacks, *Ausgewählte Dramen 2*, Berlin, 1976, pp.455-98

Franke, Konrad, *Die Literatur der Deutschen Demokratischen Republik*, München, 1974

Frede, Matthias, 'Leben, schöner als im Fernsehen: "Frauen sind Männersache" von Roland Ender in Wittenberg', *Theater der Zeit*, June 1978, p.58

Für Dich, ed., 'Interview mit Sakowski', 52/1975, pp.7-11
- 'Schreiben heißt Zu-Ende-Denken: Irmtraud Morgner gibt Auskunft', 21/1978, pp.18-20

Funke, Christoph, 'Über Helmut Baierl', Helmut Baierl, *Stücke*, Berlin, 1969, pp.235-43
- 'Heiner Müllers "Weiberkomödie" an der Volksbühne', *Der Morgen*, 20 August 1971, p.3

Gaillard, Ottofritz, *Das deutsche Stanislawski-Buch*, Berlin, 1948

Geerdts, Hans Jürgen, ed., *Geschichte der Literatur der Deutschen Demokratischen Republik* (also appeared as Volume XI of *Geschichte der deutschen Literatur*, 11 vols), Berlin, 1976

Girshausen, Theo, ed., *Die Hamletmaschine: Heiner Müllers Endspiel*, Köln, 1978 (also contains a comprehensive bibliography of plays and articles by H. Müller)

Gladkow, Fjodor, and Heiner Müller, *Zement* (contains both versions as well as a number of articles of criticism and the production notes of the *Berliner Ensemble*)

Goethe, Johann Wolfgang von, *Faust*, edited by Erich Trunz, Hamburg, 1949

Gorky, Maxim, *Mother*, *Selected Works*, 2 vols, Moscow, 1948-49, II (1949)

Grandke, Anita, *Junge Leute in der Ehe*, Berlin, 1977

Greif zur Feder, Kumpel: Protokoll der Autorenkonferenz des Mitteldeutscher Verlags am 24.4.1959 in Bitterfeld, Halle, 1959

Hacks, Peter, *Lieder, Briefe, Gedichte*, Berlin, 1974
- *Die Maßgaben der Kunst: Gesammelte Aufsätze*, Berlin, 1978

Hafranke, Ursula, *Arbeitskollektiv und Familie*, Berlin, 1977

Hager, Kurt, *Zu Fragen der Kulturpolitik der SED*, Berlin, 1972

Hanke, H., and G. Rossow, *Sozialistische Kulturrevolution*, Berlin, 1976

Hans-Otto-Theater, Potsdam, 'Heloisa und Abaelard', Programme no.7-77/78

Hardwick, Elizabeth, *Seduction and Betrayal*, New York, 1974

Hartinger, Christel and Walfried, 'Volker Braun', Hans-Jürgen Geerdts, ed., *Literatur der DDR: Einzeldarstellungen*, Berlin, 1974, pp.444-62

Hartung, Günter, ed., *Erworbene Tradition*, Berlin, 1977

Hecht, Werner, *Brecht: vielseitige Betrachtungen*, Berlin, 1969

Herminghouse, Patricia, and Peter Hohendahl, *Literatur und Literaturtheorie in der DDR*, Frankfurt am Main, 1976

Hieblinger, Inge, *Frauen in unserem Staat*, Berlin, 1967

Hiebsch, Hans, and Manfred Vorwerg, *Einführung in die marxistische Sozialpsychologie*, Berlin, 1972

Hollitscher, Walter, *Der überangestrengte Sexus: Die sogenannte sexuelle Emanzipation im heutigen Kapitalismus*, Berlin, 1975

Hörz, Helga, *Die Frau als Persönlichkeit: Philosophische Probleme einer Geschlechterpsychologie*, Berlin, 1968
- 'Die Rolle von Leitbildern im Kampf um die Gleichberechtigung der Frau im Kapitalismus', *Zeitschrift für Philosophie*, 24 (1976), pp.645-58
- *Blickpunkt Persönlichkeit: Ein Beitrag der Ethik zu Theorie und Praxis der Persönlichkeitsentwicklung*, Berlin, 1978

Humboldt, Wilhelm von, 'Über die männliche und weibliche Form', *Werke*, 5 vols, Stuttgart, 1960, I, pp.296-336
- 'Über den Geschlechtsunterschied und dessen Einfluß auf die organische Natur', *Werke*, I, pp.268-95

Hutchinson, Peter, *Literary Presentations of Divided Germany. The Development of a Central Theme in East German Fiction 1945-1970*, Cambridge, 1977

Iffland, A.W., *Über Schauspieler und Schauspielkunst*, Berlin, 1954

Institut für Gesellschaftswissenschaften beim Zentralkomitee der SED, *Zur Theorie des sozialistischen Realismus*, Berlin, 1974
- *Erkundung der Gegenwart*, Berlin, 1976

Iwanow, F.A., 'Naturalismus oder Realismus? Bemerkungen zu einer Diskussion über Rollenbilder', *Theater der Zeit*, September 1947, pp.9-11

Jäger, Elli, 'Nachwort', Stefan Schütz, *Stücke*, Berlin, 1977, pp.236-44

Jarmatz, Klaus, *Künstlerisches Schaffen im Sozialismus*, Berlin, 1976

Jhering, Herbert, *Vom Geist und Ungeist der Zeit*, Berlin, 1947
- *Theater der produktiven Widersprüche*, Berlin, 1967

John, Erhard, *Einführung in die Ästhetik*, Halle, 1972
- (as 'Leitung des Autorenkollektivs'), *Beiträge zur Entwicklung sozialistischer Kulturbedürfnisse*, Berlin, 1976

John, Hans-Rainer, 'Die Liebe von Theseus und Antiope: "Die Amazonen" in Basel uraufgeführt', *Theater der Zeit*, February 1978, pp.61-2

Kähler, Hermann, *Gegenwart auf der Bühne*, Berlin, 1966

(Kähler, H., cont.), 'Überlegungen zu Komödien von Peter Hacks', Peter Hacks, *Ausgewählte Dramen 1*, Berlin, 1971, pp.413-49
- 'Stücke eines Jahrzehnts', Rainer Kerndl, *Stücke*, Berlin, 1972, pp.351-61
- *Der kalte Krieg der Kritiker*, Berlin, 1974

Kant, Immanuel, *Metaphysik der Sitten*, edited by Karl Vorländer, Hamburg, 1954

Kaplan, Sydney Janet, *Feminine Consciousness in the Modern British Novel*, Illinois, 1975

Kaufmann, Eva and Hans, *Erwartung und Angebot: Studien zum gegenwärtigen Verhältnis von Literatur und Gesellschaft in der DDR*, Berlin, 1976

Kerndl, Rainer, 'Heiner Müllers "Weiberkomödie"', *Neues Deutschland*, 9 July 1971, p.4
- 'Konflikte genießen?', *Theater der Zeit*, February 1974, p.4
- 'Helmut Baierl: "Die Abenteuer der Johanna von Döbeln"', *Neues Deutschland*, 24 June 1976, p.4
- 'Zu Stücken von Rudi Strahl', *Theater der Zeit*, July 1977, p.52

Klatt, Gudrun, *Arbeiterklasse und Theater*, Berlin, 1975
- 'Erfahrungen des "didaktischen" Theaters: Helmut Baierl und Heiner Müller in den fünfziger Jahren', *Theater der Zeit*, April 1978, pp.52-4

Kleine Enzyklopädie: Die Frau, Leipzig, 1961, 13th revised edition 1979

Klunker, H., *Zeitstücke Zeitgenossen, Gegenwartstheater in der DDR*, Hannover, 1972

Koch, Hans, *Unsere Literaturgesellschaft*, Berlin, 1965
- *Kulturpolitik in der Deutschen Demokratischen Republik*, Berlin, 1976
- 'Kunst und realer Sozialismus: Zu einigen Fragen der Entwicklung unserer Literatur', *Neues Deutschland*, 15/16 April 1978, p.4

Kollontai, Alexandra, *Autobiography of a Sexually Emancipated Woman*, London, 1972

Kuckhoff, Armin Gerd, 'Einheit und Vielfalt dramatischer Gestaltung im Theater: Zu Fragen des Spannungsgefüges von künstlerischer Individualität und Gesellschaft beim Rezeptionsprozeß des Erbes im Theater unserer Zeit', Verband der Theaterschaffenden der DDR, *Material zum Theater*, no.94, Berlin, 1977, pp.19-45

Kuczynski, Jürgen, and W. Heise, *Bild und Begriff*, Berlin, 1975

Kuhrig, H., and W. Speigner, ed., *Zur gesellschaftlichen Stellung der Frau in der DDR*, Leipzig, 1978

Kunze, Ingeborg, 'Untersuchungen zum kulturellen Aspekt der weiblichen Gleichberechtigung: Die wissenschaftlich-theoretische und künstlerische Widerspiegelung des Frauenproblems unter besonderer Berücksichtigung der Persönlichkeitsbildung in der sozialistischen Kulturrevolution', unpublished inaugural dissertation, Karl-Marx-Universität, Leipzig, 1965

Langner, Ilse, *Iphigenie kehrt heim*, Berlin, 1948
- *Klytämnestra*, Berlin, 1949

Lauter, H., *Der Kampf gegen den Formalismus*, Berlin, 1951

Lenin, V.I., *On the Emancipation of Women*, Moscow, 1965

(Lenin, V.I., cont.), *On Literature and Art*, Moscow, 1967

Leopold, Evelyn, and Jutta Menschik, *Gretchens rote Schwestern*, Frankfurt am Main, 1974

Loesch, Ilse, *Sprechende Bewegung: Ein Studienbuch für Schauspieler und Regisseure*, Berlin, 1974

Mäde, Hans-Dieter, and Ursula Püschel, *Dramaturgie des Positiven*, Berlin, 1973

Marquardt, Hans, 'Nachwort', Johann Jakob Christoffel von Grimmelshausen, *Courasche*, Berlin, 1980

Marx, Karl, *Die deutsche Ideologie. Kritik der neuesten deutschen Philosophie in ihren Repräsentanten Feuerbach, B. Bauer und Stirner und des deutschen Sozialismus in seinen verschiedenen Propheten*, *Marx Engels Werke*, III, pp.9-530
- *Ökonomisch-philosophische Manuskripte aus dem Jahre 1844*, *Marx Engels Werke*, Ergänzungsband, erster Teil (1968), pp.465-588

Marx Engels Lenin, *Über Kultur Ästhetik Literatur*, Leipzig, 1975

Mayakovsky, Vladimir, *The Bathhouse*, see German translation by Hugo Huppert, Wladimir Majakowski, *Das Schwitzbad*, *Werke*, 5 vols, Berlin, 1974, III, pp.175-240

McPherson, Karin, 'Christa Wolf. An Interview', *GDR Monitor*, no.1 (Summer 1979), pp.1-12

Mehnert, Günter, *Kulturerbe im Sozialismus*, Berlin, 1977

Menschik, Jutta, ed., *Grundlagentexte zur Emanzipation der Frau*, Köln, 1976

Mensh, Elaine and Harry, *Behind the Scenes in Two Worlds*, New York, 1978

Mittenzwei, Werner, ed., *Theater in der Zeitenwende: Zur Geschichte des Dramas und des Schauspieltheaters in der DDR 1945-1968*, Berlin, 1972

Möhrmann, Renate, *Die andere Frau*, Stuttgart, 1977

Moers, Ellen, *Literary Women*, London, 1978

Müller, Heiner, 'Zwischenbemerkung', *Neue Deutsche Literatur*, 6 (1959), no.1, pp.120-1
- 'Gespräch über "Horizonte"', *Sonntag*, 5 April 1969
- 'Sechs Punkte zur Oper', *Theater der Zeit*, March 1970, pp.18-19
- 'Über den Dramatiker Stefan Schütz', *Theater-Arbeit*, West Berlin, 1975, pp.123-4
- 'Ein Brief', *Theater der Zeit*, August 1975, pp.58-9
- (discussion) 'Autor und Theater', *Theater der Zeit*, October 1972, p.9
- (discussion with Horst Laube) 'Der Dramatiker und die Geschichte seiner Zeit', *Theater heute*, 1975, Sonderheft, pp.119-23

Münz, Rudolf, *Vom Wesen des Dramas*, Halle, 1963

Myers, Carol F., *Women in Literature - Criticism of the Sixties*, New Jersey, 1976

Naumann, Manfred, 'Leiter des Autorenkollektivs', *Gesellschaft Literatur Lesen: Literaturrezeption in theoretischer Sicht*, Berlin, 1976

Nietzsche, Friedrich, *Also sprach Zarathustra*, Leipzig, 1904

Nippold, Erich, *Theater und Dramen: Wege zu ihrem Verständnis*, Gotha, 1949

Noll, Dieter, *Die Abenteuer des Werner Holt*, Band II, Berlin, 1964

Nössig, Manfred, *Die Schauspieltheater der DDR und das Erbe (1970-74)*, Berlin, 1976

- 'Heiner Müller: Schlacht/Traktor/Leben Gundlings . . ./Zu einer Buchveröffentlichung', *Theater der Zeit*, March 1978, p.52

Oakley, Ann, *Housewife*, London, 1974

Panitz, Eberhard, 'Frauensprache, Frauenliteratur', *Neue Deutsche Literatur*, 26 (1978), no.2, pp.70-4

Panorama, *Women and Socialism, First-hand Information* series, Dresden, 1978

Pietzch, Ingeborg, *Werkstatt Theater: Gespräche mit Regisseuren*, Berlin, 1975

- 'Rebell, der seinen Frieden macht: "Kohlhaas" und "Heloisa und Abaelard" von Stefan Schütz uraufgeführt', *Theater der Zeit*, May 1978, pp.54-6

Porter, Cathy, *Alexandra Kollontai: a biography*, London, 1980

Pracht, Erwin, *Abbild und Methode*, Halle, 1974

- 'Leiter des Kollektivs', *Einführung in den sozialistischen Realismus*, Berlin, 1975

Reimann, Brigitte, *Ankunft im Alltag*, Berlin, 1961

Rilla, Paul, *Theaterkritiken*, Berlin, 1978

Rindfleisch, Ruth, 'Erwin Strittmatter', Hans-Jürgen Geerdts, ed., *Literatur der DDR: Einzeldarstellungen*, Berlin, 1974, pp.216-41

Rödel, Fritz, 'Claus Hammel', Hans-Jürgen Geerdts, ed., *Literatur der DDR: Einzeldarstellungen*, Berlin, 1974, pp.419-32

Röhner, Eberhard, *Abschied, Ankunft und Bewährung: Entwicklungsprobleme unserer sozialistischen Literatur*, Berlin, 1969

- *Politik und Literatur*, Berlin, 1976

Rohmer, Rolf, 'Peter Hacks', Hans-Jürgen Geerdts, ed., *Literatur der DDR: Einzeldarstellungen*, Berlin, 1974, pp.408-18

- 'Nachwort', Heiner Müller, *Stücke*, Berlin, 1975, pp.390-9
- 'Persönlichkeit und Gesellschaftsprozeß', Volker Braun, *Drei Stücke*, Berlin, 1975, pp.199-209
- 'Die Aneignung der Realität auf dem Theater der entwickelten sozialistischen Gesellschaft', Verband der Theaterschaffended der DDR, *Material zum Theater*, no.94, Berlin, 1977, pp.3-18
- 'Theaterkritik - Aufgaben und Möglichkeiten' (with an appendix containing essays by Rilla, Jhering and Erpenbeck), Verband der Theaterschaffenden der DDR, *Material zum Theater*, no.108, Berlin, 1979

Sakowski, Helmut, *Zwei Frauen*, Berlin, 1959

Schivelbusch, Wolfgang, *Sozialistisches Drama nach Brecht, Drei Modelle: Peter Hacks, Heiner Müller, Hartmut Lange*, Darmstadt und Neuwied, 1974

Schlenstedt, Dieter, 'Ankunft und Anspruch: Zum neueren Roman in der DDR', *Sinn und Form*, 3 (1966), pp.832-3

Schlenstedt, Sylvia, 'Das WIR und das ICH des Volker Braun', *Weimarer Beiträge*, 20 (1972), no.10, pp.52-69

Schmidt, Heinz, *Die berufstätige Mutter*, Berlin, 1981

Schubbe, Elimar, ed., *Dokumente zur Kunst-, Literatur- und Kulturpolitik der SED*, Stuttgart, 1972

Schütz, Stefan, 'Die Schlachtung der Wörter', *Theater heute*, 1978, no.1

Schulmeister, Karl-Heinz, *Auf dem Wege zu einer neuen Kultur: Der Kulturbund in den Jahren 1945-1949*, Berlin, 1977

Schultze, F., 'Brief', *Theater der Zeit*, July 1947, p.25

Schulz, Max Walter, *Wir sind nicht Staub im Wind*, Halle, 1962

Scott, H.G., ed., *Problems of Soviet Literature: Soviet Writers' Congress 1934*, London, 1977

Scott, Hilda, *Women and Socialism: Experiences from Eastern Europe*, London, 1976

Seghers, Anna, *Über Kunstwerk und Wirklichkeit*, 3 vols, Berlin, 1971-75

Selbmann, Fritz, ed., *Die erste Stunde. Porträts*, Berlin, 1969

Showalter, Elaine, *A literature of their own: British women novelists from Brontë to Lessing*, Princeton, 1977

Sonntag, open discussion on comedy in the theatre arising out of criticisms of 'Weiberkomödie', 1 August 1971, pp.3-5; 22 August 1971, pp.3-4; 19 September 1971, pp.3-4

Sozialistische Einheitspartei Deutschlands, *Programm der SED*, Berlin, 1976
- *Bericht des Zentralkomitees der SED an den IX. Parteitag*, Berlin, 1976
- *Statut*, Berlin, 1976

Spacks, Patricia Meyer, *The Female Imagination: a literary and psychological investigation of women's writing*, London, 1976

Staatliche Zentralverwaltung für Statistik, *Die Frau und die DDR: Fakten und Zahlen*, Berlin, 1977

Stephan, Alexander, 'The Emancipation of Man. Christa Wolf as a woman Writer', translated by Ian Wallace, *GDR Monitor*, no.2 (Winter 1979/80), pp.23-32

Stephan, Erika, '"Der vierzehnte Sommer" von Rainer Kerndl, Uraufführung in Magdeburg', *Sonntag*, 7 October 1977, p.4

Stephenson, Jill, *Women in Nazi Society*, London, 1975

Stolper, Armin, *Narrenspiel will Raum: von Stücken und Stückeschreibern*, Berlin, 1977

Strahl, Rudi, 'Dialog mit Rudi Strahl', *Stücke*, Berlin, 1976
- 'Rudi Strahl und Werner Liersch im Gespräch mit Albert Wendt', *Neue Deutsche Literatur*, 26 (1978), no.4, pp.42-7

Sudau, Christel, 'Women in the GDR', *New German Critique*, no.13 (Winter 1978), pp.69-81

Surina, Tamara M., 'Die Bedeutung Stanislawkis und Brechts für das sozialistische Theater der Gegenwart', translated by W. Gruhn, Verband der Theaterschaffenden der DDR, *Material zum Theater*, no.94, Berlin, 1977, pp.46-64

Theater, das der großen Sache dient: Protokoll zum III. Kongreß des Verbands der Theaterschaffenden der DDR, 1975, Berlin, 1976

Theater der Zeit, editorials of April 1947, January 1948 and February 1949 on the place of women in the theatre
- ed., 'Alltägliches, große Form, Kampf und Glück: Ein Gespräch über "Zement" von Heiner Müller mit Rolf-Dieter Eichler, Christoph Funke, Prof. Dr Ernst Schumacher und Irene Böhme', March 1974, pp.2-6

Thönnessen, Werner, *Frauenemanzipation: Politik und Literatur der deutschen Sozialdemokratie zur Frauenbewegung 1863-1933*, Frankfurt am Main, 1969

Thurm, Brigitte, 'Theater als Geschlechterfrage? Frauen in unseren Stücken', *Theater der Zeit*, July 1971, pp.4-6

Touaillon, Christine, *Der deutsche Frauenroman des 18. Jahrhunderts*, Wien und Leipzig, 1919 (reprinted and published in 1980, Bern und Frankfurt am Main)

Trilse, Christoph, *Antike und Theater heute*, Berlin, 1975
- with Klaus Hammer and Rolf Kabel, eds., *Theaterlexikon*, Berlin, 1977

Ullrich, Helmut, 'Heiner Müllers "Weiberkomödie" an der Volksbühne', *Neue Zeit*, 8 August 1971, p.3

Vanovitch, Kathy, 'Innovation and Convention: Women in the GDR', *GDR Monitor*, no.2 (Winter 1979/80), pp.15-22
- 'Women as Social Visionaries in the Prose and Drama of the GDR', *The GDR under Honecker: 1971-1981*, conference proceedings, *GDR Monitor*, No.5 (Winter 1981/82)

Verband der Theaterschaffenden der DDR, ed., *Dialog der Regisseure: Reinhardt, Stanislawski, Meyerhold, Brecht und Piscator im fiktiven Gespräch*, text montage by Werner Heinitz, *Material zum Theater*, no.106, Berlin, 1978
- *Acht Beiträge zum Thema: Drama-Bühne-Wirklichkeit*, *Material zum Theater*, no.95, Berlin, 1977

Verfassung der Deutschen Demokratischen Republik vom 6. April 1968 in der Fassung des Gesetzes zur Ergänzung und Änderung der Verfassung der Deutschen Demokratischen Republik vom 7. Oktober 1974, Berlin, 1975

Verlag für die Frau, ed., *Frauen im Spiegel der Kunst*, Leipzig, 1972

Volksbühne, Berlin, 'Die Bauern', Programme 75/76
- 'Die Schlacht', Programme 75/76

Wekwerth, Manfred, *Schriften: Arbeit mit Brecht*, Berlin, 1975

Weininger, Otto, *Geschlecht und Charakter*, Wien und Leipzig, 1922

Wolf, Christa, 'Berührung', *Neue Deutsche Literatur*, 26 (1978), no.2, pp.53-62

Wolf, Friedrich, Prologues to the 1929, 1946 and 1947 editions of *Cyankali*, *Gesammelte Werke*, 16 vols, Berlin, 1960-68, II (1960), pp.271-80
- *Aufsätze 1945-1953*, *Gesammelte Werke*, XVI (1968)

Women in German: An Interdisciplinary and Comparative Approach. Proceedings of the 2nd Symposium, Oxford, Ohio, 1977

Zehntes Amherster Kolloquium zur deutschen Literatur: Die Frau als Heldin und Autorin, edited by Wolfgang Paulsen, Bern, 1979

Zentralkomitee der SED, 'Unsere Bäuerinnen - eine große Kraft bei der sozialistischen Umgestaltung der Landwirtschaft', 22 February 1956, *Dokumente der revolutionären deutschen Arbeiterbewegung zur Frauenfrage 1848-1974*, edited by a 'Forschungsgemeinschaft' led by Joachim Müller, Leipzig, 1975, pp.202-4

- 'Die Frau - Der Frieden und der Sozialismus', *Dokumente der revolutionären deutschen Arbeiterbewegung zur Frauenfrage 1848-1974*, pp.257-62
- 'Autorenkollektiv unter Leitung von Marianne Lange', *Kultur im gesellschaftlichen Leben*, Berlin, 1973

Zetkin, Clara, *Erinnerungen an Lenin*, Berlin, 1957

Zinner, Hedda, *Stücke*, Berlin, 1973 (contains *Caféhaus Payer*, *General Landt*, *Der Teufelskreis*, *Ravensbrücker Ballade*)

Zipes, Jack D., 'Die Funktion der Frau in den Komödien der DDR', *Sechstes Amherster Kolloquium zur deutschen Literatur: Die deutsche Komödie im zwanzigsten Jahrhundert*, edited by Wolfgang Paulsen, Heidelberg, 1976, pp.187-205

Manuscript:

Hoffman, H. Jochen, 'Das Bild der Frau im Drama der Deutschen Demokratischen Republik 1949-1971', Ph.D., University of Massachusetts, 1980

Stiewe, Gerhild Gertraud, 'Die Rolle der Frau in der DDR-Literatur', Ph.D., University of Minnesota, 1979

Vanovitch, Kathy, 'Interview with Heiner Müller', Berlin, 11 October 1977 (8 pages, transcript of cassette recording)

BRÖHAN, MARGRIT
DIE DARSTELLUNG DER FRAU BEI WILHELM RAABE
und ein Vergleich mit liberalen Positionen zur Emanzipation der Frau im 19. Jahrhundert

Frankfurt/M., Bern, Las Vegas, 1980. 280 S.
EUROPÄISCHE HOCHSCHULSCHRIFTEN: Reihe 1, Deutsche Sprache und Literatur. Bd. 390
ISBN 3-8204-6888-9 br. sFr. 55.-- *)

Einer knappen Dokumentation zur Frauenfrage folgt Interpretation ausgewählter Werke Raabes. Nachgewiesen wird eine Entwicklungslinie, die von Polarisierung im Frühwerk zu differenzierter und schließlich emanzipationsfreundlicher Darstellung führt. Ein Vergleich zeigt, daß Raabe weitgehend unabhängig von der politischen Haltung der Liberalen nach 1866 schrieb. Die Bedeutung liegt in der Entwicklung eines mündigen Frauenbildes, die als mittelbare Vorarbeit für die Gleichberechtigung der Frau gesehen wird. Die Arbeit kommt in klaren, abgewogenen Ergebnissen über ältere Behandlungen des Themas wesentlich hinaus, z.T. in Widerspruch zur konventionellen Raabe-Forschung.

Aus dem Inhalt: Einer Dokumentation zur Frauenfrage folgt Nachweis einer Entwicklungslinie von polarisierender Typisierung zu differenzierter und schließlich emanzipationsfreundlicher Darstellung der Frau bei Wilhelm Raabe.

DIESTER, MANFRED
KÖRPERGESCHICHTEN
Eine Untersuchung zum Mythosbegriff am Beispiel der Darstellung von Mann und Frau in der Kriegsliteratur von 1939-43

Frankfurt/M., Bern, 1980. 451 S.
EUROPÄISCHE HOCHSCHULSCHRIFTEN: Reihe 1, Deutsche Sprache und Literatur. Bd. 371
ISBN 3-8204-6832-3 br. sFr. 75.-- *)

Wie stellt sich aus einem natürlichen Sprachdefizit des Körpers eine physiologisch auftretende Ausdrucksform des Ichs her? Diese Form, die entlang der Sprachtheorie einer materialistischen Psychiatrie diskutiert wird, bilden die Entwicklungsgeschichten von Frontsoldaten, wie sie in der Feldpostliteratur von 1939-43 erscheinen. Die Frau dringt dabei nur in die männlich undomestizierten Randbereiche seines Lebens ein, als Restarchitektur eines Hintergrundes, den der Soldat als ziviles Leben mit der 'Feuertaufe' überwunden hat und der vom Vordergrund einer Thanatologie, die Leben und Tod identisch setzt, verdrängt wird.

Aus dem Inhalt: U.a. Literaturproduktion und Vertriebswesen in den Kriegsjahren 1939-43 - Die 'erste Produktion' des Sprechers und ihre Widersacher - Die Detonation des Körper-Ichs - Das Labyrinth männlich-weiblicher Territorien - Warum Landser lachen.

---

*) unverbindliche Preisempfehlung
Auslieferung: Verlag Peter Lang AG, Jupiterstr. 15, CH-3015 Bern

ATTAR, SAMAR
THE INTRUDER IN MODERN DRAMA

Frankfurt/M., Berne, 1980. 237 p.
EUROPEAN UNIVERSITY PAPERS: Series 1, German language and literature. Vol. 354
ISBN 3-8204-6722-X
pb. sFr. 54.-- *)

The INTRUDER is a dramatic character who appears suddenly on stage, seemingly from nowhere, unknown to the other characters, thrusting himself upon them and upsetting the status quo. The study compares twelve plays by ten major modern dramatists (Arden, Betti, Bond, Brecht, Dürrenmatt, Frisch, Gombrowicz, Ionesco, Pinter, Williams). In all the plays, as a result of the intrusion, there is a mood of uneasiness, impending social change which disturbs the socio-political equilibrium.

Contents: Introduction - The Sexual Intruder - The Ethical Intruder - The Social Intruder - The Political Intruder - Conclusion.

BECKMAN, BARBARA JOE
UNDERLYING WORD ORDER - GERMAN AS A VSO LANGUAGE

Frankfurt/M., Bern, 1979. IV, 155 p.
EUROPEAN UNIVERSITY PAPERS: Series 1, German Language and Literature. Vol. 322
ISBN 3-8204-6633-9
pb. sFr. 36.-- *)

In this work the underlying word order of German is investigated. Previous proposals for SOV and SVO bases are discussed in detail, and derivational possibilities for a variety of transformational rules from SOV and SVO as well as VSO bases are presented, analyzed and compared. It is proposed that a body of data exists that offers support for a (Prefield) VSO hypothesis over an SOV or SVO hypothesis for German to account for the extremely diverse survace configurations of verbal and non-verbal elements.

Contents: General Theoretical considerations for (German) syntax - SOV Order - SVO Order - VSO Order, Prefield and the Prefield Shift Transformation - Conclusions.

---

*) unverbindliche Preisempfehlung
Auslieferung: Verlag Peter Lang AG, Jupiterstr. 15, CH-3015 Bern